American Machine-made Marbles

Marble Bags, Boxes, and History

Dean Six, Susie Metzler, and Michael Johnson

Schiffer Publishing Ltd®

4880 Lower Valley Road, Atglen, PA 19310 USA

Dedication

David G. Hanlon
1935-2006
Dear friend, we will miss you.

Other Schiffer Books by Dean Six
West Virginia Glass Between the World Wars
Viking Glass
Lotus: Depression Glass and Far Beyond
L. G. Wright Glass. The West Virginia Museum of American Glass, Ltd.
The Black Glass Encyclopedia. The West Virginia Museum of American Glass, Ltd.

Other Schiffer Books on Related Subjects
Collecting Early Machine-made Marbles from M.F. Christensen & Son Company and Christensen Agate Company. Robert Block
Marbles Illustrated: Prices at Auction. Robert Block
Contemporary Marbles & Related Art Glass. Mark P. Block
Antique Glass Swirl Marbles. Stanley A. Block
Marbles Identification and Price Guide. Robert Block
Antique Glass End of Day Marbles. Stanley A. Block
Marble Collectors Handbook. Robert S. Block
The Encyclopedia of Modern Marbles, Spheres, and Orbs. Mark P. Block
Sulphide Marbles. Stanley A. Block & M. Edwin Payne
Marble Mania. Stanley Block, in cooperation with The Marble Collectors Society of America

Designed by Mark David Bowyer
Type set in Americana XBd BT / Humanist 521 BT

ISBN: 0-7643-2464-0
Printed in China
1 2 3 4

Published by Schiffer Publishing Ltd.
4880 Lower Valley Road
Atglen, PA 19310
Phone: (610) 593-1777; Fax: (610) 593-2002
E-mail: Info@schifferbooks.com

For the largest selection of fine reference books on this and related subjects, please visit our web site at **www.schifferbooks.com**
We are always looking for people to write books on new and related subjects. If you have an idea for a book please contact us at the above address.

This book may be purchased from the publisher.
Include $3.95 for shipping.
Please try your bookstore first.
You may write for a free catalog.

In Europe, Schiffer books are distributed by
Bushwood Books
6 Marksbury Ave.
Kew Gardens
Surrey TW9 4JF England
Phone: 44 (0) 20 8392-8585; Fax: 44 (0) 20 8392-9876
E-mail: info@bushwoodbooks.co.uk
Website: www.bushwoodbooks.co.uk
Free postage in the U.K., Europe; air mail at cost.

Contents

Preface

An abundant supply of inexpensive natural gas led to the development of a number of glass related industries throughout West Virginia at the start of the twentieth century. This included machine-made marbles.

Of the twenty-one marble-making facilities in the U.S. in the early 1950s, fifteen were in West Virginia, and of these eight were in Ritchie County, West Virginia.

Susie Metzler, Michael Johnson, and Dean Six have spent countless hours researching and assembling what will prove to be the definitive history of the machine-made marble industry.

I have had the good fortune to be associated, through my late father, O.G. Hanlon, with two of these marble factories here in Ritchie County, West Virginia (the Heaton Agate Company and the Cairo Novelty Company), and as a teenager—having worked at the latter as a grader, packer, and marble machine operator. On behalf of everyone who over the years has been burned by a hot marble, gotten cut by a broken piece of glass, had their eyebrows singed from a molten tank of glass, all while working in a marble factory, we thank the authors for telling our story.

David Hanlon
Harrisville, West Virginia
Spring 2005

Some of our neighbors from whom we learned our marble history and who were there in the days when it was happening. Left to right: Wilson Davis of Davis Marble, Mary Jane Wilson of Playrite, and David Hanlon of Cairo Novelty. Photo taken May 1999 at the West Virginia Marble Festival, Cairo, West Virginia.

Notes of Appreciation

The authors wish to thank the following individuals who gave of their time, energy, and expertise to make this project possible. If there is anyone out there who feels his or her name has been omitted, we sincerely apologize and hope the scope and length of this project will excuse our oversight. Please let us know if your name does not appear but you contributed to this project. To everyone who shared, we express our humble gratitude and sincere thanks.

Jim Arnold, Dwight Masters, Alan Basinet, Pete McMillan, David Chamberlain, The National Marble Museum, Bert Cohcn, Al Rasmus, Chris Cooper, Wayne Rogers, Jim Davis, Steve Sauer, Phil Dirkx, Paula Shepherd, Tom DeRochie, Ron Shepherd, Jack Hahn, George Sourlis, Mary Jacobs, Hansel de Sousa, Jolyon Johnson, David Tamulevich, Miranda Johnson, Susan Johnson, the late Dennis Webb, Jim King, Marjorie Webb, Colleen Kobata, Beverly Young, Neila and Tom Bredehoft, and Andrea Davis Marcinko. For special help with photography we wish to thank Jeremy Thompson.

The following individuals provided specific information for these marble companies:

Akro Agate
"Clarksburg Crow," Chris Cooper, Richard Fauss, Claudia Hardy, Roger Hardy, David Houchin, Cledith Merritt, Nina Merritt, Becky Miller, Don Miller, Bill Oliverio, Julie Nemis Oliverio, Pete Oliverio, Betty Freeman Reed, George Sourlis, Hansel de Sousa, George Williams.

Alley Agate
Sue Adcock, Frank Sellers, Betty Bills, Ruby Sellers, the late O. O. Brown, David Tamulevich, Farris A. Campbell, Jim Davis, Robert J. Dunbar, Paul Essof, Mark Feldmeier, Mary Hazelbaker, Walter S. Carpenter, Greg Melmicj, Jim King, Dr. Peterson, Rick Rine, Rick See, Chester Bills, Paula Shepherd, Jesse Brown, and Ron Shepherd.

Alox Manufacturing Co.
Marilyn Barrett, Ray Collison, Morgan Duckworth, Dotty Frier, Jack Frier, Jr., Terry Bloodworth.

Cairo Novelty Co.
David Tamulevich, Arthur Byrd, Sherry L. Byrd, Eva Jo Six, David Hanlon, June McGinnis, and Ralph Kester Six.

Champion Agate
Dave McCullough, Brian Estapp, Robert S. Michels, Dave Gardner, Al Rasmus, Hansel de Sousa, John Shackleford, Dale Simmons, Charles Stutsman, David Tamulevich, and Jim Davis.

Christensen Agate
Brian Estapp, Dave Gardner, and Hansel de Sousa.

Davis Marble Works
Marge Davis, Wilson Davis, Greg Helmick, Rick Rine, Paula Shepherd, and Ron Shepherd.

Heaton/Bogard
Jack Bogard, David Hanlon, Dave McCullough, June McGinnis, Robert Paugh, Al Rasmus, Eva Jo Six, Joanne Argabrite, Ralph Kester Six, Hansel de Sousa, and David Tamulevich.

JABO, Inc.
Joanne Argabrite, Jack Bogard, Eugene Brown, David Chamberlain, Jo Drain, Dave McCullough, Marlow Peterson, and David Tamulevich.

Jackson Marble Co.
Jim Davis, Greg Helmick, Gladys Jackson, Lehman Jackson, Norman Jackson, Rick Rine, Paula Shepherd, and Ron Shepherd.

Kokomo Opalescent Glass Co.
Ken Humphrey, Mark Reidelsperger, Hansel de Sousa, David Tamulevich, Dan Waber, and Gail Bardham of the Corning Rakow Library.

Marble King
The late Jean Howdyshell, Betty Bills, Chester Bills, Walter S. Carpenter, Blair Core, Robert Enoch, Beri Howdyshell Fox, John Lilly, Dwight M. Masters, Robert S. "Coon" Pryor, and Al Rasmus.

Master Glass
John R. Barnes, J. Fred Early, "Freeman," Hansel de Sousa, Barbara Nichols, and Bob Nichols.

Master Marble
Lawrence Cottrill, J. Fred Early, and Dave Reep.

M.F. Christensen
Michael Cohill, Brian Graham, Ed Schubert, and Hansel de Sousa.

Mid-Atlantic Glass
Connie Dale, Mike Hall, and Lewis L. Moore.

Peltier Glass
Alan Basinet, Gino Biffany, Al Rasmus, Ed Schubert, and David Tamulevich.

Playrite Marble Co.
Mary Jane Wilson, Jim Davis, Paula Shepherd, Ron Shepherd, and Sue Wilson.

Ravenswood
David Chamberlain, Chris Cooper, Charles Cox, Betty J. Fourney, Bo Hartley, Bobby J. King, Virginia King, Greg Matics, Faye Safreed Milhoan, Lori Metzler, National Marble Museum, Al Rasmus, Harry Ring, Paula Shepherd, Ron Shepherd, David Tamulevich, Rae Cox Weekley, and Roger Weekley.

Vacor de Mexico
David Chamberlain, Ron Garcia, Monica Garcia Ortega, Chelly Schmidt, and Yuriko Sutto.

Vitro Agate
William Bavin, Dave McCullough, Ron Shepherd, Eugene Brown, Becky Miller, Dale Simmons, Floyd Brown, Don Miller, George Sourlis, Chris Cooper, the late Lewis L. Moore, Hansel de Sousa, Robert Dailey, Opal Moore, Charles Stutsman, Raelyn Dolton, National Marble Museum, David Tamulevich, Robert Enoch, Brenda Lemon Payne, William Tescher, House of Marbles (England), Patty Roberts Pfalzgraff, Gary Traugh, Norman Jackson, Carmen Queen, Genie Wald, Blaine Lemon, Al Rasmus, Rolf Wald, Dustin Luckhurst, and Paula Shepherd.

Introduction and General Notes

Writing history is always challenging. Finding, sorting, determining the significance, weaving it into a pattern or story, all take immeasurable amounts of time and energy. Yet with marble history it has proven even more difficult.

Industry stories are often crafted using trade journal mentions, company catalogs, and the records left in courthouses and public records of incorporations, land acquisitions and sales, relocations, etc.

However, most marble manufacturers were not corporations but loose partnerships or sole proprietorships. These leave little or no public records. Land was owned by individuals and not in company names. Trade journals about glass largely ignored the small and nearly invisible marble factories. What remains is a mass of oral tradition. Although the American marble industry surely peaked between 1930 and 1955, within the living memory of many who were or whose families were involved, their recollections and memories present additional challenges.

At times what is recalled contradicts the scant written records found in courthouses and written documents. At times two different people recall the same event or circumstance in greatly differing ways. And at times those who have recorded the recollections of others simply failed to grasp the language of glass or marbles, failed to see what was important or the connections that should have evoked further questions. The research of Dennis Webb, a major and important earlier marble author often falls into this category. When Webb listened to and recorded life-long Marble King, Roger Howdyshell, their relative differences in understanding and language are a reminder to all of us that we come from different perspective and bring different levels and types of interest to the subject. Hopefully this book offers something to you, no matter your point of curiosity.

On Pricing

As authors our passions run to discovering new information, working the puzzle pieces of history to make a story, and to sharing. Yet a book for collectors must, to be successful on the market, also include the obligatory "Suggested Price" element. We have struggled with this at length and engaged a host of friends, quizzed strangers, sought advanced collectors, and monitored auctions and the internet sales.

The price suggestions we report here are just that, reports of possible value. Some of the figures represent what a single, actual sample of that item recently attained on the real world marketplace. Some of those real prices stunned us. Interest in nostalgic boxes and bags is at present keen and emerging. However, we have made every effort to report real prices and tried not to suggest what *we* thought the values should be.

Please be advised that the appearance of a single additional object might alter the price of some of the rarest or, with sufficient interest, bring no impact to it at all. That is to say that value can be quick to change, upward or downward, or may remain stable over the long time. No one knows. Our price suggestions are simply that: suggestions. They are not an appraisal, a definitive value, an offer to buy or a suggestion that you can rely on that figure if you sell an item. Our suggestions should not be used as investment advice. Buy what you like, pay what you deem appropriate. Use our suggestions as one reasoned guess in measuring supply and demand, both fickle elements! Whatever you do, enjoy the hobby and buy wisely.

Living Book

The authors of this book participate in a project of the West Virginia Museum of American Glass that allows the authors to post additions, modifications, and the surely rare correction to the manuscript you now hold in your hands. Those additions can be found online at www.allaboutglass.org under the Living Books icon, where books are listed alphabetically by title. Please look there for new and additional information shared over time by the authors.

Background
History, Briefly Noted

Glass spheres or marbles were produced individually and by hand in the earliest manner. By the late 1800s - early 1900s some advances toward mechanization had begun to filter into marble production. One of the earliest companies in this volume, Akro Agate, was using this mixture of hand process and partial mechanization in its early years. This era, called "transitional" at times by collectors, is the cusp of hand-made becoming machine-made processes.

To date relatively little has been written about these hand gathered, and at times machine rolled, marbles or their manufacturers. Research into glass trade journals reveals some interesting tidbits, which are shared here. Thanks are due Neila and Tom Bredehoft for sharing their research discoveries in this matter. We find these accounts, fragmented as they are, intriguing. Enjoy and be intrigued!

"The property of the defunct American Marble Co. at Steubenville, has been appraised at $1,559.98 by David Morrow, James M. Dinsmore and Samuel Irwin. The gas fires which had been kept burning under the pots at the plant since the shut down on December 22, were turned out last week." *China, Glass and Lamps.* 10 January 1901.

"The National Marbles & Specialty Co., of Steubenville, was incorporated with $100,000 capital and organized as follows last Thursday: President, F.N. Lowry, Pittsburgh; vice president J.C. McDowell, Pittsburgh; and Secretary and treasurer E.F. McDowell, Steubenville. The superintendent is J.H. Leighton, the patentee. They will manufacture exclusively imitation onyx and agate marbles, glass balls for furniture and glass bureau knobs which are now imported." *China, Glass and Lamps.* 2 May 1902.

Ed. Note: J.H. Leighton was a member of a most prestigious glass family in the US with connections to Hobbs Brockunier in Wheeling, West Virginia, and the New England Glass Co. J.H. himself participated in no less than three marble factories in Akron, Navarre and Steubenville, Ohio (Bredehoft, Neila and Tom. *Hobbs, Brockunier & Co. Glass.* Collector Books, 1997.)

"The National Marble & Specialty Co. is running right along. This is the only concern in the United States making glass marbles. The process is very novel and is not materially different from making other small articles of glass. The batch is first melted in a large pot furnace and as it is required for use it is transferred to a small working furnace in small quantities. It is then gathered on a small iron pipe in the old way and is taken in hand [not literally-ed.] by a man with a pair of pincers with which he clutches the molten glass and by pressing the pincers and revolving the rod he shapes the marble, detaches it at the same time and drops it into a pan of sand. The finisher now picks it up with a pair of pincers and holds the rough side, where it was detached from the rod, against a blow flame for a few moments until the spur is softened and then presses it with a small flat steel disc, which makes it perfectly smooth. He then drops it into an iron trough four or five feet long which carries it by gravity into a small cylindrical lehr, where it is thoroughly annealed."

"The marbles are assorted and put in packages and are ready for the market. The package contains 12, 25, 50 and 100 marbles according to size. The marbles are so hard that they can be driven through (a) inch pine board with a hammer without breaking. They turn out from 25,000 to 50,000 a day and the entire output is taken by two firms. The company propose to extend their business and have already begun the manufacturer of glass furniture knobs, fine toy sets and novelties..."

"Mr. E. F. McDowell (is) secretary and treasurer of the National Marble Works & Specialty Co." *China, Glass and Lamps.* 2 November 1901.

"Glass Marble Plant Burned. The manufacture of glass marbles in the United States has never proved a very profitable enterprise, various attempts to operate a marble factory having proved unsatisfactory. Recently the Barberton Glass Novelty and Specialty Co., at Barberton, O., has been engaged in the manufacturing of marbles, but an end was put to its operation a few weeks ago, when the factory was burned, entailing a loss estimated at $4,700. The plant was owned and operated by George N. Smith, Louis Zgorski and William Warner. The factory was insured for $1,800." *China, Glass and Lamps.* 16 May 1906.

Jumping forward to the far other end of the American marble story is the demise of twentieth century, mid-century expansion. Problems plagued the American marble industry even before a crisis developed over the question of protective tariffs and before cheap imported Japanese marbles.

An early threshold for the industry was issues of patent infringement. These plagued the emerging marble companies after World War II and complex, costly legal battles ensued. Additionally the concentration of newer factories, centered in Ritchie County, West Virginia, came up against the larger, established factories in a market battle they could not possibly hope to win. The new, small firms lacked resources, marketing savvy, trade contacts, and experience generally. Obtaining a decent marble machine, either newly made or used, was an impossible task for some. Acquiring cullet and scrap glass became almost as difficult.

Ritchie County, West Virginia, became a microcosm of the problem. By mid-1947, the price for finished marbles had already begun to fall, and, conversely, the cost for much-needed glass had risen sharply. Nevertheless, even in the face of seemingly insurmountable obstacles, the new companies in the county, Jackson, Playrite, Heaton, Davis, and Cairo Novelty, flooded an already saturated market with their production and prices dropped even further.

Compounding the issue, marble jobbers had contracts and pressured buyers not to buy, except from established manufacturers. As a result, the jobbers maintained their commissions and used their contacts in the trade to preserve sales by the old companies. During this period of turmoil, the West Virginia marble concerns held several meetings to discuss production, price, and market shares. All the newer manufacturers were represented and most of the older ones participated. According to several eyewitness accounts, neither meeting, the one in Parkersburg nor the one held in Clarksburg, accomplished anything. Chaos and bitterness are words that have been used to describe the proceedings. Certainly, the older companies, with their ninety percent share of the market had little to gain from any negotiations and much to lose.

Several of the small companies survived, for a while at least. Playrite, Cairo Novelty, and Heaton Agate (the most successful) all found buyers for their output. For Jackson and Davis, making marbles, ironically, was the easiest part. The trouble came in trying to sell them.

Everyone, it seemed, who bought marbles already had a maker under contract. In the face of this, the owners of the Davis Marble Works decided to quit – even after wholesaling their marbles to a company who sent them to Puerto Rico. Perhaps Wilson Davis expressed it best, "It was a bitter pill; we did not want to quit. The Davis Marble Works was a victim of capitalism at its ugliest. We tried, but the deck was just stacked against us."

THE AKRO AGATE COMPANY

Akron, Ohio
1910 - 1914
Clarksburg, West Virginia
1914 - 1951

Akro Agate, a variety of colors and designs.
D. Chamberlain photo.

Akro Agate selection from over time. *D. Chamberlain photo.*

Akro Agate moss agates. *D. Chamberlain photo.*

The Akro Agate Company started business in 1910, when George T. Rankin (President 1910, and died 1931) and Gilbert T. Rankin (Vice President 1910 and later President, died at age 72 on June 22, 1949), joined up with Horace C. Hill, late absconder from the M.F. Christensen Company, whose ideas, glass formulas, funds, and customer lists accompanied him into the new venture. They set up their marble retailing business in the attic above the Wagner-Marsh Shoe Store at 72 S. Main Street, Akron, Ohio. Urban renewal has since claimed the building.

Their first marbles were, ironically, purchased from M.F. Christensen and packaged for sale under the new Akro Agate logo and motto, which forever revolutionized the marketing aspect of marbles. The Christensen marbles were purchased for $3.00 per thousand, packed five to a tube, and sold for 8 cents retail. Until that time, marbles had been sold in bulk or individually in five and dime stores and hardware stores. No marble company until Akro Agate had established such a logo or had a recognized name.

In later years, Gilbert Marsh talked about how he and Dr. Rankin had built their own marble machinery and had it installed in the attic of his shoe store and how they would pack marbles until one or two in the morning.

There has been much misinformation written about Akro Agate and some of the unresolved facts may yet lie somewhere in written records. It is hard to conceive of Rankin and Marsh, successful and wealthy as they were, performing the common labor of filling bags of marbles at all hours in the attic! Such stories are repeated over time and, taking on a life of their own, become a part of the myth. More than likely it was employees in the attic in the wee hours, but we cannot know now,

nearly a century later. It is inconceivable that they actually produced hot glass marbles in such a place because of fire and other hazards. Possibly Mr. Marsh was referring to machines to make packaging materials for purchased marbles and that is reasonable, but not what has become the repeated legend.

Their logo, which they adopted in 1911, was a crow flying through a large letter A holding a marble in its beak and a marble in each claw. Their slogan, "Shoot straight as A-kro flies" appeared on many of their marble containers. Around 1912, Akro Agate moved to larger quarters in a machine shop on East Exchange Street in Akron. Only a handful of Akro packages made for them while in Akron are known to exist.

Akro mailing packet with logo and Akro, Ohio, address. *H. De Sousa collection.*

Akro Agate entry in the Clarksburg Polk City Directory for 1915.

AKRO AGATE COMPANY THE. Horace C Hill General Manager, Manufacturers of Toy Marbles, Caster Balls and Glass Balls for Lithographers use, Office and Factory Aluminum siding, B & O R R nr S Chestnut, Bell Phone 1217.

Deciding to make their own marbles, Akro sent advance man Horace Hill to West Virginia to secure a suitable location. They required an area where the chief raw materials for marbles (sand and natural gas) were cheap and plentiful. The company found an ideal location, an existing glass plant at the west end of Harvey Street (actually One Dane Street), Clarksburg, West Virginia. The incorporation date in West Virginia was October 1, 1914.

Commercial production began in late 1914, and by July 1915, the company was selling sets of five of its own marbles in red, white, and blue cardboard boxes bearing the Akro trademark. These first Akro marbles were slag-type with white striping throughout. The exact design of the striping was determined by the hand motions of the gathering boy. Gathering boys who fed the molten glass into the machines were actually adult men who were paid by piecework, per thousand marbles created.

It is interesting to note, however, that in 1918 Akro Agate was still purchasing finished leftover marbles from their old rival, M.F. Christensen, which had recently gone out of business, production having ceased in 1917. According to information in Michael Cohill's book on the M.F. Christensen Company, "The last order for toy marbles came from the Akro Agate Company. They purchased the entire remaining inventory of toy marbles which was worth $689.00."

Horace C. Hill, who had stolen so much from his former employer, M.F. Christensen, was not even moderately clever with machines and his plans for a new generation marble machine were perhaps also purloined from M.F. Christensen. He applied for a patent on a hand-fed semi-automatic machine for Akro Agate in 1912, but it was rejected by the U.S. Patent Office in February 1914, because it was not significantly different from the 1905 Christensen patent. He submitted a slightly different design that was granted a patent in December 1915 as Patent 1,164,718.

The story of Horace C. Hill and his legal problems with M.F. Christensen is more completely covered in Michael Cohill's book titled *M.F. Christensen and the Perfect Glass Ball Machine*, but the short of it was that Hill confessed his crimes and Marsh and Rankin paid restitution to Mr. Christensen and arranged that Hill did no "hard time" in an Ohio prison. As Cohill reports on page 47 of his book, "Hill was never to see a profit for his acts…. A year to the day that he was put on trial for these acts, he died of chronic Bright's disease, March 31, 1916. He was 36 years old, and Akro Agate Company had yet to make a profit."

In the following reorganization of the company, a sound core of workers and executives were assembled to meet the increasing demand for their marbles. Claude C. Grimmett was hired as Assistant Secretary of Akro in 1916 and later served as chief accounting officer. In 1926 he was promoted to general manager. George A. Pflueger became a stockholder and secretary in 1916. His marketing and promotional skills were significant to the growth of Akro in the early years.

Arnold Fiedler, a German-born and educated glass chemist, was employed until 1926. His formulas for glass color became the standard for the industry. Fiedler used the traditional glassmaker's tricks, like placing potatoes in the hot glass batch to solve the problem of "seedy" glass (air bubbles). Later Fiedler worked for Christensen Agate and the Cambridge Glass Company.

Probably the most significant hire of all was the 1919 employment of John F. Early as plant superintendent. This proved to be a positive turning point for Akro. Early's highest priority was to expand the factory and improve the production capacity of Hill's machines. J. Fred Early was interviewed by marble author Dennis Webb on June 16, 1984. From that interview we were told that when Akro Agate first moved to Clarksburg, they purchased natural gas at 3 cents per 1000 cubic feet. That was one of the significant reasons Akro had moved into the area.

John F. Early was born in Pennsylvania in 1876 on a farm. During WWI he worked as superintendent for Miller Rubber Co. in Akron, Ohio. In January of 1919 Early was hired as General Superintendent of Akro Agate in Clarksburg, West Virginia. At that time Akro had one melting furnace with four melting pots, each holding approximately 500 lbs of glass. There were twelve hand-gathering shops to produce the marbles. In 1923 he entered a ten-year contract to improve the H.C. Hill patent, and increase the production of marbles. By 1925 Early had increased the plant to eighteen hand-gathering shops, expanded the building, and im-

proved the machines to incorporate his first patent. In 1928 he developed the automatic duplex machine for use with the Hartford Empire Feeder. The Empire feeder was a patented design to force the glass (to "feed" it) from the molten tanks into the production machinery.

In 1922 Akro hired Henry Helmers as chemist. Helmers helped develop, among other things, Akro's alabaster glass.

In 1924 a one-cylinder engine powered all of the Hill machines. Early's first major improvement, the offset rollers, were installed, which increased the roundness of marbles. This machinery eliminated cold-roll marks by forcing marbles to change their axis as they came down the rollers. The original concept for this improvement was first put forward by M.F. Christensen.

During the 1920s, Akro sold millions of crystal marbles for use in the grinding of lithographic plates for the printing industry. Millions of ruby red marbles were sold for use in reflectors and in road guardrail posts. These marbles were shipped loose in wooden boxes.

In 1926, John E. Moulton was hired as sales manager. Clinton F. Israel came to Akro as a draftsman July 1, 1926. Israel drew blueprints for John F. Early's machine designs. Israel later took charge of Akro's packing department.

During the period 1926-1928, new machines designed by Early were installed that were significant advances over the earlier Hill models. The need for hand-gathering of glass prior to being placed in the marble shaping machinery was completely eliminated. Each machine was individually motorized. Early applied for a patent on his marble-making machine modifications in March 1926; it was granted as Patent 1,761,623 in June 1930 and assigned to Akro Agate. The outdated Hill machines were sold as scrap to the Osborne Machine Company of Clarksburg, West Virginia.

Included in Early's efforts to create unique marbles was work on a spinner cup mechanism to make the well-known spiral or "corkscrew" – a distinctly recognizable marble still not duplicated by any other company.

Early's second patent, number 1,880,916, was applied for in May 1928 and granted in October 1932. It was an early model of a duplex machine consisting of two sets of rollers arranged adjacent to each other and a dual feeding system that doubled the production of each machine.

In 1928 the Hartford Empire Company began supplying a glass-feeding system to Akro. These feeders contained a clay orifice and clay plunger that regulated the flow of molten glass. The feeder was fluted or channeled, allowing different colors of glass from different melting pots to be combined into a single marble. The different flows of glass were joined and were cut off by mechanical shears.

Akro Agate used a trough made of angle iron about ten to twelve feet long with a two-inch decline that transported the finished marbles to a heated bucket called a lehr, where they continued their gradual cooling. This bulky and space-wasting system was replaced when Early developed a conveyer screw to allow the marbles to cool down more slowly and save space in the work area.

In the marble grading and sorting system used at Akro, the finished marbles rolled by gravity over a wooden table while the defectives (that did not roll smoothly or had apparent visual defects) were removed by hand by girls employed for that purpose. This system was not dramatically different from what other marble companies would use for decades.

Between 1928 and 1930 Early had developed the adapter (commonly called the spinner cup) for use on the duplex machines. Between 1923 and 1930, there were many changes in management at the Akro Agate Company, as they were now making huge profits. In Early's contract, twenty percent of the company treasury stock was to be transferred to him. However, this stock was instead transferred to a new stockholder. On March 15, 1930, John F. Early mailed a letter of resignation to the Akro Agate Company. It was accepted and his employment was terminated on May 1, 1930.

In 1929, Akro Agate hired Willie Wetterau as plant manager. Personnel problems developed within the company, which led to the loss of key positions and resulted in the formation of Master Marble Company in Anmoore, West Virginia. The resignations of Early, Grimmett, and Moulton were effective May 1, 1930, and Israel resigned June 1, 1930.

Wetterau was Akro manager only until 1930. A U.S. District Court trial transcript from 1937 showing a decision in favor of Master Marble against Akro includes testimony blaming Werrerau's management tactics as a major factor in the resignations of John F. Early, Claude C. Grimmett, John E. Moulton, and Clinton F. Israel.

These four men were the driving force behind the Master Marble Company, a major power in marble manufacture in the 1930s. Clinton F. Israel later on used the assets of Master Marble to found the Master Glass Company in Bridgeport, West Virginia (see those chapters for more).

During the 1930s and 1940s Akro Agate felt the effects of fierce competition and turned to other lines of production to help boost income. Their first non-marble venture was the manufacture of large square ashtrays. Around 1932 Akro produced the first line of glass children's tea sets. Throughout the 1940s, Akro produced a wide range of glass general line items as may be seen in the book by Akro experts Roger and Claudia Hardy.

The 1941 W.P.A. Writer's Project on West Virginia describes Akro Agate thus. "Located at the west end of Harvey St., in a low, rambling building, on the bank of the West Fork River, out-of-state adults may apply at front office for admission." The interesting restriction for tours to "our-of-state adults" may have reflected a desire to keep their competitors, almost all located in West Virginia, from "spying."

Akro Agate's success as a machine-made marble company is coupled with their general line of glassware and toy dishes that in the later years accounted for an increasing presence in the Akro line. Success required physical plant growth and the sand tower was added to the building in 1946-47 and a large addition at the same time added 2,000 square feet.

From Akro authors and experts Roger and Claudia Hardy we also gather these facts: The size of plant was 100' x 1000' and 30% was for marble production. 15% was for general line production. 15% was for children's dishes, and 15% was for packaging. 20% was for storage/warehousing, and a final 5% was for office space. At the time of peak production, Akro had six to seven marble machines in operation. Any of the machines could be converted into a "Spiral" machine simply by adding the spinner cup attachment. There were 135 - 145 employees during the peak years. After World War II, unrestricted foreign competition signaled doom for many of the U.S. marble companies, which were already weakened from the seemingly endless price wars and the general decline in the interest in playing marbles. There was only one marble machine operating in 1948.

By 1949, Akro Agate was struggling. The original ownership was gone and no sound new direction for the company seems to have been formulated. They survived by selling off the remaining stock.

There seems to be some disagreement as to when all production ceased. A final sale took place on Tuesday, April 24, 1951, with Hetz Auction Sales of Warren, Ohio, conducting the auction. Edmund Burroughs was the last president and treasurer of Akro Agate.

It should be noted that the building was in use for about six months in 1951 by former Akro employees, headed by Robert Dean, making a few general line items. It is believed that no marbles were produced at this time. This temporary use of the building and business was known as the Clarksburg Glass Company.

It has been widely told in marble circles for years that Berry Pink of Marble King bought all the Akro Agate marble machines except one after the 1951 closure and that Heaton Agate bought the other. The comment by Roger and Claudia Hardy is simple: "We don't agree. Most were sold as scrap iron. Stories abound as to what really happened to them." Also, in an interview with Dennis Webb, the late Roger Howdyshell of Marble King stated that Marble King did in fact contract to buy the machines, but the sale was never transacted and the machine never came to Marble King.

Clinton F. Israel of Master Glass Company in neighboring Bridgeport, West Virginia, purchased at the auction many Akro items and the rights to the company logo, accounts, business records, and much else – the majority of which over the years has found it's way into private collections.

It has also been reported that Master Glass used Akro boxes for their own marbles and actually had Akro boxes made up in which they placed both leftover Akro marbles in with Master Glass marbles. Roger Hardy's comment is "We haven't seen a Master Glass box with Akro marbles. However, we have a box that says, "Chinese Akro Agate Checkers – manufactured by Master Glass Co., Clarksburg, W. Va., U.S.A.'.'"

A legal entity named "Akro Agate Incorporated" was chartered September 20, 1955, four years after the original company by this name had ceased to produce. This second, set up to manufacture glass products, was 90% controlled by Clinton F. Israel, once with the original Akro and by this time owner of the Master Glass Company. Five percent of the new company stock was owned each by Walter Schrader and long-time Master employee, M. P. (Pauline) Dennison. The terms of the incorporation papers declare the intent to conduct a glass business but there is no proof that any business was ever conducted or glass ever made. Roger Hardy, the author and expert on the subject of Akro Agate, has stated that during the time in question, the Akro Agate site was owned by Sutter Roofing Company and has no recollection of any marble or other glass-making activity at the Harvey Street site. It appears this was a paper company only, being a dream that never came to fruition. The company was dissolved May 13, 1957.

The actual Clarksburg West Virginia, site for Akro Agate at 1 Dane Street underwent the following ownership transfers. Prior to 1914 it was the home to an auto lens company. Akro owned the site from 1914 - 1951 when it was acquired by Clarksburg Glass Co. for a short six months. In 1952 and until 1960 the site was home to Sutter Roofing Company. In 1961 and until 1971 the site belonged to a local private individual. In 1972 and to the time of this writing the property is owned by the City of Clarksburg and has been operated by the Street Department as a garage and Public Works Center.

In 1997 the City of Clarksburg accepted bids to demolish the Akro Agate factory for scrap. City Engineer, George Duffer, reported that demolition of the building began on September 15, 1997, and that the sand tower would remain standing on the site. (*Clarksburg Telegram*, March 9, 1997)

In recent years, especially after the main building at Akro Agate was demolished, there has been much illegal digging at or around the plant site. A large section of the cement floor has been pried up. It has been estimated that several million marbles have been excavated. Some of these have been offered for sale at marble shows and on the internet as being from "experimental" runs. It is more likely that these recovered marbles were disposed of as rejects in the first place and never intended for circulation. It causes some concern that these were gathered illegally and against specific warning from the property owners. The dug Akro marbles have been observed given special names and inflated value by collectors and dealers who may have a particular personal interest in marketing them. This is a terrible disservice to the marble hobby and to history.

Finally, as with all the hundreds of millions of marbles made over the years at the various factories, Akro Agate produced many nondescript marbles, unknown and never positively identified, virtually indistinguishable from similar marbles made by other factories. The authors have been asked by several advanced collectors if it is possible to determine approximately when each type of Akro marble was first put into production. That is a difficult task for the simple reason that neither this company, nor any other company for that matter, kept accurate production records that now, many years later, are available to researchers. With that in mind, only an approximation can be made as to when certain marble types were made available for purchase. It is well known that Akro's first marbles were purchased striped onyx or slag-types from the M.F. Christensen Company and that Akro's first company-made marbles were almost identical, including the point that both companies production was then being hand-gathered.

A Thought on Urban Archaeology and Akro

When the majority of the Akro Agate building was demolished in 1997, it was hoped at that time that any recovery of artifacts from the site – if permitted by the proper authorities – would be done in some semblance of a methodological or scientific manner. That was not to be the case and much knowledge was lost. It was known or suspected by a few that when additions were made to the plant at various times, that discarded marbles were used as filler under the sections of the concrete slab. Therefore, using the approximate dates of plant additions, it could have been determined with some approximation what marbles were being produced about that time. As it turned out, a massive free-for-all ensued and illegal pillaging with reckless abandon followed. With this reality, an accurate study of the site becomes impossible and needed Akro documentation has been lost forever. An advanced collector and Akro enthusiast recently reviewed several hundred pounds of Akro diggings from the site. The question arose why little to nothing of all that was viewed is to be found in the original packaging of the company. We deemed this a good and logical question. The answer comes from former employees of all the old marble factories. The marble machines were running twenty-four hours a day – seven days a week – unless it was downtime. The workers threw all kinds of glass into the mix – whatever was available and anything or nothing could come of it. Millions of really awful or uninspired marbles, or simply random and accidental marbles were the result. Some beautiful marbles too came from this practice of unbridled production. Many of these were simply tossed out into the dump, into the parking lot, into the yard, and not recycled or marketed. At Akro they were destined to the possibility of being landfill the next time the plant was expanded. Marbles, made quickly and inexpensively, were at times dealt with as a disposable commodity at the factory site. This was particularly true of slightly imperfect marbles or ones of dubious coloration.

Akro Agate Marbles Produced

The Akro Agate Company throughout the late 19-teens and through most of the 1920s reigned supreme in the marble world with little competition. During these years no other company produced a comparable quantity, quality, or variety of toy glass marbles.

We list many Akro sizes based on the data given by the company as advertised, however, many in-between sizes or irregular sizes do exist. The same is true for colors.

Carnelians and Cornelians: These marbles are rarely found in general circulation but were originally packaged in beautiful boxes and labeled as such. Carnelians were manufactured in sizes 0, 1, and 2 and are marbles with translucent orange, white, and oxblood in a random pattern. Cornelians are a dark red, almost oxblood color that is opaque.

Glassies: The Akro company name for their clear or transparent marbles. These marbles were produced in 00, 0, 1, 2, and 4 sizes and in the following known colors: clear, light blue, green, amber, and red. These marbles are best identified from their original packaging. They are usually free of bubbles as Akro practiced the age-old glass tradition of adding a potato or a piece of pinewood to the molten glass to remove the bubbles from the molten glass batch.

Imperials: Certain Akro company letters show a box of marbles called Imperials and these seem to be rather nondescript. More importantly, Roger Hardy tells that he has learned from former Akro employees that Imperial was not the name of a specific marble, but rather a generic name Akro gave to their fancy marbles. Indeed, there are many original Akro boxes with the word Imperial, but it does not pertain to any particular marble.

Opals: The Akro company name for solid opaque marbles. These were produced in 00, 0, 1, 2, 3, and 4 advertised sizes and in the following colors: red, white, blue, green, yellow, black, although through the years various shades of red, blue, green, and yellow were produced. Many Akro opaques are identifiable by a tiny dot-sized spot of clear at one pole. Original boxes of Akro Chinese Checker marbles give clues to their various colors. The lighter blue is a remarkably beautiful marble. Within the Akro opaque family, the greens, yellows, blues, and reds do come in several different shades. Generally though, as with the Glassies, they are not easy to distinguish from the solid one-color opaques produced by other companies.

Striped Onyx: The name given by Akro to their slag-type marbles was Striped Onyx. These are a transparent-base marble with white striping that can swirl deep into the marble and also appear on or near the surface. They were produced in the following colors – rarest being first: orange, Vaseline (yellow), clear, aqua, red, green, blue, purple, root beer (brown). The red slags were often packaged in special boxes and were called Cardinal Reds. The Akro slags lack the soft feathering of Peltier slags and the recognizable seam that appear on both Peltier and Christensen Agate slags. It should be noted that, like the M.F. Christensen slags, the Akro slags were hand-gathered and examples of the familiar "9" and tail pattern in the white striping have been found at an early factory dump site. Akro striped onyx marbles were produced in the following advertised sizes: 00, 0, 1, 2, 4, 5, and 6.

Spiral: Perhaps the most recognized Akro Agate marble is the so-called corkscrew or barber pole design. The Company name was Spiral, but other names were given such as Ace Agates, Tri-color Agates, Prize Name Agates, and Onyx Agates, depending on glass type. Other names have been given by collectors and dealers to identify specific types. This company-unique marble was the result of work by John F. Early, who designed the spinner cup attachment that combined and twisted the colors before they hit the rollers.

Dave McCullough, marble-maker at JABO, Inc., has suggested that some random swirl marbles from other companies seem to present a corkscrew pattern, but that is because the marble machine's cutting blade was dull and the glass was twisted as it hit the rollers; not a true spiral. True Akro Spirals are known to have opaque, translucent, and transparent base glass and spirals of one, two, three or more colors in a seemingly endless variety of styles and color combinations. Experimentals and hybrids enhance the collectibility and value of this popular marble. It is not uncommon to see advanced collections of this type marble with over 100 different varieties. Some will be fluorescent and many high-prized spirals contain oxblood glass. These marbles come in all the eight regular sizes, although the twenty-eight known orange and blue of a size ranging from 1-1/4" to 1-3/8" were probably experimental as all were found in an Akro dump site and appear to have been too large for the rollers as they are not completely round. Regular production spirals of any size larger than 1" are extremely uncommon.

Spirals of 1/2" or less are extremely uncommon and, despite years of searching, the authors have personally found only one in general circulation. Spirals that generally are two-color opaque were called "Prize Name" by the company and those of three-colors were called "Tri-Color Agates," advertised in sizes 0, 1, 2, 4, and 6 but odd sizes are known. The Spirals of three, four, or even five distinct colors are hard to find, especially the four or five color types that are not blends. For example, a red and green corkscrew that blend into a third color (yellow) does not make it a three-color Special, it remains a two-color Prize Name. There is some lingering controversy in the marble world over this issue, but it is generally accepted as such. True four and five color spirals are very much prized by collectors, especially if the fourth or fifth color is not white or clear. A nice example might be; red, green, blue, brown, yellow. There are many possible combinations of color. All are uncommon and priced accordingly.

There are other types of spirals as well that have company names. The Ace is a milky white base marble with a colored spiral. A truly great Ace would have a second color spiral. These have been advertised as being offered in sizes 0, 1, and 2, but much larger ones are known. Another factory named spiral is the Onyx, which features a transparent base with an opaque white spiral. There is a very pretty spiral with the adopted name of Snake, which is a transparent with the spiral near the surface. A so-called ribbon is also a transparent, but the spiral is usually thicker or more toward the center of the marble. It is sometimes called an auger. A very uncommon example of either of these types might be an Oxblood Snake in a clear glass base. Only a few are known to exist.

Popeye (a type of Spiral): A favorite and easily recognized spiral among collectors is the Tri-Onyx; commonly called a "Popeye." It takes this name because it is associated with the red box that has printed on it a picture of the comic character, Popeye. This marble may be described as a clear base with white filaments floating in it plus two other colors. More colors in the Tri-Onyx, such as oxblood, pink, or any other color would be considered a hybrid. These marbles are usually found in sizes 0, 1, and 2. A few have been found that are a bit larger, but these would be very scarce. The Tri-Onyx, a truly beautiful marble, having been described by some as "the perfect machine-made marble," may have only a small area of clear with many white filaments to being very clear with only a few wispy white filaments. The most common to least common color combinations are: red/yellow, green/yellow, red/green, dark purple/

yellow, dark blue/red, red/orange, black/yellow. Often the yellow in "Popeyes" is fluorescent.

Yet another level is a variation of the "Popeye" is called the "Popeye Patch." It is a marble with the Tri-Onyx color combinations but that does not spiral. The spinner cup attachment was not in use when these marbles were made. A few years ago, these were considered rare and enjoyed a brief and expensive popularity. Now they are known to be more common and both popularity and value have fallen.

Ade (a type of Spirals): A very collectible type of spiral is popularly known as an "Ade." They have a translucent milky white base and the spiral will be opaque to translucent in the following colors: yellow, "lemonade," green "limeade," and "Cherryades." "Orangeades" are also found. Sometimes the yellow and green "ades" will also have a spiral of oxblood glass. Oxblood on the other "Ades" is less common and this color appears more often on the lemon than on the lime.

Oxbloods: It should be said that almost any marble containing oxblood colored glass has an inflated value. It was once thought by many that Akro Agate was the only company to use this color. That has been found not to be the case. Other Akro marbles featuring oxblood glass will include those spirals with clear-glass base, oxblood on a milky white base (Milky Oxblood), oxblood on translucent wispy white (Silver Oxblood), and oxblood on an opaque brown base (Chocolate Oxblood). Oxbloods on a milky translucent white base with yellow are "Egg yolk Oxbloods." Collector fascination with assigning names seems to be endless.

Blue or black spirals on a white opaque base with a shadowing of oxblood underneath are called "Bluebloods." These combinations of colors will also appear on patch marbles as well as in random pattern swirls.

Swirls: Random-pattern swirl marbles from Akro Agate rarely have more than two or three colors and, unless trademarked with the recognized brilliant Akro colors, are difficult to distinguish from the swirls made by other companies. It is thought by some that swirls, quite often white based, were produced during the later years of the company.

Patches: Beyond the "Popeye Patch," Akro also produced many other two and three color patch marbles. Many patch marbles have the same color combinations as the spirals but were made without the presence of the spinner cup attachment.

Royal is yet another Akro patch type. This is a two-color patch that is featured in company literature from at least the 1930s. They are found in sizes 00, 0, 1, 2, 4, 5, and 6, and are in the following color combinations: black/white, red/yellow, blue/white, black/yellow, red/white. Other color combinations exist that are factory diggings: blue/yellow, green/white, yellow/white. Collectors call red/yellow Royals "Pumpkins." Another factory-named patch is the "Unique". It is boxed the same as the "Tri-color Agate." These are actually identical marbles that are three color patch marbles although an extra color or two and sometimes a blend may be found, especially in the larger sizes.

Uniques are also found as patch marbles with an opaque white base with a kind of burnt orange or brown-brushed patch covering less than half the marble. The company named "Hero" marble is of the same type, though variable in color, but has little or no white.

Collectors have given certain patch varieties of "Uniques" and "Hero's" bird names such as "grebe" or "brown thrasher" and others, but these are not original with the factory. Uniques, Heroes, and Tri-color Patches are thought by Roger Hardy to be late-production items, probably from the 1940s.

Moss Agate (a type of patch): Moss Agates were produced by many of the marble companies, including Akro Agate, whose literature states that these marbles with a milky base and colored translucent patch covering about half the marble were produced in sizes 00, 0, 1, 2, 4, and 6. Some Akro varieties have the milky base in a color other than milky white.

An Akro marble known as a Hy-Grade usually has a blue, brown, green, or clear base glass with a patch of brushed or wispy opaque white covering about 1/3 to 1/2 of the marble. Master Marble and Master Glass, also of Harrison County and controlled by ex-Akro employees, produced pretty much the same marble. Akro expert Roger Hardy says they are virtually indistinguishable by company.

There remains controversy surrounding a patch marble known as a "Helmet Patch." Often described as looking like a football helmet –

thus the name given by collectors – it has a transparent base, usually clear, with an opaque colored patch covering about half the marble with a colored stripe in the middle of the patch. Marbles matching this description have also been found at the Vitro Agate factory sites in both Vienna and Parkersburg, West Virginia.

Sparkler: Some have deemed Akro sparklers among the most beautiful marbles of the mid-machine-made era. It was Akro's peer to a cat's eye marble even before cat's eyes were made. In the Sparkler are threads of colored glass that were injected into a clear glass base. According to marble expert, Rolf Wald, the Sparkler must have at least five different colors of filaments to be ranked as a true Sparkler. Examples with six colors are known. There was a similar marble produced by Master Marble called a Sunburst, but it is much more opaque, duller in color, and usually has no more than three or four colors in fall-of-the-year tones. Generally Sparklers are seen in various color combinations of red, white, blue, orange, green, yellow. Occasionally filaments of pink, purple, brown, and black are seen. These internal filaments form bright bands of color and are sometimes close to the center of the marble and sometimes close to the surface. Sparklers were advertised as being available in sizes 0, 1, and 2.

Moonies: Akro Agate made several types of marbles known as "Moonies." One type is a translucent white, opalescent glass that seems to glow as an orange color when held up to a light. Other types of Moonies are called "Flinties" and come in colors of blue, green, yellow, and red. The red ones were given the factory name "Fire Opals." Many of the Akro opalescent marbles have a small clear spot surrounded by the main color.

Ringer: Collector and authority George Sourlis relates that Vitro Agate made a marble called a Ringer but Akro Agate never did. Castle and Peterson coined the term for Akro after they found a bunch of those marbles in a Ringer box. The term was never used by Akro, unless it was used in connection with the game of Ringer or the Ringer boxes made by Akro. It designates no specific type of Akro marble.

Experimental Types: Roger and Claudia Hardy have discovered several marbles at the Akro site during the time of their permitted digging which may be classed as true experimental types: the Akro "Steelie" and the Akro "Metallic Stripe." The Steelie and Metallic Stripe marbles were actually experimental versus accidental creations. The Hardy's learned this from interviewing former company employees. As they were not accepted for mass production, the samples made were reportedly discarded. At times the difference between discarded experiments and discarded mistakes may blur after the many decades. The Steelie is coated in a metallic looking surface chemical treatment that gave the mirrored look of glossy steel. The Metallic Stripe has a translucent white or blue base with a thin metallic strip circling the marble at the equator.

Akro Agate Marble Identification Tips

All About Marbles is described as "A Little Book for Boys" and is in reality an advertisement for Akro Agate Marbles. It was published in 1926 and does contain the rules for marble tournament play, but more importantly it describes the Akro marbles then available. The pictures and text show and describe Striped Onyx, Cornelians, and Cardinal Reds – all attractively packaged.

The Akro Agate Jobber's Confidential Wholesale Price List for July 1929 shows the following marbles being available: Striped Onyx Agates, Cardinal Reds, Akro Moonies, Akro Imperials, and Akro Flinties.

The marble-naming contest that resulted in the naming of the new Akro "Prize Name" spiral is from a May 1930 dealer flyer. The implication here is that the spinner cup attachment modification engineered by John F. Early must have been in use shortly before that. This seems significant in dating the most recognizable of all Akro marbles. Interestingly too, from a historical standpoint – this timeframe approximates almost exactly when Mr. Early left Akro to help found the Master Marble Company.

An Akro advertisement from 1931 announces that "The Akro Agate Line is Complete." This ad shows a much expanded offering, which included not only the striped onyx, but also the following new listings: Moss Agates, Ace Agates, Prize Name Agates, Sparklers, Spirals, Glassies, and Special Royals.

Some Akro stock boxes contain instructions, entry forms, and prize lists for various Akro contests. The form for naming of new marbles was one of these paper inserts and is in its own right collectable.

E. Schubert, a marble collector and dealer from Chicago, has reported that "Prize Name" and "Special" boxes have been known to contain "Sparklers" and the factory-named "Tri-Onyx" (Popeye) marbles found in "Ringer" boxes. Other anomalies do exist. As with the Akro children's dish sets, when there was a shortage of some boxes, Akro used what they had available. Several factory packaging workers have stated that oftentimes they put whatever items were available into whatever packaging was available.

Akro Agate Packaging

One of the most prolific of marble packagers was the Akro Agate Company. In fact, this company had the first universally recognized name, logo, and slogan: "Akro Agate", the crow, and "Shoot straight as A-kro flies." Akro used virtually all types of packaging, from cardboard, to tin, to mesh. Akro used limited polyvinyl bags as that company went out of business before poly bags came into general use. A few heavier plastic or poly Akro packages are known to exist.

The earliest Akro packages date from the early years in Akron, Ohio, ending around 1914 when Akro marbles moved to West Virginia. These boxes and sleeves are extremely rare and only a few are known to exist. They contain marbles manufactured by M.F. Christensen. These packages carried the Akro crow logo and were in many cases coffin type boxes. The sleeves held five onyx-type slags and sold five for eight cents. See the images.

A wider range of packaging was added after the move to West Virginia in 1914 and the earliest ones are uncommon. Stock or display boxes for sale in retail stores became popular and were used throughout the rest of the company history. These very collectible boxes usually held 25, 40, 50, or 100 marbles of standard sizes. They were often stenciled on top with the crow logo and other writing as well as having end-paper labels identifying the marble type, size, and number of marbles. Striped Onyx, Moss Agates, Prize Names, Specials, Opals, Hero's, Uniques, Royals, and Glassies were most often packaged in this manner.

An interesting little tidbit of information comes from advanced collector Hansel de Sousa who brought to our attention the misspelling of the word "onyx" on the Akro "Striped Onyx" boxes. This has been seen on the #2 boxes and possibly others as well. Someone, somewhere spelled the word "onyx" as "oynx!"

Akro's smallest box, and by far one of the most uncommon, is the single marble box that usually held a shooter size Cardinal Red. Chicago World's Fair 1933 gave us these Tiny Akro boxes (one marble). It has been reported that these tiny boxes were handed out when one paid at the gate to attend the fair. Depending on which entrance gate one went through and when, fairgoers got some kind of promotional gift and each item promoted a store or company.

Small boxes and sleeves include the #112, #A-112, #A-16, #20, #32, #44, #64, and #88. Some of the #16 sleeves contain various types of advertising on the bottom.

Marble historian George Sourlis has made a comprehensive study of Akro's smaller boxes. He found that "Akro's sleeve boxes can be categorized in several ways. There is a single width sleeve box like the #16 box, the double width box like the #32, and the one and only triple width box, #64. Some sleeves are numbered and some are not. Akro put numbers on its boxes starting in 1927. Prior to that, the numbers did not appear on these boxes. The #16 and #112 sleeve boxes are examples of long-lived sleeve boxes that cross this date line. Unnumbered boxes usually come with slags (striped onyx). Numbered boxes may come with slags or corkscrews (Prize Names). Sleeve boxes from the 1940s may contain Akro patched marbles – Royals or Tri-colors."

There is a small group of these boxes that we call center-hole sleeve boxes. These boxes contain assorted sizes of marbles, and all are double-width boxes. One is unnumbered and is shown in ads from the early 1920s. The small #112 box has a numbered and unnumbered version. The #88 box and the #A-112 boxes do not appear to have unnumbered versions. Up to this time, only these four boxes have been discovered in this category.

As shown in factory ads, the large center hole was to be blocked by a #2 or #4 size shooter – lest the smaller marbles fall through the hole. This must have been a nightmare for packers.

Fancy boxes of twenty-five marbles, sometimes referred to as presentation boxes, were often labeled as Imperials, Moonies, Flinties, Cardinal Reds, Carnelians, or Cornelians. Striped Onyx marbles as well as the Gropper and Sons Cerise Agates jobber boxes also contained twenty-five marbles.

Uncommon boxes of this approximate size include the cellophane top #15 containing twenty-five striped onyx marbles and a #25 cellophane top containing thirty striped onyx marbles.

Gift boxes include the #125, #230, #250, and #300. These are colorful cardboard boxes and, except for the small #125 box, usually had a picture of children playing marbles. Some #300 boxes have flashy foil lids or Art Deco diamond (strained glass) designs. The #125 box sometimes contained a marble bag. The #230 and #250 contained bags and the #300 box contained either a bag or a kneepad. Several examples have been seen containing both. There is at least one #230 box known with the marble game scene on the lid featuring the central figure of a girl instead of a boy. The #225 box contains a marble bag and an assortment of thirty-eight Akro Agates.

The marble numbers for these boxes are as follows:

#125 contains 25 of size No. 0.
#230 contains 6 of size No.2 and 21 size No.0.
#250 contains 6 of size No.4, 8 of size No.1, and 40 of size No.0.
#300 contains 4 of size No.6, 10 of size No.4, 20 of size No.2, and 60 of size No.0.

As a general rule, older boxes of these types contain fancier marbles and value of the original boxes and contents vary greatly: i.e., a box containing all oxblood marbles would be valued higher than a box with two-color opaque.

Several #300 boxes have been found containing a bag with a V printed on it and with the Morse Code for V as well. Everett Grist suggests that this particular box could have been made around the time of World War II when the Allies used the V sign meaning Victory made famous by Winston Churchill.

Tin gift sets: The lid has a marble game scene and the background color ranges from light to dark blue. Both gift sets contain a marble bag. The #150 bag is often marked with the company name while the large bag in #200 tin is usually not so marked.

Tin Gift box #200 contains 4 No.3, 4 No.2, and 70 No.0 for a total of 78 marbles.
Tin Gift box #150 contains 4 No. 3, 25 No.0 and 5 No.00 or 19/32" and rules for the game of Ringer with a marble total of 34.

Several books on machine-made marbles show a #200 tin with a marble bag with the word "LIBERTY" printed on it. Don Miller reported in the West Virginia Marble Club newsletter of January 2004, that he has researched this particular #200 box with the "LIBERTY" bag. From evidence he has uncovered, it is apparent that these tins were given to boys and girls in the 1930s for selling *LIBERTY* magazine. The printing of "LIBERTY" on the bag and magazine title is the same. The prize catalog shows a #150 tin but the actual prize was the larger #200 tin. It is interesting to note that Akro would custom print advertising on marble bags for their customers upon request – at added cost to the buyer. These special LIBERTY bags may or may not have been imprinted at the Akro Agate factory.

Another Akro box that has achieved some recognition in recent years because of its scarcity is the #123 Ringer box. It has a picture of children playing marbles on the lid and the same picture on the marble bag. The box contains 18 No. 0 Akro marbles. Akro did not make a specific marble called a Ringer.

A great gift box from Akro Agate that has only previously been seen in Hardy's book on Akro Agate is the "O'Boy!" box, which contains a bullet pencil, bow tie or necktie, a handkerchief, and a #16 box of marbles. These are scarce indeed when found complete.

Yet another unusual Akro box is the counter display "Bubble Gum" box. This box contains 100 sticks of gum, 100 No. 0 marbles plus one large shooter. A small printed sign reads: "One stick of gum and one agate 1 cent. Large agate free with last stick purchased."

The well-known "Popeye" boxes are both very rare and highly collectible by both mibophiles and collectors of Popeye memorabilia. These are #116 boxes; one is red and the slightly rarer one is yellow. Both contain pictures of the famous sailor on the lid as well as on the bag and both contain fifteen marbles. The correct styles are: red box: fifteen assorted colors of tri-onyx (commonly called "Popeye") marbles; yellow box: silver oxbloods, lemonade oxbloods, and limeade oxbloods.

Recently several larger size "Popeye" boxes have been found and both are red and one is marked #236 and the bag has a picture of Popeye. The other one is unmarked and has a plain bag. Each box contains 36 tri-onyx marbles.

Chinese checker boxes: Probably the easiest Akro boxes to find, suggesting they were the most often sold in their day, are the 60 count Chinese checker boxes containing ten each of six different colors in size 00 or 9/16". The older boxes in red or tan command a slightly higher price than the white boxes. All the boxes have "Chinese Akro Agate Checkers" written on the lids.

A few different Akro Chinese checker boxes have turned up with 100 count #00 marbles. To avoid repetition of exact colors (from the six basic colors), the blues, greens, and sometimes other colors are used in different shades. All boxes of this type that are known are red.

Two previously unknown Akro Chinese checker boxes have been found. One is tan and looks exactly like the regular Akro Chinese Checkers boxes, but is slightly larger and contains 60 - #0 5/8" opaque marbles in six different colors. The box is only slightly larger and the difference in size almost unnoticeable. This box has T-2102 stamped on one edge. The other box also contains 60 - #0 Chinese checker marbles with the number T-2102 stamped on the edge. However, this lid has the stock box "Shoot Straight as A Kro Flies" circular logo on it.

There are other 100 count or 50 count opaque one-color boxes put out by Akro that contain just one color marble, be it blue, black, green, etc.

Within the last ten years, Roger and Claudia Hardy have found a one-of-a-kind Akro box (#228) that has "Choice of Champions" written on the lid as well as on the marble bag. The box contains: 28 - #0 Akro marbles of several different styles.

Another Akro box seen first in Hardy's first edition Akro book is the 1932 Grand Army of the Republic promotion box, which contains red, white, and blue opals in a shooter size. There exists another unusual Akro marble box that is 4" square and 1-7/8" deep and contains assorted Akro marbles.

Games: Box #40, Click: Retail price 50 cents. This box contains directions for several different games, contains 40 No.1 Prize Name marbles.

Box #41, Kings: Retail price 50 cents. This boxed game is described as "fast and intense", contains directions, and 40 No.0 Akro Agates.

Akro Solitary Checkers: Meant to be played by one person. This handsome box with a Chinese dragon motif on the lid contains a nicely lithographed game board and 25 one-color marbles – one of which is a different color from the other 24.

Mesh Bags exist with both red mesh and yellow mesh and with paper headers that are either red or tan. Marbles of many styles have been found included in these such as Ace, Prize Name, Moss Agates, Brushed Patch, Royal, and Unique. Headers will read "Akro Agates," "Hot Shot," or "Hy-Grade." All Akro mesh bags are hard to find.

Sample boxes and bags are all uncommon to rare. The small sample boxes generally contain 25 assorted Akro Agates in several sizes and types. A cloth sample bag is known to exist with an attached address label.

The large salesman's sample case is a beautiful box and clearly shows, by factory name, various types of Akro Marbles. There are now known to be about twenty of these that have survived. The most well known Akro salesman's sample box is owned by Roger and Claudia Hardy. It was used by Akro's top salesman, Ralph Heatherington. Akro Agate had sales representatives located all over the world and it may be assumed that salesman's sample boxes went with the territory. Two have been located in Mexico, one in New Zealand, two in Australia, one in Hong Kong, two in England. An exact number of these sample cases may never be known and even the discovery of one or two more would not affect the value substantially.

Collector Hansel de Sousa has an original sample box that contains later-year production Akro marbles including, "Tri-colors," "Royals," "Glassies," and "Opals."

Jobber boxes: Gropper and Son of Ottawa, Ill., bought Akro marbles and marketed them in Gropper boxes. No doubt other jobber companies also purchased and privately packaged Akro products that were sold under the jobbers name.

Polk's "Clarksburg City Directory for 1939" Akro Agate Co. Roll Call for 1939. AKRO AGATE Co. Wm. C. McConnell, gnl. Mgr. Toy marbles mfrs. Harvey at B. & O. RR.

Allen, Donald J. (Laborer); Ayers, Jas. R. (Polisher); Bacchus, Jack W. (Operator); Bartlett, Walter (Grader); Beasley, Dennis (Batch Mixer); Bohenski, Josephine (Packer); (See p. 42 Hardy book); Britton, G. B. (Grader); Burnett, Homer (Batch Mixer) (See pp. 6-7 Hardy book); Bush, Milton L. Jr. (Operator); Carson, Lloyd W. (Tankman) (See Box #64 on p. 23 of Hardy book); Coffman, O. E. (Helper); Collins, H. Max (Operator) (See p. 6 Hardy book); Criss, H. L. (Operator); Delaney, Chas. L. (Mold Maker); Delaney, J. H. (Operator); Donnald, Robt. H. (Chemist); Elliott, Dewey C. (Foreman); Gibson, R. E. (Operator); Gregovich, Anna M. (Packer) (See p. 42 Hardy book); Grilli, Isabel (Packer); Gulas, Mary (Packer); Harnish, Douglas H. Jr. (Carry-In); Hester, Blaine H. (Operator); Hester, Hugh (Ware Inspector); Heatherington, Ralph (Sales Manager) (See p. 17 Hardy book); Hedge, Thomas P. (Foreman); Howell, David L. (Mold maker); Hughes, Carl E. (Ware Inspector); Hughes, George D. (Operator); Hughes, John R. (Foreman); Hughes, Ronald L. (Glass worker); James, G. Harold (Tank man); Javo, Stella (Packer) (See p. 42 Hardy book); Jeffries, Paul B. (Bookkeeper); Jurcak, Agnes L. (Packer); Kemp, Guy L. (Purchasing Agent); Kemp, Paul W. (Polisher); LaChapelle, George E. (Grader); Lantz, Howard R. (Operator); MacGregor, Lottie (Stenographer); Malone, Vance E. (Operator); Masters, Susan (Packer); Matheny, Harvey W. (Ware Inspector); McClain, J. Guy (Operator) (See p. 24 Hardy book); McConnell, W. C. (General Manager); McQuay, D. O. (Mold maker); Miller, Martin P. (Glassworker); Morrison, Charles A. (Glassworker); Neutzling, Frank J. (Operator); Nutter, Ira (Watchman); Nutter, R. T. (Glassworker); Nutter, Robert N. (Inspector); Oliverio, Angela A. (Shipping Clerk); Oliverio, Anna V. (Floor woman) (See p. 40 Hardy book); Oliverio, Dominic D. (Foreman); Oliverio, John O. (Shipping Clerk); Oliverio, Peter R. (Shipping Clerk); Oliveto, Philomena (Packer); Oliveto, Rose (Packer); Page, E. W. (Mold Maker); Patterson, Charles E. (Foreman); Patterson, Edward M. (Carry-In); Patterson, L. T. (Shipping Clerk); Patterson, R. W. (Carry-In); Payton, Bernard (Carry-In); Petrigal, Eska (Packer); Phillips, M. E. (Carry-In); Plecker, Adam G. (Packer); Radcliff, Okey F. (Polisher); Reger, D. C. (Carry-In); Russell, Paul (Operator); Russell, Ralph (Carry-In); Smith, Burton D. (Carry-In); Strosnider, George J. (Purchaser); Swisher, Olin (Foreman); Wallace, Harold G. (Operator); White, Emma C. (Packer); Wise, Marlow (Factory Superintendent); Wise, Romeo (Operator); Wittman, George L. (Mold Maker); Zimmer, Charles N. (Foreman).

Also listed are three former AKRO AGATE employees from page 6 of the Hardy book: Early, J. F. (V.P. Master Marble Co.); Grimmett, C. C. (President Master Marble Co.); Israel, Clinton F. (Sec. Tres. Master Marble).

Authors note: We may have overlooked some Akro employees for that year, but there were "hundreds" of people listed as glassworkers with no company listing, and over the many years possibly many hundreds of people worked at Akro Agate – a complete listing may never be known.

"Akro Agate gang" is the inked inscription on this circa 1942 photo of ladies from the factory.

Still photo created from a rare moving picture about West Virginia Industries filmed in 1946. Rarely were cameras of any kind allowed inside Akro Agate. This image of an unidentified operator shows the rollers of the Akro marble machine. *Image made possible by the WV Department of Culture and History.*

Another still photo created from a rare moving picture about West Virginia Industries filmed in 1946. The ladies in the image, sorting marbles, are Julie Nemis Oliverio on the left and Betty Freeman Reed on the right. *Image made possible by the WV Department of Culture and History.*

Akro Agate factory interior at time of demolition. September 1997.

Akro factory site as it appeared April 1999. The broken floor is the result of looters breaking and raising cement floor slabs to access possible shards and marbles covered by expansion construction in decades past. It has been declared unlawful pillage and theft by the sites owners but continues at the time of this writing.

What has become a near icon in the marble world is this fading Akro Agate sand tower with the company name. Photo May 1994.

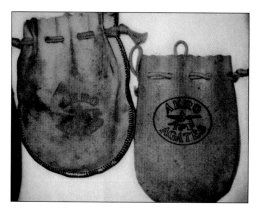

Akro Agate logo marble bags. *Hardy Collection.* Each, $150-200.

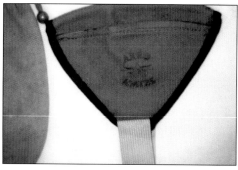

Akro Agate logo kneepad. *Hardy Collection.* $125-150.

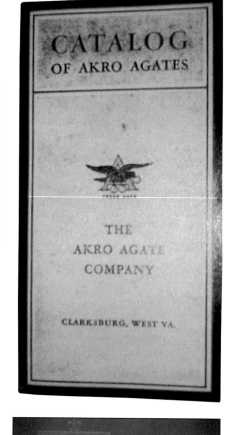

Akro Agate catalog. $200.

Akro Agate store display. *Hardy Collection.* $4,000-5,000.

Akro Agate Kings Game. Cardboard game set; lid and game interior/board. *Hardy Collection.* $1,200-1,400.

Akro Agate Solitary Checkers. Copyright 1937. $50-75.

Akro Agate gift set. Contains bullet pencil, bowtie, and #16 box of Akro Agates. *Hardy collection.* $2,000-2,500.

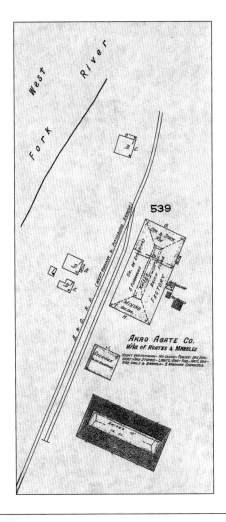

Sanborn Fire Map of Clarksburg, West Virginia, for 1916, showing the factory and site of Akro Agate at that time.

Akro Agate catalog, page two of four.

Akro Agate catalog, page three of four.

Akro Agate catalog, page one of four.

Akro Agate catalog, page four of four.

Early Akro box with Akron, Ohio, address in lid (same box as in early newspaper ad). Marketed by Akro, the box contains M.F. Christensen marbles. *H. de Sousa collection.* Scarce. No value determined.

Early newspaper ad for Akro Marbles from Akron, Ohio. *Courtesy H. De Sousa.* Note the box.

Akro Agate. End of early stock box containing 50 #2 striped onyx. Box undecorated except for end as shown. Note misspelling of onyx. *H. de Sousa collection.*

Akro Agate #16 sleeve with advertising for other business. *H. de Sousa collection.* $150.

Akro Agate sleeve with striped onyx marbles. *H. de Sousa collection.* Scarce. $1,300.

Akro "1915" sleeve showing side of box and contents.

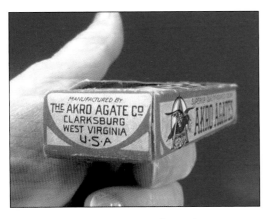

Side and end flap of same Akro Agate sleeve.

Akro Agate No. 32 box containing ten #0 prize name spirals. $150.

Akro Agate #44 sleeve with striped onyx marbles. Scarce. No value determined.

Akro Agate sleeve "copyrighted 1915" containing striped onyx marbles. Possibly the marbles are from M.F. Christensen? The end flap shows a Clarksburg, West Virginia, address suggesting the possibility that these are Akro production from Clarksburg. *H. de Sousa collection.* Scarce. No value determined.

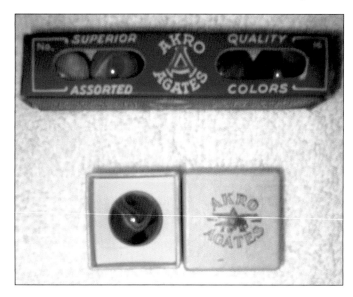

Akro Agate No. 16 sleeve, $100-150. Single marble box. Scarce. $1,200-1,400. *Both Hardy Collection.*

Akro Agate: left: No. 112 box unnumbered, $200; center: No. 88 box, scarce, no value determined; right: No. 112 box numbered, $180. Priced with marbles. *H. de Sousa Collection.*

End of above shown boxes.

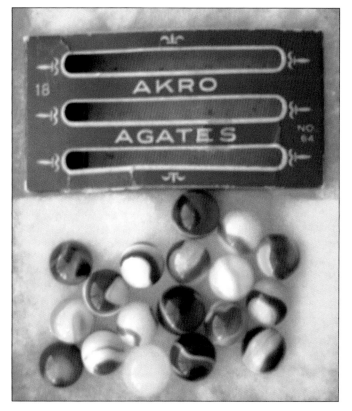

Akro Agate No. 64 box containing 18 marbles. *Photo courtesy National Marble Museum.* $180-200.

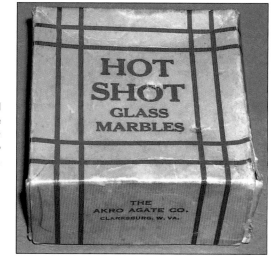

Akro Agate, unusual deep box with stripe design lid. *H. de Sousa Collection.* No value determined.

Akro Agate No. 25 containing No. 1 marbles "Universal Assortment." *H. de Sousa Collection.* Scarce. No value determined.

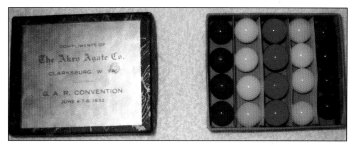

Akro Agate presentation box and lid containing 20 Opals. Grand Army of the Republic Convention, Clarksburg, W.Va., 1932. Note the patriotic red, white, and blue marble selection. Only a few examples of this box have been reported at this time. *Hardy Collection.* $1,000-1,200.

Akro Agate presentation box containing 25 No. 0 Cardinal Reds. *H. de Sousa Collection.* $500.

Akro Agate, unusual deep box with color graphic lid and later production marbles. *Hardy Collection.* $740-760.

Akro Agate presentation box containing 25 No. 1 Carnelians. *H. de Sousa Collection.* $1,500.

Akro Agate gift box and lid containing 16 Royal Blue and Red. *Hardy Collection.* $3,500-4,500.

Akro Agate presentation box containing 25 No. 1 Carnelians. $550.

Akro Agate presentation box containing 25 No. 3 Cornelians. *H. de Sousa Collection.* $2,000.

Akro Agate 25 No. 1 Flinties in green presentation box. Transparent red. *E. Schubert Collection.* $1,000.

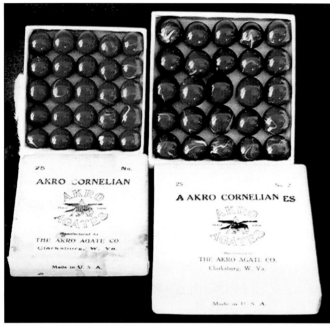

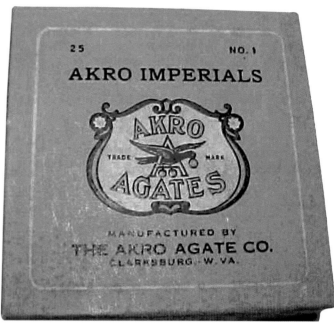

Akro Agate on left presentation box containing 25 No. 1 Cornelians, $1,500; right presentation box containing 25 No. 2 Cornelians, $2,200. Note relative box and marble size for both. *Both H. de Sousa Collection.*

Akro Agate presentation box containing 25 No. 1 Akro Imperials. Box with oxblood marbles, $1,800-2,200; with marbles but without oxbloods, $900-1,000.

Akro Box sample label info inside lid. See above.

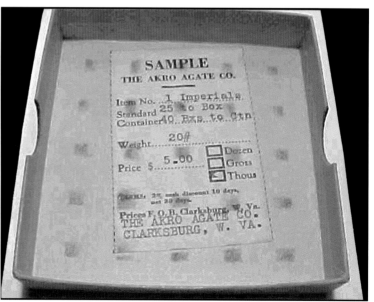

Akro Agate 25 No. 1 Akro Flinties in green presentation box. Opaques. *H. de Sousa Collection.* $1,500.

Akro oxbloods inside box shown above.

Akro Agate 25 No. 2 Akro Imperials. *H. de Sousa Collection.* No price determined.

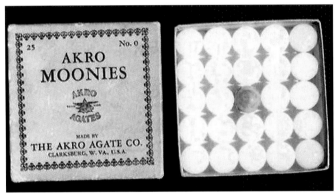

Akro Agate white presentation box containing No. 0 Moonies. *H. de Sousa Collection.* $1,800.

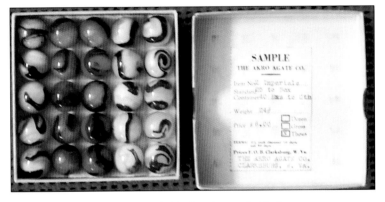

Inside lid of above Akro Imperials No.2 with sample labeling.

Akro Agate green presentation box containing 25 No. 1 Moonies. *H. de Sousa Collection.* $2,200.

Akro Agate white presentation box containing 25 No. 1 Akro Flint Moonies. *H. de Sousa Collection.* $3,000.

Akro Agate green presentation box containing 26 No. 2 Akro Moonies. *Hardy Collection.* $1,500.

Akro Agate stock box of 100 No. 1 Prize names in logo box. $1,400.

Akro Agate. Unlike Akro packages most often used, "Visi-Paks with removable covers" *H. de Sousa Collection.* Scarce. No value determined.

Akro Agate stock box containing 100 No. 0 Spiral Agates (box may also contain sparklers). *Hardy Collection.* $1,200-1,400.

Akro Agate red lid box of 100 Chinese Checkers. Known only with red lid. $400.

Akro Agate 50 No. 2 striped onyx marbles in logo box. $1,200-1,500.

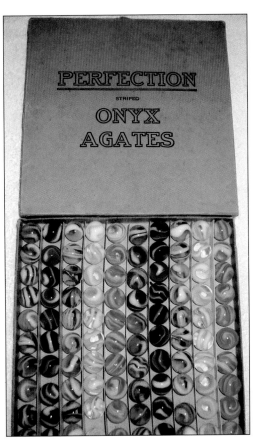

Akro Agate box containing 60 Chinese Checker "game" marbles. One of the most common Akro boxes. $25-60 depending on condition.

Akro Agate stock box containing 100 No. 0 onyx agates. *Hardy Collection.* $2,200-2,500.

Akro Agate box containing 60 Chinese Checkers. Note absence of size (No. 00) that appeared on above similar box lid. $30-60.

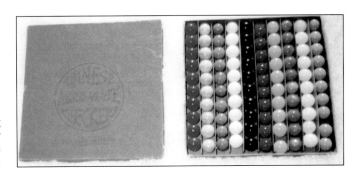

Akro Agate stock box containing 100 No. 00 Chinese Checker game marbles. Lid known only in red. $450.

Akro Agate stock box lid for box containing 100 No. 0 assorted glassies. $250.00

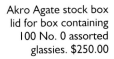

Akro Agate glassies in box, lid shown above.

Akro Agate Chinese Checker red and yellow lid containing 60 marbles. $40-80.

Akro Agate logo lid stock box containing 50 No. 2 opals. $200.

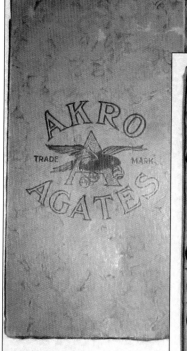

Akro Agate logo lid stock box containing 50 No. 2 Tri-Color Spirals. $1,500-1,800.

Akro Agate logo lid stock box containing 50 No. 4 Glassies. Box shown in poor condition. As shown, $250.

Akro Agate logo lid stock box containing 50 No. 2 tri-color agates. $400-500.

Akro Agate empty stock box for 100 No. 1 Tri-Onyx (Popeye) marbles. Note penciled price of 2 for 1 cent. As shown, $300.

Akro Agate stock box containing 100 No. 00 Chinese Checker game marbles. $300-400.

Akro Agate stock box containing 50 No. 4 Uniques. Lid with logo. *H. de Sousa Collection.* $2,400.

Akro Agate "Click" Game, box with lid and marbles. *Hardy Collection.* $450.

Base of above box containing the 50 Uniques.

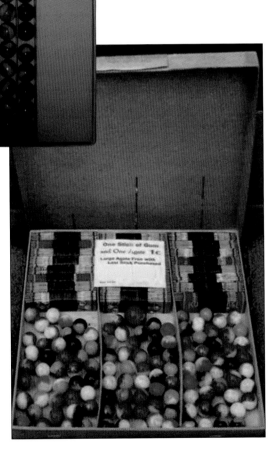

Akro Agate stock box lid and bottom containing 50 No. 4 Heros. *Hardy Collection.* $800-900.

Akro Agate counter display, "One stick of gum and one agate for 1 cent." *H. de Sousa Collection.* As shown, with gum and marbles, $4,000.

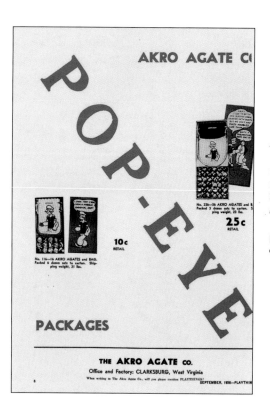

Akro Agate Popeye gift set with red box containing Tri-Onyx (also known as Popeye) marbles. Printed Popeye bag. *Hardy Collection.* $1,200-1,400.

Akro Agate ad showing Popeye illustrated marbles bags and marbles. Appearing in September 1936 issue of *Plaything* magazine. Note 10 and 25 cent retail prices for sets. *Image courtesy H. de Sousa.*

Akro Agate large red Popeye gift set with unmarked marble bag. *H. de Sousa Collection.* $10,000-12,000.

Akro Agate Popeye gift set with yellow box. Original marbles: 5 limeades, 5 lemonades and silver oxbloods. $1,600-1,800.

Akro Agate #232 Popeye red gift set, one of two known. This set has printed bag and number for gift set; the other example has neither of those elements. *Hardy Collection.* $12,000.

Akro Agate game of Ringer gift set. Original bags have children playing the game printed on them. *Hardy Collection.* $1,800-2,000.

Akro Agate "Choice of Champions" gift set. Logo box lid and printed marble bag. *Hardy Collection.* Scarce. $3,500-4,000.

Akro Agate gift box No. 125 with bag. Logo lid. *H. de Sousa Collection.* $1,200.

Akro Agate gift box No. 225 with bag and logo lid. *H. de Sousa Collection.* $3,500.

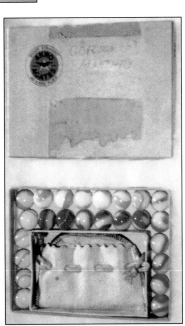

Akro Agate Box 125. Most frequently found with bag and 24 marbles. $350.

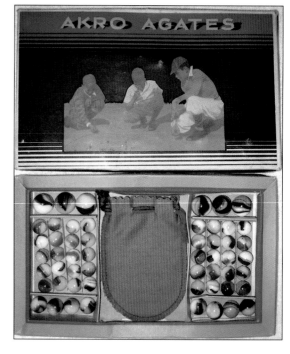

Akro Agate gift box No. 250 with oxblood patch marbles. $500-600.

Akro Agate gift box No. 230 with bag and printed lid. Lid similar to those following, but this features a girl as the central marble shooting figure. Only four known to the authors. *H. de Sousa Collection.* $5,000.

Akro Agate gift box No. 230, the more commonly found version with three boys on lid and bag. This set has moss agate marbles. As shown, $450-550.

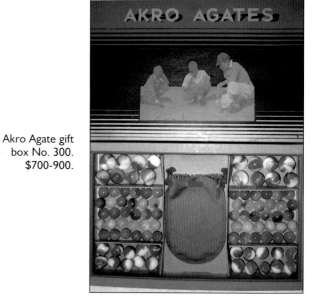

Akro Agate gift box No. 300. $700-900.

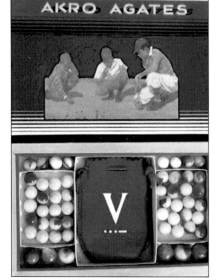

Akro Agate gift box No. 250 with less common Wartime (Victory) bag. *H. de Sousa Collection.* $1,800.

Akro Agate gift box No. 230, an early version. With oxblood marbles and two-tone bag. *Hardy Collection.* $2,500-3,000.

Akro Agate gift box No. 300, an early version. *Hardy Collection.* With oxblood marbles and two-tone bag, $2,000-3,000. Without oxbloods, but other marbles, $850-900.

Akro Agate gift box No. 250, an early version. Contains bag and kneepad. *H. de Sousa Collection.* $2,500.

Akro Agate gift box of moss agates and bag. Graphic lid. Condition as shown, $650.

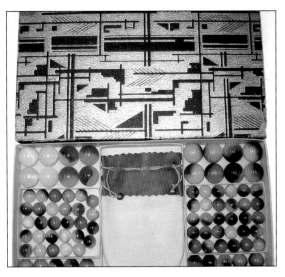

Akro Agate gift box No. 300 with bag and moss agate marbles. Graphic lid. *Hardy Collection.* $1,200-1,500.

Akro Agate gift box with bag. Graphic lid. *H. de Sousa Collection.* No price determined.

Akro Agate gift box with bag. Graphic lid. *H. de Sousa Collection.* $3,800.

Akro Agate tin box No. 200. *D. Miller Collection.* See below for possible interior and contents.

Akro Agate tin box No. 150. An exceptionally illustrated lid. See below for variations on the interior and contents utilizing this box.

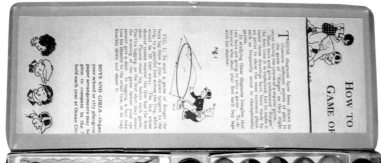

Akro Agate tin box No. 150 with logo bag and original rule sheet interior. As shown, lid illustrated as above. $700.

Akro Agate No. 200 tin with moss agates and logo bag. $500-600.

Akro Agate tin box No. 150 with bag. *D. Miller Collection.* No value determined.

Akro Agate No. 200 tin containing 60 No. 0 Prize Names, 4 No. 2 opals and 4 No. 4 Flinties with logo bag. $800.

Akro Agate No. 200 tin with Liberty bag (see text). *Miller Collection.* $1,200.

Akro Agate salesman sample box. Contains later era marbles. *H. de Sousa Collection.* $8,000.

Akro Agate No. 200 tin with yet a different marble selection. As shown, $700-900.

Akro Agate salesman sample box. As shown, $10,000.

Akro Agate medium sample case, lid not shown. *Hardy Collection.* This item has undergone price adjustment as a few are now known. The power of the Internet continues to find new variations of boxes and other changes that adjust our awareness of what is out there. $1,500-1,800.

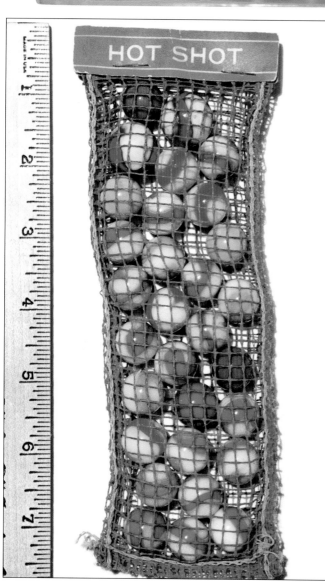

Akro Agate Hot Shot mesh bag with red header and reverse. *E. Schubert Collection.* $200.

Akro Agate mesh bags. Hy-Grade and larger bags, $150; Akro Agate red ink header, $100.

Akro Agate mesh bags. Red ink small bag, $100; Hot Shot, red label, $200. *Hardy Collection.* Note: there are no Akro poly bags, only mesh known.

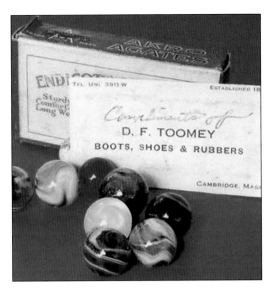

Akro Agate box No. 112 with advertising printed on the plain white bottom. Scarce. No value determined.

Examples of Akro Agate production include these attractive tri-color spirals. *E. Schubert Collection.*

Akro Agate example of one of the "not marble" production lines. Glass Tea Sets for children were a significant part of Akro production and they are numerous in size, packaging, etc. Shown here is Larger Interior Panel in lemonade and oxblood. Note that colors used for children's dishes and marbles are the same. $1,400.

Akro Agate mailing box. Scarce. No value determined.

Akro Agate tea set box lid for set shown above.

Akro Agate examples of diverse marble production. *D. Chamberlain photo.*

ALLEY AGATE
and THE COMPANIES OF
LAWRENCE E. ALLEY

Paden City, West Virginia 1929 - 1931 as The Lawrence Glass Novelty Co.
Sistersville, West Virginia 1931 - 1932 as The Lawrence Glass Novelty Co.
Pennsboro, West Virginia 1931 - 1937 as Alley Agate Co.
St. Marys, West Virginia 1937 - 1948 as Alley Agate Co. until 1947 when it became Alley Glass Manufacturing.

Alley Agates produced at Pennsboro, West
Virginia. *D. Chamberlain photo.*

Alley Agates produced at St. Marys,
West Virginia. *D. Chamberlain photo.*

Any attempt to adequately and accurately document the fascinating career of Lawrence E. Alley is fraught with seemingly insurmountable obstacles. The official family story submitted by Lawrence E. Alley III is as follows:

Lawrence E. Alley, Sr. was eighteen or nineteen when he went to work for Fostoria Glass. He started as a carry-in boy. The boy who started the same day with him, Mr. Dowzell, became the president of the company. Years later, Lawrence amazed the salesmen there when he was able to buy glassware at less than wholesale cost. In 1910 he went to Huntington Glass in Huntington, W. Va. This may be where he learned to cut glass. Next he did cutting on quality glassware at Fenton Art Glass Co. in Williamstown, W. Va. Next he started his own business at Kingwood, W. Va. It was a complete glass factory and cutting shop, but it did not prosper fast enough to satisfy the investors and it was closed. He went back to Williamstown for a year and then to the St. Marys Glass Co. as a cutter. At this time (1919), his son Lawrence Jr. was six years old. They next moved to Moundsville, W. Va. and Lawrence Sr. worked in Cumberland, Md. for a while. Next he was general manager of Picquet Glass in Shinnston, W. Va. After designing a sand blasting machine for glass, he started a sand blasting and cutting shop of his own (in Shinnston). Then he moved and merged with the Salem Glass Co. The company had financial problems before the merger and closed soon afterwards. After some other jobs he worked at Akro Agate Co. Then he started a company at Ravenswood, left it and in 1930 started a plant at Sistersville with a partner, and then sold out to the broker. Then he started a plant at Parkersburg. Finally he started the Alley Agate Co. at Pennsboro in an inadequate building and moved soon after to St. Marys. He owned this plant until he retired in 1948. Lawrence, Jr. started working for him in 1935 in Pennsboro. The St. Marys plant was a partnership between them. The name was later changed to Alley Glass and Manufacturing Co. Their products were mainly marbles, toy dishes, small

glass figures of animals and electrical insulators. In 1948, it was sold to Marble King Co. Later the building burned and the business moved to Paden City.

The authors point out the interesting absence of mention of Alley having a marble factory in Paden City, but the claim of employment with Akro Agate and in a Parkersburg, West Virginia, factory, neither of which we were able to document.

Lawrence E. Alley was born April 16, 1882, married Bertha Weekley in 1904, and they had three children: L. E. Alley, Jr., Mrs. Adrian Belt, and Naomi Alley Sellars. Lawrence Alley died March 31, 1952.

Lawrence E. Alley set up his first marble factory in a building just south of the Wissmach Glass Company plant in Paden City, West Virginia, around 1929. This was far from his first glass factory or involvement in a glass start up but seems his first marble effort. The building that was to become Alley Agate marble factory in Paden City was built in 1903 as a powerhouse for the Wetzel-Tyler Railway Co. (a streetcar line that operated between New Martinsville and Sistersville). In 1911, McKee and Bliven Button Co. started a button factory in the building, cutting buttons from mussel shells taken from the Ohio River. Around 1915 the building was bought by The Bowers Sales Corporation and was used to manufacture concrete blocks. Around 1929, Lawrence E. Alley started a marble factory in the building. All the marble machines were built and installed there and the marbles were gathered by hand. In 1946 the building was occupied by a company known as Cecil-Bosma, Inc., General Building Contractors. That may have been the last business to occupy the building. It was later used for storage until it was raised.

Alley was, according to his daughter, Naomi Alley Sellers, an accomplished glass cutter, mold maker, and machinist. He made his own rollers and marble machine parts at the Skaggs Machine Shop in Sistersville. He called his business "The Alley Agate Company".

Soon after start-up, when the future "marble king", Berry Pink, joined the company, the name was changed to "The Lawrence Glass Novelty Company". Besides producing marbles, they also made "moon balls", large glass globes used in street lamps.

Mr. Feldmeyer, of Wissmach Glass, couldn't remember the exact dates of Alley's marble operation, but stated that it was in the late 1920s or early 1930s. As a boy, he used to sneak over and pick up marbles – lots of them – and sold them to other boys in town.

Today, nothing remains of the Alley building in Paden City. Several sources have stated that the company was moved down the highway to Sistersville, about four miles away, in the summer of 1932 because more space was needed. The Glass Factory Annual Directory notes that the Lawrence Glass Novelty Company was in Sistersville in 1931.

Next we find Alley in Sistersville, West Virginia. The Glass Factory Annual Directory lists The Lawrence Glass Novelty Company, Inc. as being located on Railroad Street, Sistersville, West Virginia, for the years 1931 and 1932.

A deed, dated October 16, 1930, states that the McJunkin Machine Company sold the lease of land and one building to The Lawrence Glass Novelty Company. The partners were listed as Lawrence E. Alley and Dewey Hibbs. Curiously, Berry Pink is not listed as a partner. The deed states, "For $100.00 and other good and valuable consideration…, a lot 100 feet wide and 114 feet long on the east side of the Baltimore and Ohio Railroad. The Grantees will promise to pay the further sum of $1200.00 in 24 payments with each having $50.00 with interest until paid in full. The last note being due and payable on the first day of November, 1932."

"The grantor does not own the land, but is occupying said land and by virtue of a ground lease and hereby transfers unto the Grantees all its rights in and under the lease."

During the time in Sistersville, Alley was producing a wide variety of colorful marbles. According to Paul Simon Essof of Sistersville, Berry Pink, when he visited from New York, used to stay at the fashionable Wells Inn. Mr. Pink had bottled water delivered to his room from the Essof Grocery Store. He didn't want to drink the river water. Apparently some legal problems developed while in Sistersville and Berry Pink left the company. Mr. Essof stated that Pink left as a result of a dispute over a marble packaging machine.

It was probably in 1931 while still operating the Sistersville plant that Alley opened a new marble factory in Pennsboro, Ritchie County, West Virginia, again because more space was needed.

The Sistersville factory is now long gone, with no known picture available. It was sold, according to a bill of sale dated March 27, 1940, to the Bowser Sales and Trading Corporation. The bill of sale reads in part: "In consideration of the sum of $15.00 and other valuable considerations…the party of the first part does sell, assign, and convey….two factory buildings, both situated upon real estate belonging to the heirs of Maud Thistle Neuenschwander. 1. That a certain one-story, wood and sheet iron shop building used by the party of the first part as its office and factory building; and, 2. That a certain one-story wood and sheet iron shop building used by the party of the first part as its packing plant building; and both of which afore mentioned buildings constitute the entirety of the shops and buildings in which the party of the first part formerly conducted its marble-making and packaging business."

The Pennsboro Alley facility was located in an area once called "Glass Factory Hollow." The marble machines used at this site were probably the same ones used earlier, or if additional ones or parts were needed, they were made by Mr. Alley at the Skaggs Machine Shop in Sistersville. The machines produced 165 marbles a minute; a quantity not achieved by any others at the time. In 1935, while in Pennsboro, a patent for a glass shearing mechanism for use in marble machines was granted to Russell Adams and Clyde Hibbs and assigned to Alley Agate.

An annual trade directory listed Alley in Pennsboro in 1933 as "Alley Agate Co., The. Pennsboro, West Virginia. L.E. Alley owner, 2 day tanks. Marbles." In 1934 there were 4 day tanks, but 1935 reported only 2 again.

The authors interviewed Robert J. Dunbar (April 1999) and he stated that he was employed at Alley Agate in Pennsboro from May 1933 to January 1934. Alley had been in business at that location for some time before he went to work there. It was an established business. He was paid 20 cents an hour right out of high school for a ten hour shift. He worked as a go'fer. Dunbar said he mostly kept the bins full on the packaging machines and carried the marbles in nail kegs. He stated that the packaging machines worked on a radial axle with five or six sections which would fill up and drop the proper number of marbles of the chosen color into troughs which would guide them to the waiting mesh bags.

Dunbar further stated that Alley had a rough time marketing his marbles at first, but later a contract with Pressman Toys of New York saved his business. He described Lawrence E. Alley as a man of compassion. He treated folks well. At Pennsboro, Alley operated two and possibly three machines. It was, as marble factories always are, a 24 hour a day operation. To save money on the electricity bill Alley set up a gas generator. It disrupted production for several days, but it did ultimately save some money Dunbar reminisced.

Dunbar described a large room with bins filled mostly with Chinese checker marbles. The glass for these came from Clarksburg and Paden City. He believes they used scrap Vitrolite as well.

The reason Alley moved around so much, according to Dunbar, was because of his basic inability to manage his business affairs. Some employees felt disgruntled at his inconsistent ability to pay his payroll, drayage fees, and pay vendors. Some people left Alley because of these complications. Many stayed because he kept them working – and it was The Great Depression, times were tough almost everywhere and they liked Alley.

The office manager in Pennsboro was Irene Snider, who later married Palmer Hill of Champion Agate. Irene Snider was good at business matters. Alley was not. However, Dunbar said, if anything went wrong, "Alley took care of it."

Mary Hazelbaker, an Alley employee, said that she was grateful for the employment she got there and that Alley was a good man who loved to give marbles to children.

In 1999, Mary Domler reported that her husband, Pearl, worked for Alley Agate in Pennsboro from 1934 through 1936 and ran a machine that made the toy dishes. Domler is the one who had kept a fine group of Alley marbles made in Pennsboro for years until she sold them to Jim Davis, the Pennsboro marble artist. These marbles made quite a stir when exhibited at several marble shows. Many of the marbles from this group are now owned by the National Marble Museum, donated by Barbara Banas. Another known Alley employee was Mary Stuart Campbell.

In the book West Virginia Glass Between the Wars (D. Six. Schiffer Publishing. 2002) we read, "That Alley made children's dishes at this Pennsboro site cannot be questioned. Locally it was referred to as "the dish factory," and not a marble factory as the name Agate implies. I have listened to several elderly ladies who report on passing the site as youths when an adult presented them with toy dishes from the cullet piles. Another lady shared her story of being given a set of boxed children's glass dishes when she visited the site."

It was long believed that competing Akro Agate made most, if not all, of the glass children's dishes, but discoveries in a previously unknown Alley dump, oral traditions of Pennsboro, and the complete absence of the "J.P." marked pieces from the extensive digging done over time at Akro all point to Alley as the manufacturer. Today we know Alley had a close business relationship with J. Pressman, the J.P. mark on the Alley child's dish line. It seems indisputable the JP children's dishes are Alley products from Pennsboro and St. Marys and perhaps, in limited numbers, other Alley sites.

In a September 20, 1984, interview with marble author Dennis Webb, Naomi Alley Sellers, a daughter of Lawrence E. Alley, recalled that, "The postmaster in Pennsboro, West Virginia, when sorting mail, by request, usually discarded junk mail intended for my father, came across a letter which looked to him like junk mail and almost threw it in the wastebasket without putting it in my father's box as there was no home or business delivery in those days. People had to go to the post office for their mail. But he thought, perhaps I should put it in Mr. Alley's box, so he did. The letter was from J. Pressman in New York, a broker for a toy company. So with that letter my father became acquainted with Mr. Pressman and eventually sold all his marbles to him."

In 1937, the Alley Agate Company moved to a huge facility in St. Marys, West Virginia.

In early 1996, the old Alley building in Pennsboro, which had operated for many years as Pennsboro Glass Company, was purchased by Helen Michels of Champion Agate. She continued hot glass production at the business site under the name Champion Glass, with production being mouth blown and later some pressed ware. No marbles were made by this company, called Champion Glass. In March 2003, a heavy snow caused the collapse of a large section of the roof. The building was partly razed in 2004, but that stopped for unknown reasons, leaving a partly destroyed, partly abandoned, partly gone site. At the time of this writing, the Pennsboro site has been sold at tax auction to a speculator who then sold it at public auction. It is undergoing evaluation for dangerous chemical or site contamination by the Environmental Protection Agency. It's future seems complex and very unsure.

Alley's time in St. Mary's is noted in the 1949 souvenir program celebrating 100 years of St. Marys, West Virginia, entitled "The Bells of St. Marys", describes The Alley Manufacturing Company in this way: "Situated in the lower end of town, the Alley Manufacturing Company was purchased from the Gilligan Glass Plant in 1936. Their chief industry is making marbles, being the largest producer of marbles in the United States. Marbles from this factory are shipped to all parts of the country and abroad. Children's dishes, made of colored glass, were made until 1948, when this industry was dispensed with. Officers of this company are: L. E. Alley, Sr., President; L. E. Alley, Jr., Vice President; Kramer Sellers, Treasurer; and Mrs. Adrian Belt, Secretary."

A deed found in the Pleasants County Clerk's office, dated November 21, 1936, states: "R. W. Douglas, Trustee, (deeded to) L. E. Alley, for the sum of $4,800 cash in hand, for certain parcels of land in the city of St. Marys, County of Pleasants, West Virginia, as a lease….The tract of land is subject to the rights of the Cleveland Stone Company under a lease to said company by H. A. Carpenter, bearing the date of November 9, 1920."

Pleasants County historian, Walter S. Carpenter, stated that the Koonz family built the original building in 1919 and made terra cotta tiles there. Mr. Carpenter's father bought the land and building and used it for sorting and packing fruit from his orchard and the lease, later granted to Gilligan Glass, was sold to L. E. Alley in 1936. Carpenter further stated that none of the earlier Alley operations were profitable and that Alley had to put cardboard in his shoes to cover the holes.

Better times were ahead, however, because of the arrangement with Pressman Toys. This turned out to be a major boon for Alley, finally making his business profitable as Pressman agreed to market his entire marble output.

Over the next few years, The Alley Agate Company became one of the largest marble makers in the world. One of Pressman's marble games was Hop Ching – a popular brand of Chinese Checkers, a game that at that time was causing much excitement in the toy world. Among the known colors for that game, from marbles still in the possession of the Alley/Sellers family are: red, turquoise, black, green, white, and purple. At one point, Alley shipped fourteen million of these marbles in six months.

A small booklet entitled "History of Pleasants County, West Virginia," describes L. E. Alley as having developed a new technique for multiple striping of marbles and a cut-off device that was new to the glass industry. According to Chester Bills, a St. Marys antique dealer who as a boy visited the Alley factory, there were seven to ten marble machines operating at any given time at the St. Marys site and that a railroad spur ran right up to the side door.

At the height of production, Alley employed about 125 people. The plant was a busy place with all the phases of the business being carried out under one roof. In addition to marbles, Alley produced and boxed the "Chiquita" and "J. P." toy dish sets. A general line of small glass animals, small flower pots, and possibly glass insulators of various styles rounded out the factory's production.

In another part of her interview, Naomi Sellers described how the St. Marys marble factory was set up, saying "Father had a very good manager in St. Marys, 'Pete' Oliver Roseman Hill. I think 'Pete' needs to be recognized. He turned the Alley plant in St. Marys into an assembly line system because each man and woman had his or her job to do. There were batchmakers, the carry-in boys, and the machine workers. The finished marbles were put in bins, some of which were as big as twenty-seven by fifteen feet. From there they were taken to the room where women put them into bags that had been made in an upper room – a sewing machine shop."

There was an article in National Geographic in August 1940, which stated that Alley (St. Marys) was producing 2,625,000 marbles a day. A beautiful photograph of a girl bagging marbles has created a novel mystery to researchers. Her identity remains unknown and the Pleasants County Historical Society, after considerable searching, has been unable to identify her.

In the mid-1940s, The Alley Agate Company underwent a modest corporate change. Originally incorporated in 1937 as The Alley Agate Company, on November 15, 1946, corporate reorganization documents were filed making it a family owned business with authorized capital of $50,000 in shares as follows:

L. E. Alley, Sr., 260 Shares
L. E. Alley, Jr., 120 Shares
Bertha L. Alley, 120 Shares

The company was renamed "The Alley Glass Manufacturing Company." These documents were recorded in The Pleasants County Court Clerk's Office on January 14, 1947.

Actual working family members included son, L. E. Alley, Jr.; daughter, Naomi (Alley) Sellers; and son-in-law, Kramer Sellers. Mrs. Sellers mentioned several Alley employees that she thought should be remembered. Irene (Truscott) Snyder Hill worked at Alley in Sistersville, Pennsboro, and St. Marys as secretary. She retired in 1940 to work at the A & P. She married Palmer Hill of Champion Agate. Her brother, Fred Truscott, worked at Alley in St. Marys for many years. Her brother-in-law, "Pete" Oliver Roseman Hill, was the plant manager in St. Marys.

In 1949, because of ill health, Lawrence E. Alley sold out to his old partner, Berry Pink, and Sellers H. Peltier, and several other minor stockholders. Mr. Peltier was the son of Victor Peltier, who founded The Peltier Glass Co. of Ottawa, Ill.

On June 1, 1949 the deed to the marble factory in St. Marys was transferred to Berry Pink "for the sum of $5.00 and other good and valuable considerations…" The description of the property was the same as when it was transferred to Alley in 1936 and was signed by L. E. Alley, President, Alley Glass Manufacturing Company, attested to by Naomi E. Sellers, Treasurer and acting secretary.

At a meeting in the City of St. Marys, State of West Virginia, on the 27th day of June 1949, a resolution was passed that "the Alley Glass Manufacturing Company, a corporation created and organized under the laws of West Virginia, does hereby discontinue business as a corporation and surrenders to said State its charter and corporate franchises." This document was recorded in the office of D. Pitt O'Brien, West Virginia Secretary of State, November 21, 1949, and recorded in the Pleasants County Clerk's Office November 25, 1949.

Frank Sellers, a grandson of Lawrence E. Alley, mentioned in an interview that he recalled that his grandfather enjoyed a vacation in Clearwater, Florida, every year. He also noted that around 1950 or 1951, the U.S. Government asked Alley to go to Japan to help them set up factories to make marbles. Alley declined because of failing health.

ALLEY Companies
Marbles Produced

Clear is absolutely bubble-less.
Clear with opaque or translucent patch.
Moss Agates.
Opaques in various colors.
Opaque Swirls.
Transparents in various colors.
Translucent Swirls.
Transparent Patch.
Transparent Swirls.

Alley Marble Identification Tips: It should be noted that some Alley marbles are fluorescent under a black-light, but not all.

Moss Agates: Found in blue, red, yellow, orange, and green, the green has two shades, one of which is not seen from any other factory. In general, one could think many Alley marbles to be Akro Agate, Ravenswood Novelty Works or Christensen Agate. There are perfect color matches for many of these marbles, though the patterns may differ.

A few Alley marbles are known to contain oxblood, while a rare type appears to have a metallic substance.

As with many marble types, unless they are in original or identifiable packaging, Alley marbles may be difficult to identify. Much research into the types of marbles produced of the various Alley sites has been conducted in the last four or five years and it may be stated with some confidence that many Alley marbles are as outstanding in color and quality as any marbles produced anywhere. The sizes range from 9/16" to 1".

Swirls: White-based swirls come with a variety of second and even third color combinations. Often the second color is two-toned or blends into the white. The color combinations seem almost endless and the patterns range from broad lazy striping to fantastic flame patterns.

Flames: Recent discoveries indicate that the Alley flame patterns, very reminiscent of those of Christensen Agate and Ravenswood Novelty Works, were site specific as to size. It appears that Alley two-color flames, mostly white based, in sizes 9/16" to 5/8", were made at the Pennsboro site and the 1" flames, again mostly white, based, were made while at St. Marys. A few 5/8" flames have been found at the Sistersville site.

The Alley Packaging

The Alley/Sellers family has several examples of Alley marbles in packages distributed by the J. Pressman Company. These include the "Hop Ching" Chinese checker box and the small red and white box containing three marbles. The printing says "Allies" and "Marbles" on three sides with the fourth side containing a cut-out area to reveal the marbles inside.

Descriptions exist of red mesh bags being used by Alley at his various locations. While examples are known, none of these were available for photographing for this book. Alley marbles have also been identified in early Marble King packaging, perhaps as leftover Alley stock from 1949.

Several advertising packages have been found, again possibly distributed by Marble King, as they are in early poly bags. These include bottle hangers from Tower Root Beer and B-1 Lemon-Lime. Alley marbles are also found in Hot Shot jobber boxes from Pressman. The same box was used to package Heaton Agates.

The abandoned and partly razed Alley/ Pennsboro Glass factory, May 2003.

Alley Agate factory, Pennsboro. This site operated as Pennsboro Glass, producing mouth blown crystal, from 1948 until 1990s.

Lawrence E. Alley

Alley employee at the Pennsboro factory, Mary Hazelbaker. Shown holding Alley Pennsboro marbles. West Virginia Marble Festival, Cairo, West Virginia, 2002.

Alley Factory, St. Marys, West Virginia, later the site of Marble King. *Image from Dennis Webb collection.*

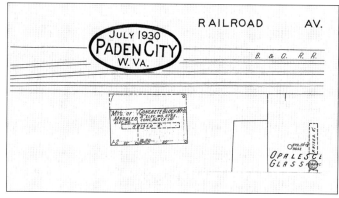

Sanborn Fire Map for the town of Paden City, West Virginia, showing the marble factory site as it appeared in July 1930.

THE LAWRENCE GLASS NOVELTY CO.
MANUFACTURERS OF
MARBLES AND BALLS
ALL COLORS
L. E. ALLEY, Manager
PADEN CITY, W. VA.

Letterhead for Lawrence Glass Novelty Co. noting production of marbles and L.E. Alley as manager.

Wissmach Glass factory on left and Alley/Lawrence Glass Novelty factory in Paden City, West Virginia, on right. *Image from Jesse Brown collection.*

Sistersville, West Virginia, Alley site as it appeared in 1994. The building to the left in the image is not related to the marble factory that is now gone.

Paden City, West Virginia, Alley/Lawrence Glass Novelty site in 1994. Note cabbages growing in the garden where once the factory was.

Frank Sellers, L.E. Alley's grandson, chats at West Virginia Marble Festival, Cairo, West Virginia, 2003 with Robert Dunbar, Alley employee at Pennsboro in the 1930s.

Alley Agates, Pennsboro, West Virginia.

Alley Agates, Pennsboro, West Virginia.

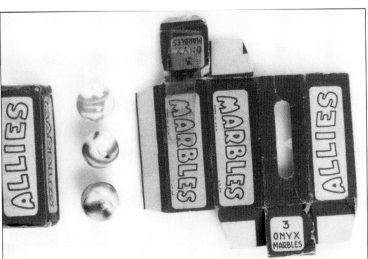

Two Alley boxes made to contain "3 onyx marbles." Top image is box assembled, lower box unfolded to show all sides.

Alley Agates, Pennsboro, West Virginia.

Alley Agates, Pennsboro, West Virginia.

Alley Agates, Pennsboro, West Virginia, production. Note variety of sizes. *D. Chamberlain photo.*

Alley, St. Marys, West Virginia.

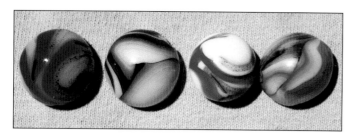

Alley agates, Sistersville, West Virginia.

Alley family collection includes photo, boxed marbles, Hop Ching checker board with marbles, cup and saucer, and in the foreground glass "toy" animal, bowl, "marble tops," fused misshaped marbles from factory, and a small child's tumbler.

Alley agates, Sistersville, West Virginia.

Alley children's dishes recovered at Pennsboro, West Virginia, Alley site, 2004, by R. See.

Alley agates, Sistersville, West Virginia.

Alley St. Marys marbles packaged by Marble King after they purchased Alley. Noted that Alley is not known to have used any poly bags and only one style of red mesh bag, of which the authors have yet to see an example. Tower Root Beer or B-1 Lemon Lime bottle hanger bags, $20 each.

ALOX MANUFACTURING COMPANY

St. Louis, Missouri
1919 - Ceased production circa 1946 - 1949

Alox Manufacturing Co. selection of marbles. *Photo by D. Chamberlain.*

The Alox Manufacturing Company, a named derived to obtain good alphabetical placement in phone directories, was founded in 1919 in St. Louis, Missouri, by John Frier. Alox began as a shoelace and corset lace making operation, and in the years that followed expanded to also manufacture carnival canes, yo-yo's, tops, kites, jacks sets, and Chinese checker boards, among other things. Frier began the business using money from the buying and selling of inexpensive railroad stock while in the U.S. Navy during World War I. Jack Frier, Jr., speaking with the authors in a telephone interview in 2002, further explained that the Alox company mission was to make low-end products by piecework, hiring only fast workers so that the company and its employees could prosper.

John Frier was reportedly not only a clever businessman, but a man full of ideas. Some of the kites produced by Alox under the brand name of American Eagle were of an elaborate five foot box-kite design that Frier developed himself, and some of his kite designs are those still used by kite makers today. One such kite was commissioned to promote the National Recovery Act in the 1930s. During World War II, Alox kites caught the eye of the U.S. military, who commissioned a foil kite to attach to balloons as radar targets.

Before becoming manufacturers of marbles, Alox purchased fifty pound boxes of 9/16" Chinese Checkers to sell with their boards from an unnamed West Virginia company. Alox was making and selling 10,000 boards every day, and needed 60 marbles for each board. The unknown supplier, after proving somewhat inconsistent in filling marble orders, went out of business in the late 1930s. Jack Frier, Sr., needing to ensure a steady supply of Chinese Checkers, purchased seven marble machines in West Virginia from a source that the younger Frier no longer could identify when speaking with the authors. Alox, he recalls being told, hired two experienced marble workers from West Virginia, recalling nothing else about them, to set up shop making their own marbles in the Butler Building on Pennsylvania Avenue in St. Louis, Missouri.

Unlike West Virginia companies, which were fortunate enough to have plentiful and cheap natural gas available, Alox rigged their tanks to run on fuel oil. Although seven marble machines were purchased, they had only two tanks, so could run only two machines at a time. Over the years, some of these machines were cannibalized for spare parts. Machines were run five days a week and the marble machines were shut down on Friday night for the weekend to be used again the following Monday – the glass furnaces would have required constant firing to keep the glass hot, molten, and useable when the marble machines resumed operation. As with most of the Alox toy line, marbles were manufactured during the winter months for spring and summer sales.

Alox purchased both new cullet and scrap glass for their marbles. They used Seven-up bottles for green, beer bottle for brown, Milk of Magnesia and similar bottles for blue, and cold cream jars for white, and other scrap glass. This scrap glass was purchased from junk dealers who kept the colors sorted recalled the younger Frier.

Jack Frier Sr. created a rotating wheel to count marbles and deposit them in bags, which were then stapled by female pieceworkers. Marbles were sold both in the now familiar "Tit-Tat-Toe" boxes with ten marbles in two color schemes, and in mesh bags, later replaced by poly bags. A 1946 wholesale catalogue prices 40 count bags of marbles at $6.40 per gross, and bags of 5 shooters at $6.75 per gross.

Marble production halted temporarily during World War II, and then resumed. Problems with the aging machinery kept coming up in the late hours of the night, and in the postwar years the company quit marble production altogether, sometime after 1946 and before 1950 as recollected by Frier, Jr.

John Frier Jr. joined the company upon finishing college in 1950, and kept the business running until he retired in 1989, selling the properties. Though marble production had ceased before the younger Frier joined the company, marble sales increased dramatically when he began making trips as far west as San Diego, California, and Seattle, Washington, selling to retail stores and chains. Though most larger retail outlets were not interested in such low-end commission merchandise, enough sales were made to keep the small company afloat. Still, the leftover inventory of marbles lasted many years, selling in mesh bags, and later in plastic bags when the supply of mesh was exhausted.

The saga of the marble machines brought by Alox to St. Louis from West Virginia does not end here. Of the seven machines originally purchased, all but two were scrapped in 1975, and those two were sold to an amusement park in Branson, Missouri, called Silver Dollar City, strictly for display purposes. At that time, two gifted machinists, Claude Miller and Joe Wiley, now deceased, were working at the park. These two men, and a Terry Bloodworth, a glass worker who told the authors this story, undertook an amazing project. Never having seen such a machine before, they worked with the machines and salvaged working parts from each in order to come up with one working marble machine, scrapping the rest of the parts. They found that the machines incorporated an old auto transmission to control the speed of the head and rollers. Upon closer examination, they were able to identify the transmission as being from 1920s era Hupmobile. Once the three men got the machine running, they wanted very much to prove to themselves it worked. Though pressured by their employers to stop wasting time, Bloodworth torch-melted some crystal Fenton cullet in a crucible, which he dropped onto the moving rollers, and about a half dozen final imperfect marbles were made on this wonderful West Virginia machinery. Bloodworth divided these few marbles with the machinists, and eventually gave the others to his children – none of the Branson made marbles are known to exist today. In the 1980s, the machine was shipped from Branson to Dollywood Park in Pigeon Forge, Tennessee. The authors have been able to confirm that this well traveled marble machine still rests in Tennessee, perhaps dreaming of more productive days.

Alox Marbles Produced

Clearies: This type is found in several pale shades of glass and range from clear, bubble free glass to rather seedy.

Opaque: Many Alox Chinese checker marbles appear to be solid color in a clear matrix that is not completely mixed and actually appears to be a type of swirl. They occur in various shades of yellow, green, blue, and red, along with a white swirl and black. Although Alox produced many Chinese checker (opaque) marbles in several sizes to meet the demands of that game, they were not the only marble product of that company.

Opaque Swirls: The opaque swirls often have a white base glass with blue, green, or red striping. Other base colors include a light brown, blue, purple, and green. Only about ten percent of the Alox marbles examined by marble collector David Chamberlain a few years back were found to fluoresce under a black light. Most of these were white based opaque swirls. Many of these opaque marbles have very eye-catching wavy lines.

Striped or Brushed Patch: Transparent marble with white opaque striping covering roughly one half of the surface of the marble.

Translucent Swirls: Usually these have a milky white, translucent blue, green, or light root beer base with red, green, blue, or white striping. These marbles are very pleasing to the eye and often resemble marbles made by the small factories of Ritchie County, West Virginia, during the late 1940s.

Transparent Swirls: The clear base glass is sometimes seedy with the bubbles adding to their beauty rather than being a distraction. The transparent base is often a bright green, medium cobalt blue, or light root beer. The striping is usually white.

It has long been generally accepted that Alox marbles were of a fairly uniform 5/8" size. Recently marbles have been shared by the owners of the company that are a magnificent 1" size. These marbles range from clear to opaque, with some having opaque striping on the surface resembling a Master Marble Sunburst or Akro Agate Sparkler. These are truly marbles of beauty. Marbles of a nice 3/4" size were also released in opaque and translucent with either random swirls or wide stripes that appear to be more of a patch. The owner indicated that marbles were also made at Alox in a size as small as 1/2".

Alox Packaging

The most recognizable Alox package is the "Tit-Tat-Toe" game box. Usually these red, white, and blue cut-out top boxes come with ten marbles in two opposing colors along with instructions for playing the game. The end flap on the box does not indicate the number of marbles enclosed.

There is another version of this box, quite scarce, that is known as the sample box and contains thirty marbles and this number is shown in red on the end flap. This box, with company fliers, was sent out to prospective customers upon request.

Marbles were also sold in yellow mesh bags of twenty marbles. The headers were white with a red picture of boys playing ringer. The writing says "Alox Agates" and "Alox Mfg. Co. St. Louis, Mo., U.S.A.".

Poly-vinyl bags with counts of forty, thirty, nineteen, and fourteen were sold with three-color (white, red, and green) headers. Alox also sold bags of five shooters.

In recent years three poly style bags have appeared on the market with white headers and black writing labeled Army, Navy, and Air Force. The fake labels say Alox Agates but the marbles inside are recent Marble King.

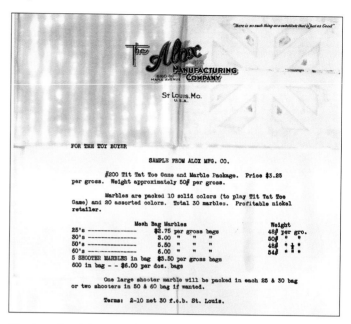

Alox letterhead showing wholesale marble offerings. Found as insert in a sample Tit-Tat-Toe box.

Illustrated Alox toy catalog sheet. Note marbles at end of listing and poly bag filled with marbles and three larger sized marbles beside bag.

John Frier, Alox founder. *Photo courtesy Jack Frier family.*

Alox marble factory as it appeared in November 2002. 1600 block of Pennsylvania Ave. Pagedale, MO. The garage doors were added more recently to the existing building, known as the "Butler building." *Photo provided by of Jack Frier family.*

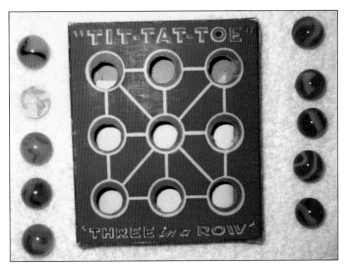

Alox "Tit-Tat-Toe" three in a row standard box. Game with ten marbles and instructions. $30.

The Alox machine as it sat in Pigeon Forge, Tennessee, recently. *M. Duckworth photo.*

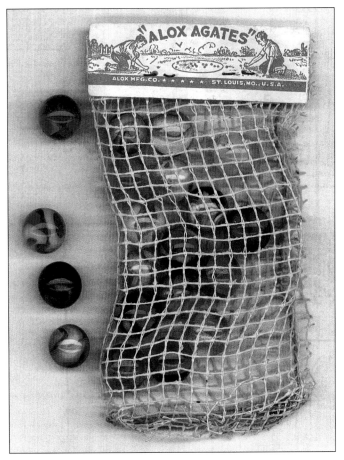

Alox Mfg. Co, Mah Tong Chinese Checker box. As shown, $50.

Alox Agates yellow mesh bag with header of two boys shooting marbles. "Alox Agates. Alox Mfg. Co., St. Louis, MO., U.S.A." Original contents. *Collection of West Virginia Museum of American Glass.* $30-45.

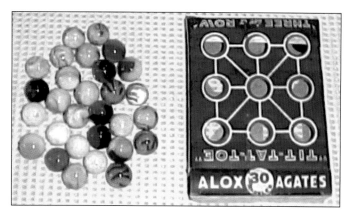

Alox "Tit-Tat-Toe" box, showing end with Alox Agates visible and the 30 marbles count. Less common in this count. *R. Collison collection. C. Kobata photo.* $150.

Alox. *D. Chamberlain photo.*

Examples of Alox production, 5/8 to 3/4 plus inches. *D. Chamberlain photo.*

Alox 1" marbles. *D. Chamberlain photo.*

Examples of Alox production in several sizes. Note the flame pattern on the red/orange marble in front and the green on white flame in the rear left.

Examples of Alox production. *R. Collison collection. C. Kobata photo.*

C.E. BOGARD & SONS
The BOGARD CO.

Cairo, West Virginia
1971-1983
Cairo, West Virginia, and Nutter Farm, West Virginia
1983 - 1986
Reno, Ohio
1986 - 1987

C.E. Bogard Cat Eye marbles.

In 2004, Ms. JoAnn Argabrite of JABO, Inc., related the story of how the Bogard family got into the marble business. She wrote: "Jerry Bogard heard Heaton Agate in Cairo, W. Va., was for sale through his work at Plastic Kote. Jack Bogard was driving a truck at the time and he and Jerry discussed the purchase of the Heaton Agate Co. Jack went to his father and asked for a loan to do the purchase, Dad said no. So Jack went to his mom. She told Jack, I will ask your Dad, Clayton E. Bogard, to do this but the company will need to be owned equally with your brothers: Jim, Joe, Jerry, and yourself. Jack said ok but he would need a buffer between the sons, someone who could resolve disputes if the need arose. We will have Dad own the majority of the shares and have the final say so. This is how C. E. Bogard & Sons was started. Jim and Joe sold out after a few years and went back to Florida, then Jerry sold out in the early 1980s, leaving Jack as the only Bogard remaining in the marble mfg. business."

Oddly the C. E. Bogard and Sons, Inc. was chartered on June 10, 1967, with the following shareholders:

C. E. Bogard of Medina, OH owning 52 shares
James Bogard of Medina, OH owning 12 shares
Jack Bogard of Medina, OH owning 12 shares
Jerry W. Bogard of Medina, OH owning 12 shares
Joseph Bogard of Medina, OH owning 12 shares

Although existing as a corporate entity since 1967, it was not until 1971 that Clayton E. Bogard and his sons purchased the Heaton Agate Company in Cairo, West Virginia, and changed that company and facility name to C. E. Bogard and Sons, Inc.

Jerry Bogard was plant manager for Plastico Paint Co. and Jack was hauling marbles from Heaton Agate, but has said he was tired of driving trucks – that gave them the inspiration to go into the marble business.

When the Bogards purchased the company, all of the equipment stayed with the plant, including a 3/8" machine that Heaton had used to make pee-wee marbles. The Bogards eventually traded that machine to Roger Howdyshell of Marble King.

David Tamulevich interviewed Jack Bogard in 1998 and was told that Heaton was about out of business by the time Bogards appeared. The plant was beginning to get run down. Even all the windows had been broken out. There were few Heaton marbles in the factory when the Bogards bought the place – maybe about 100 boxes – some of those were already bagged and labeled. The Bogards had some labels printed up and stapled right over the existing Heaton labels. Bill Heaton told the Bogards that they would go broke making industrial marbles – they needed to make cat eyes and Chinese checker marbles. The Bogards tried several types of cat eyes with varying degrees of success and they tried a machine-made onionskin.

As part owner, Jerry Bogard was company manager and Jack became a truck driver (so much for being tired of driving a truck!). His own truck became the "common carrier" transporting the marbles from the factory to their destination, thus saving several thousand dollars a year in transportation cost. Jack and Jerry Bogard became sole owners in July 1983, after Jack bought out the other family members. The name was changed to The Bogard Company.

Before he bought the company outright, Jack Bogard bought cans of spray paint and started calling the manufacturers regarding their use of marbles. Plastico and Krylon, Heaton's only industrial marble accounts, weren't even using twenty million marbles a year – a very low number to keep a marble company in business. Jack spent six years going to Rustoleum and they finally ordered but insisted on having the marbles shipped to them in steel drums. This proved too expensive for both parties and Rustoleum eventually accepted the marbles in cardboard boxes. Jack Bogard had been, all along, the chief activist in convincing the aerosol can industry to utilize marbles instead of metal balls as agitators in spray cans. Since that time, the aerosol can producers have been a major consumer of industrial marbles. Jack reported traveling far and wide in this endeavor, sometimes living out of his car while on the road to establish a firm base in this market. Jack Bogard's industrial marbles were all single color as it was feared that mixed color glass might shatter when agitated in the spray cans. Jack preferred the industrial marble trade as he found at the time less competition than there was in the toy marble industry.

Mounds of broken and shattered fluorescent light tubes were once found at the site in Cairo. This was glass being recycled into industrial marbles and it came from a factory in Fairmont, West Virginia. It was favored for cullet because it was easy to handle as hand shoveling was required and the small fragments were easy to shovel.

Bogard made cat eye marbles and Chinese checker marbles for several years but got few orders. Jack Bogard put together the "Mountaineer Shooter" blister packs of cat eyes in an effort to market the toy marbles they produced. When they came out, the cost to produce them was about 4 cents each and they reported they couldn't even sell them for 5 cents a package. Dean Six recalls buying his packet at the state park gift shop a few miles from Cairo, where they sold for about $2 per package, suggesting a wholesale price of one dollar or more, not the 5 cents wholesale that Bogard recalled. At the over two dollar price they were indeed then slow sellers!

Cat eye marbles were purchased from Marble King from time to time to package and resell and Bogard made industrial marbles for Marble King. Bogards reported that Roger Howdyshell didn't want to be bothered with industrial marbles. At one point in the mid-1980s, Bogard was making one million industrial marbles a month for Marble King.

In the mid-1980s, Consumer's Gas raised the price of natural gas in Cairo from $3.00 to $6.24 so Jack Bogard closed production in Cairo and moved his industrial marble works to an unused farm site along old US Hwy. 50 near the small community known as Nutter Farm and a few miles from Cairo. There they produced clear and light blue industrial marbles from 1983 through 1985.

They had three marble machines going at the Nutter Farm site. There were problems with the rustic site including pipes freezing in winter. During that time, they used the building in Cairo for packaging and storage. In 1985, Jack moved his machines back to Cairo and dealt with the high natural gas price, which forced him to leave Cairo in the first place. He used a recuperator that serviced all three machines. This is a system that preheated the tanks by re-circulating the exhaust air and actually saved 15 percent to 20 percent on energy costs. Significant savings, but not enough.

In December 1986, the Bogard Company moved out of Cairo and out of West Virginia. It set up shop in Reno, Ohio, where the natural gas was only $2.80 per 1000 cubic feet.

In 2005 Jack Bogard was semi-retired from the marble business but at the time of this writing maintained a consultant role in JABO, Inc. in Reno, Ohio, a successful marble company he and C.E.O. JoAnn Argabrite put together.

The building in Cairo, West Virginia, that once held both the Heaton Agate and the Bogard companies is still standing and was sold at public auction in February 1988.

BOGARD Marbles Produced (Cairo, Nutter Farm Road, and Reno locations)

Cat Eye.
Imitation Onionskins.
Opaque.
Opaque Swirls (Reported by Dennis Webb).
Pink Transparents (Reported by Dennis Webb).
Transparent Industrial Marbles.

BOGARD Marble Identification Tips

The Bogard cat eye marbles are virtually indistinguishable from those of Heaton Agate as they were made on the same machinery within a relatively confined time frame. The colors include light blue, yellow, light green, red, white, and black. Dennis Webb reported that some of the yellow cat eyes are brighter than the other colors because the yellow glass was obtained from Champion Agate.

Jack Bogard once threw out a whole run of green cat eye marbles. He didn't like how they turned out. Many were fractured and the whole run looked like Peltier green bananas. Unacceptable at the time to Bogard but appealing to today's collectors when found!

Author Dennis Webb reported that Bogard made opaque swirls, but none have been individually identified as such. Webb also reported that Bogard made a few pink transparents using glass from the Federal Glass Company in Columbus, Ohio. The design was not entirely successful as the color was difficult to perfect and it was not a big seller. Webb further reported that Bogard made opaques (Chinese checker) marbles during the years 1971 - 1978.

A very scarce Bogard marble is the machine-made onionskin. It may be described as a clear transparent marble with wisps of brushed color intended to duplicate the nineteenth century hand-made onionskins. The striping of Bogard's onionskin marbles tended to run toward the center and the design was run only for a short time.

The color combinations of black/red/clear; red/white/clear; orange/white/clear; green/white/clear have been found.

Both Bogard companies at all three sites produced millions of single color transparent industrial marbles; these were used in spray cans and in various types of filtering operations.

BOGARD Packaging

After the Bogards bought Heaton Agate in 1971, they continued the use of polyvinyl packaging. In fact, their earliest packages were merely already packaged marbles to which they stapled Bogard labels over the Heaton headers.

When those supplies ran out, the packages were labeled with usually blue or purple graphics on white paper showing a cat on the left side and the words "CAT EYES The cat's eye in glass" along with the marble count. The other side reads " C. E. Bogard & Sons, Inc. Agate Company Cairo, West Virginia 26337 United States of America." Most packages were in counts of 10, 22, 25, 50, and 60 in sizes of 5/8". There are other packages of 4 or 6 shooters, but the marbles appear to be either Marble King cat eyes or unknown opaque patch marbles.

One of the most well-known C. E. Bogard packages is the blister pack called "Mountaineer Shooters." This package features a whimsically illustrated mountaineer lounging on the package. Most packs contain either 19 or 20 cat eye marbles.

The Bogard Co. factory site, utilized 1983-85. Old U.S. 50 near Cairo, West Virginia. *Photo 1997 by S. Metzler.*

Bogard Cairo site after production ceased, Cairo. West Virginia.

Bogard poly bag of
Cat Eyes. $10.

Bogard label stapled
over Heaton label.
Cat Eye poly bag.
$25.00

Bogard poly bags, either, $10 each.

Bogard 50 count poly bag, Cat Eyes. *J. Thompson photo.* $10-15.

Bogard Cat Eyes poly bags, "C.E. Bogard & Sons. Inc Agate Company Cairo, West Virginia, The Untied States of America." Left 20 count, right 10 count bags. Either, $10-20.

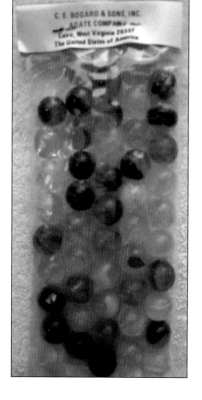

Bogard 50 count Cat Eyes, reverse of above.

Bogard Cat Eyes poly bag of 19 and 20 count. *D. Six collection.* Either, $10-20.

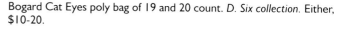

Bogard Cat Eye bag with a corner of a label turned up to reveal the Heaton label over which Bogard added their label! *D. Six collection.* $10-20.

Bogard Hybrid Cat Eyes. *D. Chamberlain photo.*

Bogard cat eye packages, including some packages with marbles other than cat eyes! The variety of these packages in size and content and the as of yet reasonable pricing makes this an ideal starting point for newer collectors. All $10-15 each.

C.E. Bogard and Sons blister pack "Mountaineer Shooters." $15-25.

CAIRO NOVELTY COMPANY

Cairo, West Virginia
1946 - 1952

Cairo Novelty marbles. Note the green striped marble second from left and others as good examples of Cairo Novelty Snakes. *D. Chamberlain photo.*

The year was 1946. A group of boys were playing marbles in Cairo, West Virginia. They paused when the man who owned the local drug store walked across the railroad tracks towards them. As he got closer, they could see that he was carrying bags of marbles. He handed the bags out to them saying, "You might as well have these. There won't be any more marbles sold in Cairo." He pointed to a new building being constructed just up the tracks on the east side of town. It was to be the site of the Heaton Agate Company, and the drug store owner knew that in no time at all the local kids would have access to more free marbles than they could shoot. A common practice was that flawed and at times excess marbles were simply dumped on the factory grounds. As a child, one of the authors made repeated trips to the sites to scoop up such discards.

One of those boys was David Hanlon, whose father, Oris Hanlon, was in partnership with his brother-in-law, William Heaton, and it was they who were building the new marble factory in Cairo that would become Heaton Agate. The Krupp's and Wilson's who operated the Playrite Marble Co. in nearby Ellenboro (then Lamberton) were relatives of these two men and were already in the marble business and doing fairly well, it appeared.

The partnership between Bill Heaton and Oris Hanlon was short-lived. They had a falling out. There are several local stories yet floating around as to the nature of the dispute, but none have been confirmed or positively documented. It is likely at this juncture that we will never know why the partnership failed. Bill Heaton was married to Oris Hanlon's sister, making the business and family connections further complicated. Once the Heaton-Hanlon partnership ceased, Oris Hanlon decided to start his own marble factory on the other side of the small town of Cairo, in Carrol Addition. The Hanlons had, at one time, lived in Pennsboro where Oris Hanlon worked for a marble factory (presumably Champion Agate). They moved to Massillon, Ohio, sometime prior

to Pearl Harbor. The family moved to Cairo in 1946 and the partnership with Heaton commenced said David Hanlon.

The Cairo Novelty Company had its origin in U.S. Patent 2,422,413 filed May 23, 1944, to Oris G. Hanlon, then residing in Massillon, Ohio. On June 17, 1947, he received his patent for a glass marbles manufacturing machine. The actual use of the Hanlon machine seems to begun prior to the granting of the patent. The 1940s saw many new entries into the marble manufacturing business and the concentration of this was most heavily centered in Ritchie County, West Virginia. As technology created machines to make marbles faster and thus more profitable, the business seemed more and more likely to generate a good return for owners. It was in such a time and place that Hanlon, a West Virginia native, was inspired and motivated to build his unique machine.

On the 26th of June, 1946, a corporate charter was granted for Cairo Novelty Company to Oris Hanlon, John H. Sandy, and Dennis Farley, each then residing at, and doing business in Cairo, West Virginia. They subscribed to 33-1/3 shares each at $100.00 per share. Land was acquired in 1946 adjacent to the B & O Railroad line. In all, six lots were conveyed by the Cairo Board of Trade to attract the new business.

Hanlon's 1947 patented machine was the only one used by the company. This machine, a unique design, was nevertheless a cause of constant frustration because of mechanical problems. However, David Hanlon has stated that his father was so proud of his marble machine patent that he carried a copy of it in his pocket throughout his life.

Don Murphy made the original machine in George Murphy's machine shop in Ellenboro, West Virginia (then Lamberton), recalled Dave Hanlon. The cutting bar wouldn't make more than one marble at a time even though the machine had a double set of rollers. Hanlon called machine shop owner George Murphy, who took one of his machinists to the Cairo factory to have a look at it. They reworked the mechanism to more closely match Hanlon's original design and it worked, making twice the number of marbles of any other machine of its time, although it was so complicated that there were constant adjustment problems with it. The George Murphy machine shop also made a set of rollers at $2.00 an hour for machine work and it took 21 hours to make a set of rollers. Another problem that was overcome was to devise a way to separate the steel rollers from the brass gearing because the latter wore out every few months and were expensive to replace.

Dave Hanlon reminisced in an interview with David Tamulevich recorded in May 1996 that the company equipment consisted of (besides the one marble machine), two sets of rollers: one for bigger marbles, one for smaller ones. They were half again as long as standard rollers used by others in the industry. Cairo Novelty had a grader and sizer with holes in it through which marbles would drop by size. Someone would sit there and pull out the imperfect marbles. The other two items they had were a counting machine and a bagging machine. All the ideas were Hanlon's, who was a creative person. There was no sales person but Oris Hanlon. Every so often he would go up to New York where there was a man who had the market on tops and show him his newest marble designs. This man marketed Cairo Novelty marbles. The biggest customer was Woolworth's and they sold Cairo marbles nationwide. The marbles were packaged in mesh bags with Woolworth's labels on them. David enjoys recounting the time there was a fluke with the machine and for one eight hour shift it made small black doughnuts with white stripes. Oris Hanlon sent some out as samples and got some orders, but could never get the machine to make them again.

An uncommon insight into employment in the local marbles factories is found in employee check stubs existing from Cairo Novelty for June McGinnis as early as 1946. By May 1947, one stub shows 66 hours worked in a two week period at forty cents per hour. McGinnis told the authors that she left the employment of Cairo Novelty Company when the "other" Cairo marble manufacturer, Heaton Agate, offered fifty cents per hour for the same labor. She bagged, stapled, and at times graded marbles at both Cairo sites over three decades.

Glass for Cairo Novelty Company was delivered by truck. Cairo Novelty got no glass in by train, although it was a few yards from the Baltimore and Ohio tracks. Cairo Novelty shipped by truck and train, using the train depot in town for rail service. Near the end, the railroad mandated that they could ship only full boxcar loads and since that great a volume was no longer possible, they used only trucks after that.

Marbles were made with the colors and kinds of glass they had on hand. Their machine tank was set up for a two-color operation with only one striping tank. This was located in front of the main tank and it was filled from the back using a long-handled metal shovel to put the proper color glass in it. They didn't need a lot of glass for the striping bank as it lasted quite a while. Marbles of more than two colors were created when a third or fourth color was added to the striping tank. At one time they had tons of cathedral glass (probably Wissmach). That is where many of the multi colored marbles came from.

Disaster struck Cairo Novelty on June 25, 1950, when the nearby rain-swollen Hughes River overflowed its banks and much of the town of Cairo was terribly flooded. Homes washed away and flood damage was extensive. Things were bad at Cairo Novelty in Carrol Addition, which was a low-lying area along the river. Water rose to a point much above the roof level of the Cairo Novelty building and damaged the machinery as well as taking out a large marble order packaged waiting shipment.

When the flood hit in 1950, the Hanlons were living in a house across the street, very near the factory. David remembers the water being so high that they climbed out onto the porch roof. They got into a rowboat and were rowed up the hill behind the factory to the railroad tracks and safety. The town was under water.

By mid-1950, Cairo Novelty was broke and there were many creditors reports David Hanlon. One party had even gotten a judgment against the company. On top of everything else, the newly-imported Japanese cat eye marble was beginning to cause real concern to all the American marble companies. Co-owner Dennis Farley was working sixty hours a week keeping his Cairo store going and had no time for marbles. The other owner, John Sandy, had sold his business in Cairo and moved to Parkersburg and was also not available nor interested in daily operations.

After the flood, Hanlon decided to repair what he could and re-open the factory. The in-stock inventory and the packaged shipment were a total loss. The boxes had fallen apart and the contents washed away or buried in mud.

In a conversation with David Hanlon held August 1997, David Tamulevich recorded the fact that David Hanlon worked at Cairo Novelty during his junior year in high school, doing the four p.m. to midnight shift and the young man was usually there all by himself. The marble business was doing poorly at the time and Oris Hanlon got a job at Electra Metallurgical Company between Belpre and Marietta, Ohio, to bring in much needed cash. Cairo Novelty at that time would run for three or four weeks, then shut down for two weeks, to do packing and shipping. Then they would fire up again to make marbles for three or four weeks. The longest straight stretch they ran continuously was for about six months.

Oris Hanlon gave his brother, who worked for their brother-in-law Heaton, all the Woolworth information so that Heaton could try to get the account. Woolworth had been Cairo Novelty's biggest customer.

After the flood, what marbles that were not washed away or buried in mud were simply strewn out all over the parking lot. The Cairo Novelty Company never fully recovered economically, but Hanlon hung on for two more years, finally closing for good in 1952, the majority of the business now going to Heaton Agate.

Local resident, Ralph Six, reminisced that "A trucking company, Burke, Parsons and Maddox, in 1953 or 1954, rented the site from Oris Hanlon. Later this company moved to Reedy, Roane County and is now a multi-million dollar business. When in Cairo they brought in green, newly cut pine trees and they had a machine with heavy rollers – after debarking they used a yellow treatment spray and ran the logs, under pressure, through the rollers to preserve them. The logs were sold to the State Hwy Dept. for highway posts. Their trucks carried out at one load about four hundred logs, which weighed about ninety pounds each. The debarked/peeler they used uniformly sized the logs. The Cairo Novelty Company site was swampy in the front anyway and the tons of wood chips filled in the area to a depth that is at points nearly three feet. The marbles at this site were buried underneath."

Danny Bircher, a member of the family that has owned the site for several years shared with the authors that "In the winter of 1993 - 94, three feet of snow collapsed the building. In the spring of 1995, I came in and hauled away most of the building. The building had stood nearly intact, but crumbling, until a bad winter took it down."

Examples of slag type colored sheet glass collected in the 1970s at the factory site by West Virginia glass historian Dean Six leads to the belief that one source of glass for Cairo Novelty striping was Wissmach Glass of Paden City, West Virginia. Additionally much Vitrolite flat architectural glass was found at the factory site as well as milk glass from Hazel-Atlas and an amazing variety of colors of scrap glass from light green depression era type glass to darker opaque shards. Six has an extensive collection of shards from the site.

Writing about Cairo Novelty Company, Dennis Webb in Greenberg's Guide to Marbles (First Edition), and elsewhere by others, suggested that Cairo Novelty Company did not make marbles for play, that only industrial marbles were produced for use in the oil industry. West Virginia glass historian, Dean Six, found this objectionable to read in print and provided confirmation to the marble community beginning in 1991 that Cairo Novelty had in fact made marbles for play. This was done by site finds and interviews with locals, including his grandmother June McGinnis who had worked there. She vividly recalled sorting and packaging marbles in bags for children's play and Six recalled seeing the wooden marble sorting machine in the old factory in the 1970s, a piece of machinery useful only in preparing toy marbles for bagging. Dennis Webb reported this revision in Greenberg's Guide to Marbles, Second Edition, 1994, correcting his earlier statements and illustrating the marbles Six had sent him from Cairo Novelty. Webb had relied on local residents who shared with him their recollection, albeit faulty recollections, about Cairo Novelty production. Again this source for fact reveals one of the potential pitfalls of oral history.

Following on the 1980s and 1990s activities of Six and his grandmother, Susie Metzler and Michael Johnson made additional discoveries at the site in 1994 and 1996 while David Tamulevich and his daughter, Molly, did some detailed excavations in 1995 and 1996. Since that time this team, as well as others, have brought to light many thousands of Cairo Novelty Company marbles that are now fully recognized as such. Digging by the authors was done with the express consent of the property owners.

In addition to Cairo Novelty marble names used by locals, other names for these marbles have been invented by David Tamulevich and his daughter. He says it makes them easier to discuss and recall (giving them an individual character) and as most names just came to mind, he used them. The Byrd family of Cairo, residents near the factory site, and other neighbors, have excavated and documented many marbles from this site in the 1990s. Many of those marbles have made their way into collection across the country.

There are very few one-color opaque or clearies and no cat eyes present at this site. It cannot be definitely stated why there is a lack of one color marbles. Perhaps they are buried in areas that have not been explored.

David Tamulevich, reported that "Many marbles recovered from the site are rejects for one reason or another such as not being round, hybrids, split, cracked. But one of the exciting things about the Cairo Novelty Company site is that it has contained many examples of many different color combinations. There may have existed hundreds of thousands of marbles there of types that were boxed, ready for shipping that, after the flood, were simply buried because it was not economically feasible to gather them up, clean up, and repack them."

A conversation with David Hanlon in May of 1996 recorded by David Tamulevich states that Oris Hanlon was a dreamer type person. He first made a mock-up of the marble machine as he saw it in his mind by welding steel plates together. Eventually he went to a machine shop to get the working machine constructed. Where other machines had two holes for the glass to go through in the cutting bar, this one had three, so he could make marbles fifty percent faster than other machines. They only made one size marble at a time. There were few orders for peewees, which were just as much work to make, but less profitable. Also, there were few orders for larger marbles.

They re-melted a lot of marbles too, especially the defective ones, former employee June McGinnis also stated that she used to take whole buckets of defective marbles and dump them in the parking lot out front.

Sometimes when they had a lot of orders, they would run three shifts around the clock making marbles. The most people they had working there was eight to ten persons when busiest.

Inside, the factory building had wooden bins, each with different marbles in it. When they got orders, a certain number of this color and a specific number of that color were gathered and a simple machine counted out the right number of marbles. It consisted of several steel drums with ten holes punched in them. Marbles were poured in the back and came out the other side. If the order called for five red marbles, five holes were plugged with paper and only five marbles would come out. These would come down a spout into a mesh bag that someone was holding over the opening. When the marbles were in, a label was put over the top of the bag and put in the stapler machine and a foot pedal was pushed to staple it. The completed bag was tossed into a bin and the process repeated. This was slow, hand labor.

CAIRO NOVELTY Marbles Produced

The local name for this company's marbles, reports Dean Six, was "clouds" or "cloudy days," and "snakes," although the company had not given specific names to their marbles.

Clearies are found in the colors of green, blue, amber, and clear and in sizes from 3/8" to 13/16".

Opaque marbles of two color, three color, four color varieties are found with the latter being quite uncommon.

Random Pattern Swirls are in sizes 3/8" to 7/8"; transparents are mostly two color and very slag-like; translucents are mostly two color, while some three color are found.

Solid One-Color Opaques are found in red, blue, white, black, green, faun-brow, and yellow-gold and sizes from 1/2 to 5/8".

In general, marbles sizes range from 3/8" to 7/8" and the vast majority are close to 5/8". Peewees seem to be extremely uncommon, as are 7/8" marbles. A size not quite so rare but hard to find is 13/16".

Some Cairo Novelty Company marbles are found to glow under a black light, a function of the varying sources for scrap glass from which they were produced.

Cairo Novelty employees included Catherine M. Chapman, June McGinnis (both of whom went to work at Heaton Agate after the flood), Pearl Reed, Troxell Skidmore, and the Sandy sisters.

Most of the information for this chapter was collected and compiled by David Tamulevich, David Hanlon, and Dean Six.

Cairo Novelty Marble Identification Tips

It is relatively easy to spot many Cairo Novelty Company marbles after one has seen and handled thousands of them, but most of us will never have that opportunity. There are characteristics in the color combinations that are distinguishable. It is true that there are striking resemblances to many of the other Ritchie County, West Virginia, marble products. As the marble machines were largely built by the same machine shop and the marble companies there bought the majority of their scrap glass from the same source such similarities seem inherent.

With no original Cairo Novelty packaging containing marbles found to date, one must rely on marbles found at the site and/or having strong local provenance to make attributions. There are characteristics that seem to be inherent in many marbles produced on Hanlon's unique machine. David Hanlon, son of factory owner Oris Hanlon, noted: "As Cairo Novelty never bought, sold, or traded marbles with other companies – a common practice among many companies – this means that the marbles taken from this site are pretty much verifiable as being made by Cairo Novelty Company."

In addition to following the Wissmach color palette, Cairo Novelty marbles have at least one and possibly two frequently occurring characteristics: a snake-like stripe on the exterior. It seems that the machine that rolled the marbles by using the Hanlon patent created a snake-like stripe on a limited side of the marble. This reappearing characteristic is not on all Cairo Novelty marbles, but neither has it been observed in the production of any other manufacturer.

A secondary characteristic seems to be a mark that appears like a tiny clear-glass window into the marble and extends away from the center of the surface of the marble as a clear-glass slash from a quarter to a half an inch.

As with all the marble companies, Cairo Novelty Company produced a seemingly endless number of non-descript, off-color marbles and fairly common two-color opaque white-based swirls in green/white; blue/white; red/white. The same is true with both translucent and transparent swirls. Some appear to be very common while others are remarkably rare and pretty.

Clearly one third of all Cairo Novelty marbles are virtually indistinguishable from those produced by other marble companies, particularly those in Ritchie County during the same time period.

The majority of uncommon three-color swirls are opaque and those in translucent bases are distinct and beautiful. Among the most colorful of all swirl marbles are the extremely uncommon four-color Cairo Novelty marbles, the majority of which are opaque.

Cairo Novelty had no recipe glass, they did not make their own glass. All of the glass used was scrap they purchased. Much of it came from a vendor of scrap glass in Washington, Pennsylvania. They got it from other sources as well. The color red they got from scraps of broken car tail lights and was used for striping. Once they got a shipment of construction-block glass and whatever was between the glass layers gummed up the machine. It had to be completely dismantled. Pieces of this laminated glass were found at the site decades later by Dean Six.

Cairo Novelty Packaging

To date, the only known original Cairo Novelty Company marble packaging is owned by co-author Dean Six, who lives and works in the town of Cairo. It is a cardboard box with cut-outs and a scene with two pyramids. The writing on the box says: "Pyramid Play-Time Marbles" and the words "Cairo Novelty Co., Inc. Cairo, West Va." The box appears faded and was found flattened, unused, and contained no marbles when found in the factory many years ago.

A board game utilizing marbles as game pieces, called "Trap the Fox," was produced by Cairo Novelty. David Hanlon believes the company marketed this game themselves. Few of these games have been found and production and distribution may have been limited. The cardboard boxed game is approximately thirteen inches square and features a colored fox hunting scene-type illustration on the cover. The underneath of the lid states the rules for play and says, "Copyright 1946 Cairo Novelty Company, Cairo, West Virginia." There are three cardboard pieces: the printed lid (color outside, ink text inside), the colorful printed game board, and the plain box bottom. For the "Trap the Fox" game, they specifically made black and white swirl marbles for the hounds. The fox was a solid-color opaque. The game was marketed as late as Christmas 1948 and 1949. Six found boxes in the rafters of the abandoned factory in the 1970s, years after the factory closed and was then being used as a oil field machinery work site.

David Hanlon has stated that, as a young man still in high school, he worked at the factory and remembers stapling mesh bags using several different headers. One was a header saying "Woolworth's" and the other was a header with the name, "Cairo Novelty Company," on it. To date, one of these mesh bags has been found.

A bag and header, using Cairo Novelty marbles, was made by Dean Six and his grandmother, June McGinnis, who worked at the factory. These bags were signed by both of them as containing verified Cairo Novelty marbles and sold nationally. Dean Six, writing about his grandmother and this experience says, "When I first dug at the Cairo Novelty site, she was there and dug beside me (although approaching eighty then). I packaged some with a header telling the tale and signed them as authentic Cairo Novelty. Grandma signed them as an ex-factory employee to add authenticity. These packages were limited to less than thirty signed packets and were marketed through one of the national marble newsletters by a classified ad. My goal was to place some good looking Cairo Novelty marbles in the hands of those most interested and to further dispel the erroneous belief that only industrial marbles came form Cairo Novelty."

Cairo Novelty two and three color swirls. *D. Chamberlain photo.*

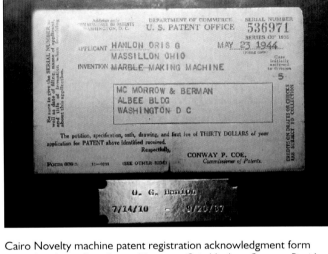

Cairo Novelty machine patent registration acknowledgment form carried in the wallet of proud inventor Oris Hanlon. *Courtesy David Hanlon.*

Cairo Novelty's Oris Hanlon. *Photo courtesy David Hanlon.*

Cairo Novelty factory site, Cairo, West Virginia. The building as it stood in disrepair in 1992. *D. Six photo.*

Cairo Novelty factory Cairo, West Virginia, as it appeared in July 1950, after the devastating flood. In the foreground is a young David Hanlon, son of one of the owners and a part time laborer while in High School.

Cairo Novelty pay stub for June McGinnis, dated May 10, 1949. Note the rate of pay is 40 cents per hour.

Cairo Novelty box. The only known example of the only know Cairo Novelty packaging. No price determined. *D. Six Collection.*

Cairo Novelty board game box lid for Trap The Fox. Scarce. *Game owned by C. Haga.* $500 to market.

Cairo Novelty Trap The Fox board interior.

Two of the roughly 30 packages created by Dean Six in 1991 to combat the belief that Cairo Novelty made only industrial marbles. Shown here is front and reverse of header. Most of these after market packages contained two each of six types of marbles. Each packet individually signed. These two were retained for the family. No value established.

Cairo Novelty examples of production. 3/4" to 13/16". *D. Chamberlain photo.*

Cairo Novelty examples of production. Can you identify the snake marbles? *D. Chamberlain photo.*

Cairo Novelty Cloudy Day marbles. These distinctive marbles contain blue whisps on and throughout a clear base.

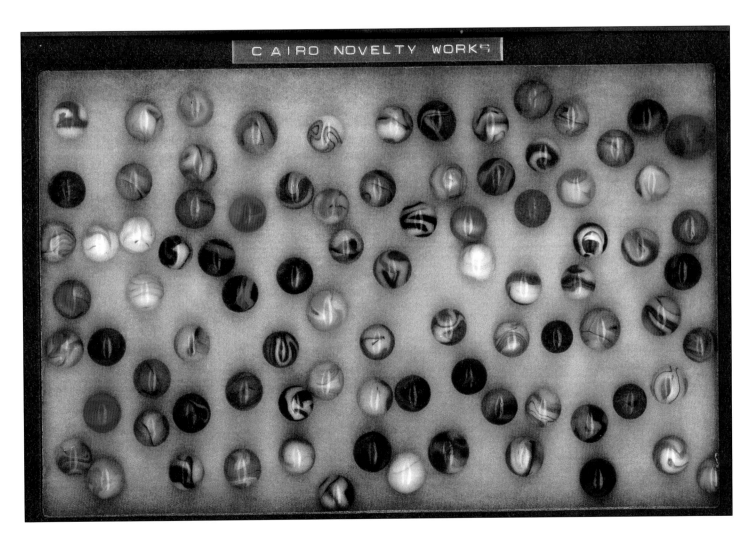

Cairo Novelty typical production examples.

CHAMPION AGATE

Pennsboro, West Virginia
1938 - operating at the time of publication

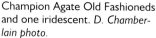

Champion Agate Old Fashioneds and one iridescent. *D. Chamberlain photo.*

Champion Agate Wire Pulls. *D. Chamberlain photo.*

A partnership agreement was entered into bearing the date of January 18, 1938, and that is the earliest known reference to a company that would come to be known as Champion Agate. In that agreement, Ralph R. Michels, Roy S. Michels, J.R. Murphy, and Lawrence "Jacup" (pronounced Yaccup) Jones formed a working partnership to form a marble company. This significant agreement is known today only because of its mention in the partnership dissolution (Ritchie County West Virginia Deed Book 109 at page 584).

Members of the Michels family, Bob (Robert J.) and Sam Michels, have expressed the belief that before anything was ever put on paper, the partnership was informally known as Jones and Michels Marble Company.

In the *Glass Factory Yearbook*, an annual trade directory, Champion first appears in 1940 where the listing reads: "Champion Agate Co., Pennsboro, W. Va., J.B. Murphy, president, general manager and sales manager; Roy S. Michels, secretary; Ralph R. Michels, treasurer; Lawrence Jones, factory manager. 3 small continuous tanks, 1 day tank. Glass marbles."

According to Sam Michels, the background of only one of these men included marble-making. Lawrence (Jacup) Jones had worked at the Alley Agate Company in Pennsboro as a handyman and mechanic. He had developed a unique glass-cutting mechanism for use in marble machines that was never patented. After Alley relocated to St. Marys, West Virginia, in 1937, Jones used to hang around Ralph (Pat) Michels drug store. Ralph Michels was the youngest of five brothers, a college graduate and pharmacist. Roy S. Michels owned the Pennsboro Hardware Store.

Jones, the family says, convinced Michels to start a marble factory in Pennsboro. According to Sam Michels' account, Ralph talked to Pennsboro city officials and they struck a deal on land and a small building owned by the city as a way to create a local jobs and business.

This original Champion factory site is located on Industrial Avenue, Pennsboro, West Virginia, at the west end of town near what was once the Baltimore and Ohio Railroad mainline. The area is locally known as Glass Factory Hollow, a reference to the presence of two large window glass factories that dominated the area in the early twentieth century and the continued presence of some form of hot glass production there for over a century. After the window glass factories closed, the last in 1928, Alley Agate Company occupied a site in Glass Factory from around

1931 until 1937. It was the relocation of Alley to St. Marys that seem to have inspired the formation of Champion Agate. The Champion site is diagonally across the street from the old Alley building.

The four original partners in Champion Agate obtained the land by a September 3, 1940, deed from the City of Pennsboro under the condition that it was a conveyance only "so long as used for manufacturing." (Ritchie County West Virginia Deed Book 108 at page 94).

Early on, Lawrence "Jacup" Jones designed a new machine and it was built in Murphy's machine shop. It reportedly produced 180 marbles a minute. Over the next few years five additions were made to the existing Champion building, which gave it a strange and rambling appearance that is retained even today.

A major development occurred in 1942 and is know to us today because it was part of the legal agreement contained in a deed. It was written and recorded that: "This agreement shall dissolve and forever terminate the partnership composed of Ralph R. Michels, Roy S. Michels, J.B. Murphy and Lawrence Jones effectuated by that certain agreement of partnership dated the 18th day of January, 1939, between the last mentioned persons, and that from and after this date the said Lawrence Jones is to have no further interest in the business or property of the said partnership but it is agreed that the said Ralph R. Michels, the said Roy S. Michels and the said J.B. Murphy as to the three last mentioned persons the said agreement of partnership will remain in force and effect, and that the partnership agreement made by the said agreement of partnership shall be continued as to the last three mentioned parties upon the same terms and conditions, except that there shall be no officer known as plant manager. As a part of this agreement, the said Lawrence Jones promises and covenants that he will not divulge any information whatsoever relative to the manner of construction or operation of a machine and tank with which the said partnership manufacturers a three-eights (3/8) inch marble, the said method of construction and operation of the said machine being a trade secret." (Ritchie County West Virginia Deed Book 109 at page 584).

The deed and agreement bearing the date March 11, 1942, had the effect of Lawrence Jones and Lillie, his wife, conveying their undivided 1/4th interest to Ralph R. Michels, Roy S. Michels, and J.B. Murphy for a tract of land in Pennsboro, W.V. The deed was for the tract the four men had acquired from the City of Pennsboro in 1940 (Ritchie County Deed book 108 page 94). But in transferring that tract the same agreement also conveyed much more and tells us much about what was happening there in 1942. The agreement transfers "all machinery, equipment, fixtures, cullet, marbles, packing supplies, tools, tanks and all other personal property of every kind and character now situate on or used in connection with the real estate mentioned or the business thereon conducted. All book accounts...claims and bank accounts or other tangible assets of the partnership known and operated as the Champion Agate Company. The exclusive right to use the name, the Champion Agate Novelty Company, and the right to manufacture and build any machine, tank or equipment like or similar to any machine, tank or equipment now used on the premises..."

Noted that the consideration received by Jones in the 1942 deed for his share in the land, partnership, machinery, trade secrets, and a promise to not divulge information or compete was seven hundred and fifty dollars. The dissolution of the initial partnership was soon reflected in the Annual Glass Trade Directories. All four men appear as noted above in the 1940-1942 issue of the *Glass Factory Yearbook*. In the 1943 edition, Jones and his position no longer are listed, exactly as the court documents reveal. Champion Agate was a partnership owned by Roy Michels, Ralph Michels, and J.B. Murphy as of March of 1942.

Jones brought into the partnership his skill as a machinist and designed the original Champion machines. In the years to come, it was these Jones designs that became known to others in the immediate community and were copied or closely replicated in the several start-up marble companies that later sprang up in Ritchie County. The resignation of Lawrence Jacup Jones in 1942 was a significant departure.

Perhaps Lawrence Jones was never really quite out of the picture. Sam Michels reported to the authors that during the mid-1940s a now unemployed Lawrence Jones used to hang around the Eagles' Club in Pennsboro and often talked around about how much money could be made making marbles. Both Robert and Sam Michels remember hearing of this boasting. It is fact that Champion machine operator, Carroll Jackson, left Champion around 1945 to start his own marble manufacturing company. Jackson's departure might have been induced by a combination of Jackson's firsthand observation and his belief, as Jones was saying, that there was good money to be had making marbles. Could others in Ritchie County, where so many small marble factories spring up, have had their aspirations fed by hearing Jones?

At this time Champion and other larger, better established marble manufacturers were pressuring jobbers and other marble buyers not to deal with the newcomers. They were striving to make it difficult for the newer concerns to obtain the scrap glass, called cullet. Champion was at that time acquiring it's glass from nearby Williamstown (the location of Fenton Art Glass) and from the H. M. Gabbert Glass Company, a Parkersburg, West Virginia, scrap glass vendor.

An article in the local Sunday newspaper, *The Parkersburg News* (December 12, 1954), related that during World War II marbles became an important item in the national defense with the men and women at Champion Agate working around the clock seven days a week. This generally sounds impressive and is often a boast of the effort on behalf of the war. Keep in mind that due to the extreme heat and energy required to convert and retain glass in a liquid state, marble furnaces generally run twenty-four hours per day, every day of the calendar year. It was the interesting and adaptive uses of Champion Agate marbles during this time that is noteworthy. There was an allocation of all available metal to military armament products. Champion marbles found their way into airplane instruments, where they appeared in turn-and-bank indicators. In uses where physical pressure was adequate, glass marbles were substituted for steel ball bearings.

After the war, according to both Robert and Sam Michels, Champion hired a New York firm to broker their marbles. Champion furnaces ran, like most marble furnaces, seven days a week. Operators logged in for twelve hour shifts and rotated to work around the clock until all orders were filled. Champion then shut down until more orders were accumulated. This was a fairly typical mode of operation during those years and is still used today as melting tanks and other equipment need overhauling and replacement during down times.

In the early 1950s, disaster struck the domestic toy marble industry. Robert J. Michels reported a theme that was repeated all over the post World War II U.S. marble industry. Michels relates that the U.S. government, anxious to encourage industry in Japan and trade with that country, requested that Champion and his father allow a Japanese delegation to tour the Pennsboro factory. The visitors took no notes and no photographs, but returned to Japan and built marble machines that Michels believes were identical to those at Champion based on the marbles they produced.

Champion joined forces with other U.S. marble manufacturers in an attempt to stem the flood of cheap import marbles but to no avail. The *Parkersburg News* of December 12, 1954, chronicles the bleak circumstances that followed the abrupt turn of events that came after World War II to the marble industry. Champion Agate had been moderately prosperous until the Japanese products began to appear. However, during this time in 1954, the *News* article states "within the last ninety days, the situation has become so serious in the American marble industry, that plant payroll had to be cut as much as sixty percent. At Champion, peak employment had been cut from more than forty persons to eighteen. At the time, these eighteen were not assured continued employ-

ment beyond a few months as the American marble business faces dissolution."

Many American marble companies indeed went out of business in this era. Jackson, Playrite, Davis, all small concerns and all located near Champion, closed. Several of the major and long standing marble producers also closed: Akro Agate in 1951 and Ravenswood Novelty Works in 1955. A few held on, including Champion Agate, hoping for better times.

By 1953 the next change appears in the *Glass Factory Yearbook* entry with the note that Champion operates four furnaces, an addition of one over the prior years, and only Roy S. Michels is listed, giving his title as president. It is not known what, if any, change in ownership or control this reflects at that time, but a slight increase in production is suggested with the addition of another furnace.

In 1957 the *American Glass Review* listed Champion's officers as J.B. Murphy, president; Roy S. Michels, vice president and sales manager; R.R. Michels as secretary-treasurer; and Roy S. Michels as general manager. It cites 4 continuous tanks and 5 machines making 6/16ths to 1" marbles.

By 1964 the *American Glass Review* entry lists only Ralph R. Michels as general and plant manager and purchasing agent. They had cut back to 3 continuous tanks and listed marbles only in the sizes of 3/6th to 3/4ths.

Industry directories, such as the one cited, give valuable insight not only into the general health of the industry, but also that of individual companies. While the marble factories that do appear in glass trade directories give us interesting year by year details, those are limited. Much relevant information is lacking today. Looking back, we wish for more details such as ownership changes and plant managers' names, etc. Regardless, they are a major, and often the only, source tracking annual affairs of the marble factories such as Champion.

On November 12, 1964, J.B. Murphy, Roy S. Michels, Ralph R. Michels, and their respective wives sold to Palmer and Irene Hill the real property that was the site of Champion Agate. At this time, J.B. Murphy signs the deed from Lake County, Florida. (Ritchie County West Virginia Deed book 149 at page 512) A few days later, on the 17th of November of 1964, Palmer and Irene Hill conveyed the same to Champion Agate, a corporation. (Ritchie County Deed Book 150 at page 514). A short few months later in April of 1965, Palmer Hill, as president of Champion Agate Co., conveyed the property to Donald G. Michels for the sum of $5,000. Once again, Champion Agate was back in the hands of the Michels family.

Donald G. Michels was the son of Ralph "Pat" Michels. He was the owner of a coffee shop in West Union, West Virginia, and had no previous experience in the glass industry. On April 20th, 1965, Donald G. Michels, DBA Champion Agate Co. and Helen his wife, borrowed $50,000, signing only in their individual capacity and not as corporate officers. The transaction suggests that Champion is not a corporation at this time but a partnership or sole proprietorships as they did not endorse the legal document in any capacity as corporate officers. (Ritchie Co. West Virginia Trust and Mortgage book 50 at page 418).

The *American Glass Review* annual directory for glass factories lists Champion Agate in 1969 through 1972 as "Donald G. Michels, owner, sales and plant manager; Mrs. Georgia Miller, secretary. 4 cont. tanks, 1 day tank, 4 roller machines."

The next change we find is in the 1976 *American Glass Review*, where there is a listing for Champion Agate that states "Donald G. Michels, president, sales and plant manager, Mrs. Helen Michels, treasurer." The production information remains unchanged: 4 continuous tanks, 1 day tank and 4 roller machines. This is the first year Helen appears in the list. Helen was known as a former schoolteacher in their home community of Doddridge County, West Virginia.

In 1975, Champion Agate became incorporated, having operated for most of four decades as a partnership or sole proprietorship. Once Champion becomes a corporation, the ownership becomes murky and difficult to follow in the 1980s.

From 1983 through 1985 the *American Glass Review* trade directory lists Champion Agate, Inc. with "Donald G. Michels as president, sales and plant manager; Mrs. Helen Michels, treasurer. Four continuous machines, one day tank, and nine roller-type machines." Note that there were four roller machines (marble machines) listed in 1976 but nine by 1983, seven years later.

Dave McCullough joined Champion in 1980 to run the day-to-day operation, but as plant manager he does not appear in the trade directories. Dave's recollections are that Helen Michels took control of Champion in 1982 and retained him as plant manager.

The 1986 through 1993 *American Glass Review* trade directory lists Champion Agate, Inc. 107 Industrial Ave., Pennsboro, West Virginia, with Helen Michels, president, sales and plant manager. The production information remains unchanged: "4 continuous tanks, 1 day tank, 9 roller-type machines. Marbles for toys and games, industrial balls."

The confusing question of company ownership came up in a June 2005 interview with Sam Michels. He stated Don had given Helen the marble factory at her demand. While there are endless local accounts of tension between the Don and Helen, this too is complicated. Reportedly Helen told workers there to not allow Don on the property and no one recalls seeing him there again. Some reports include a divorce and the marble factory transfer as part of that proceeding but we were unable to find any record of divorce or legal documents reporting the actual transfer of the marble factory property. The Michels family says there was no divorce.

Helen Michels, suffering with a debilitating illness, ran Champion Agate by telephone from her home. She assumed control in 1982, recalls Dave McCullough, though it took until 1986 for her name to appear as president in the trade directories. Helen got her son-in-law, Dan Christian, to work under Dave McCullough to learn the business. McCullough produced the "Whirlwind" and "Old Fashioned" marbles during this circa 1984-1988 time. It has been noted elsewhere that those marbles appear to be an attempt to duplicate the older style of Ravenswood Novelty marbles. It is noteworthy that at some time Champion did acquire an old Ravenswood marble machine.

Dave McCullough reports that during this era, the management situation at Champion became difficult as he found himself answering to two people. Further, Helen Michels was unwilling to allow McCullough to "do his own thing" with new colors or designs. Even under these circumstances, Champion continued and prospered. In 1987, Champion had grown to thirty-seven employees and worked two-twelve hour shifts each twenty-four hours, seven days per week, making approximately two million marbles in the two shifts, fourteen million per week. John Shackelford, a Champion marble machine operator, reported working twelve hour shifts, from 4:00 a.m. to 4:00 p.m. with a two man crew for each machine during this era. A significant seller in 1987 was the Chinese checker type opaque marble used for the then popular Pac Man board game.

While at Champion, Dave McCullough had built a marble machine based on blueprints designed by Bill Heaton of Heaton Agate and given to McCullough by Mrs. Bill Heaton. There was a single striping pot, the source for adding the color stripes to marbles, at the front of the hot glass tank and near the cutter. It was on this machine that the Whirlwind and many of the Old Fashioned marbles were produced. McCullough recalls producing these marbles at Champion from 1981 until 1984 or '85. Vitro Agate, in nearby Parkersburg, West Virginia, was having financial difficulties at that time and the House of Marbles, an English distributor, turned to Champion Agate to fill the gap resulting from diminished supply from Vitro. The vast majority of Champion's Whirlwinds and Old Fashioneds went to this large British distributor. However, some found their way into the U.S. market by way of Charles Stutsman and Ralph Neat. McCullough had made a second Heaton designed marble machine while at Champion. This featured two striping pots – one at either side of the front of the tank. This machine never worked well as one color tended to dominate the other and the desired effect was not fully achieved.

McCullough also discovered how to make a good ruby glass. About 1984, McCullough was running a tank of red Chinese checker marbles. McCullough instructed the man responsible for that machine to add one level shovel full of a certain glass into the tank each hour. The operator thought he was told to add eleven shovels full each hour and proceeded to do so all through the night. McCullough recalled that he was angry the next morning before he realized what the result was. He has been making ruby glass in that same manner since that time. Before

and after the discovery of the new red, Champion was known for the type of burnt orange which they called cranberry. McCullough does not reminisce long about the marble industry without his repeated quote "A lot may be learned by accident or mistake in this business."

In or about the year 1988, a new building was constructed to house Champion Agate. It was a short few hundred yards up Glass Factory Hollow and on the opposing side of the small valley. The original building continued in use but production was largely relocated to the newer structure. This semi-circular roofed metal building was built by the Jackson brothers whose father, Carroll Jackson, had once worked at Champion Agate and in the 1940s started his own marble factory on the opposite side of Pennsboro.

During McCullough's tenure as Champion's plant manager, Champion began producing their version of flats or gems. The flat, rock-like glass stones are made for crafts, game pieces, and other uses. Flats or gems became a major part of Champion production after relocation to the new building. Champion continued to produce various marbles for industrial and commercial applications in addition to the much smaller output of toy marbles for play.

In 1991, Dave McCullough found employment with marble maker JABO, Inc. in Reno, Ohio, and left Champion Agate. McCullough continued his exceptional exploration of color and design at JABO.

Between 1991 and 1996, Don and Helen Michels' son-in-law, Dan Christian, ran the business. The 1994 *American Glass Review* trade directory lists Champion Agate, Inc. with Helen Michels as president, sales manager, and plant manager. Dan Christian is shown as general manager, and again, the production information had not changed. With the addition of the name Dan Christian, it was the first time in some years that a name other than Helen Michels appeared in the directory. The information in the 1995 directory remained the same. This was the last year Champion Agate was listed in the directory.

March 19, 1996, there is taken a tax lien against Champion Agate Co., Inc. for corporate income tax in the amount of $318. It is paid and released by August but may have been seen as some indication of the cash flow or attention to business that Champion is receiving at that time. In 1996, expansion of the company came with the purchase of the adjacent Pennsboro Glass factory, being the same structure that had been the old Alley Agate building. Champion had at the time been renting part of the Pennsboro Glass site for storage. The new building was soon to hold a business operating as Champion Glass that tried its hand at pressed glass and other glass products. Champion Glass was short lived, operating a few years only. The 1996 *American Glass Review* trade directory lists Champion Glass (across the street address), Inc. with "Helen Michels, president; Rick Morse, general manager." There is no mention of Champion Agate in the industry trade annual that year.

The year 1996 saw reuse of the original Champion building for production. New tanks and renovated marble machines were put to work in the old building. Once production was underway in the old building, the machines and tanks were repaired in the newer, metal factory that had been built in 1988. They were long overdue for serious overhaul. One employee, exaggerating, described the tanks at that time as having "walls so thin that one could almost see through them." Intense heat and years of service takes a toll on glass house machinery.

In 1997, according to family member Sam Michels, Helen Michels passed away of an undisclosed illness in California. Both she and Donald G., who died several years later, are buried in unmarked graves near Crystal Lake in West Union. As per request, there was no actual public or family funeral, no guests, and no flowers were accepted.

By 1997 the *American Glass Review* trade directory lists Champion Glass and again there is no mention of Champion Agate. However, Donald H. Michels is president, and the product line is hand blown glass with a George Street, West Union address. This is the Michels family home address.

Donald H. is the son of Donald G. and Helen and grandson of Champion co-founder Ralph "Pat" Michels. The business was now being operated by a third generation family member. This is something perhaps unique in the American marble industry. Donald H. drew a paycheck from the family owned business as early as September 1971 when he was issued Champion paycheck #2874 on September 9, 1971, for $146.89. (David Tamulevich Collection).

In 1997, the new building was the site for production of both flats and marbles; the old building was used only for storage. Employees repeated to the authors at that time that the old building was only temporarily down and would soon again be producing. In that year, two machines were at work (May), one each for flats and marbles. Another furnace was cooking glass. Recent years have seen very little production in the old building and observations at the site proved that it was indeed used to store marble machine parts, tools, and for general storage. In 1998 and 1999, Champion Agate was again not listed in any trade directory.

Sam Michels reported that due to the failing health of the parents (Donald G. and Helen), Donald H. (called Donny by the family) has actually run the business from the family home in West Union since about 1995. It was 1997 that Donald H. first appeared in the trade directories. Donald H. has continued to run Champion in the same manner as was done by his mother, by telephone from the family home. He is not known by the employees or residents in Pennsboro or at the factory. Daily operational questions at Champion have been handled for some years by Barbara Barker, also not a resident of the Pennsboro community. The Michels family shroud of privacy and near secrecy continues. As of 2005, Barbara continued at the factory and was overseeing daily operations. The connection of Donald H. Michels from the family home in West Union can only be assumed and that is by the appearance of that West Union, West Virginia, address on the labels for bags of Champion marbles, suggesting that business should be directed there, to the home and not the factory.

In 2001, 2002, and early 2005, Champion produced three different types of Old Fashioned marbles for play, all having an element of purple/amethyst to them. Several boxes of these were donated to the West Virginia Marble Festival in Cairo, West Virginia, and a small handful was given to each attendee of the event. Examples of these marbles have been saved for the permanent collection of the West Virginia Museum of American Glass, the Marble Festival sponsor.

On a visits in 2003, Champion machines were observed idle for several months, but by June, one machine was observed working in the new building and was producing flats/gems. Production continued, but erratically, into 2005. In 2005 production of a different version of the purple/amethyst marbles commenced and nearly one hundred pounds were donated to the West Virginia Marble Festival in Cairo and given away there.

The year 2005 revealed other Champion developments. A nylon mesh bag of colorless marbles was recovered from the old Pennsboro Glass/Champion Glass factory. This bag has a label imprinted with the U.S. mailing address of the company being given as West Union, West Virginia, and naming the maker as Champion Agate. This was the first time an actual Champion Agate bag label had been seen for over fifteen years.

Saturday, June 25, 2005, saw the auctioning off of the contents of the Champion Glass building (formerly Pennsboro Glass, and Alley Agate). Very little of a marble-related importance was in the building, but the owner promoted it as the sale of a marble factory, based on the considerable inventory of recent Champion gems and marbles stored there. This caused speculation and rumor across the marble collecting community but was disappointing in its marble content or marble artifacts. No marble machinery was in the sale, as had been suggested in advertisements for the auction, but there was machinery for hand blown glass production, not related to marbles in any way.

A visit in 2005 revealed only one marble machine was operating at Champion Agate (in the new building) and eight workers employed. The old building on the site is of wooden frame construction with an outer shell of corrugated tin. Special roof vents, called lanterns – typical of glass houses, cap the roof's crest. These function to help dispel the intense heat the glass furnaces generate inside the building.

Within marble collecting circles, a story has grown around the so-called "Pit" at Champion Agate. In truth, The Pit was storage inside a building that Jim Davis reports was once a small garment factory. It was across the street from the original Champion building. It took its name from the dilapidated condition of the structure, as Champion employees referred to it. Tales of a massive hole in the floor or anything similar that has been created in people's minds should be dispelled. The storage building was used from the mid-1970s until late 1994, when it burned.

In 1976, as Champion was preparing to market American Bicentennial packaging, they let it be known that they were seeking a variety and diversity of marbles to fill these bags. Dave McCullough recalls an overwhelming response to this informal appeal. People cleaned out barns, garages, basements, and other storage spaces and came to Champion with their older marbles. Boxes in cars and pick-up trucks came. Marbles from several of the then defunct factories thus made their way into the mixture that filled the Champion plastic Bicentennial bags. This circa 1976 appeal for marbles is tied to the otherwise confusing presence of marbles from various manufacturers that came from Champion and The Pit.

Dave McCullough recalls that shortly prior to his leaving Champion, everything deemed to have value was taken out of the building. Several boxes and loose marbles were left behind. Many loose marbles had fallen through the floorboards. Charles Stutsman, a marble dealer from Indiana, bought many "odds and ends" from The Pit and is reported to have crawled under the building to gather marbles. After the building burned in late 1994, the site was dozed and fill dirt added to level it.

One Champion Agate warehouse and shipping facility consists of a single pre-fabricated, light yellow, metal building located at the extreme eastern end of Ellenboro, West Virginia, along Old US Route 50. On June 7, 1977, Champion Agate acquired land along Old Route 50 at the east-end of Ellenboro for $67,000. Ellenboro is a short few miles west of Pennsboro. A packaging and storage operation warehouse was maintained at this site by Champion. In the 1977 purchase, Donald G. signed as president and Helen as secretary. (Ritchie County Deed Book) Since 1994, at least, this building has seen the swing of activity from absolute desertion to a hustling activity and near overflow. It should be noted that these observations were made during the spring of each year and may not reflect the flow of activity at other times of the same year.

On a 1994 visit, an employee stated that most Champion marbles were "made up to order" and largely in bulk, "for shipment all over the world and to the U.S. and Texas". At that time there were fifty pound boxes, twenty-five pound boxes, pint plastic jars, and bags of marbles (bearing no labeling of any kind). He told us that he could hardly remember the last time he saw bags of Champion marbles that had their own labels on them. During the next several years, the authors observed erratic activity at the warehouse, from deserted to bustling. The years 1996, 1997, 1998, and 2002 saw considerable activity. A visit in 2003 revealed literally thousands of packages from Michaels Hobby and Craft Stores. These were scattered about the facility. The facility looked otherwise deserted. In 2004, however, there was much activity and open doors revealed five or six employees busily packaging marbles, with hundreds of cartons of Champion products clearly visible, stacked on pallets, ready for shipment. A visit in 2005 saw a return to the 2003 conditions.

CHAMPION AGATE
Marbles Produced

It is difficult to positively identify the early marbles from Champion Agate. One source states Champion first produced only opaque and transparent marbles. If so, those are virtually indistinguishable from the production of several other companies at that same time.

In later years, opaque, transparent, and translucent swirls were introduced and little is known about early packaging that would allow positive identification. With few clues, it is not possible to make a positive attribution for the early Champion production. Further complicating the issue of identification is the close proximity of Champion to the early Pennsboro location of Alley Agate. A few yards separate the two locations. Over the years, many marbles from both companies have been scattered over the area, making attribution based on industrial archeology impossible. (That is to say, you cannot say who made what is dug anywhere near there!) One reliable source for attribution is marbles in the collections of ex-employees with credible histories for coming directly from the factory. One such collection for Champion marbles is owned by Dale Simmons, son of Pete Simmons, a Champion employee from 1949-1951.

Collectors once viewed Champion Old Fashioned and Whirlwind marbles as attempts to reproduce earlier marbles and thus they were held in some disdain. In recent years, these products are gaining appreciation in their own right, as well they should, for being attractive marbles regardless. The most commonly seen Champion Agates are the Old Fashioned and Whirlwind marbles of the 1980s. These marbles are in fact often mistaken for and identified as older swirls and often attributed to Ravenswood. Some possible clues to distinguish them might be that the Champion products can have an oily surface appearance, may be slightly out of round, and can include minor fractures or obvious crimp marks.

Many of these marbles are colorful, pleasing to the eye, and perfectly round. It may sound like we are describing seconds or rejects dug from the site. Generally, however, these marbles, in various conditions, were shipped in bulk cartons ungraded and were entered into the world "as is".

Backlash: In 1988 a marble machine operator accidentally dropped a welding rod into the melting tank/furnace of clear class. This resulted in a kind of metallic wire pull. Author Dennis Webb named these Backlash marbles due to the similarity in appearance to a fly fisherman's silken line about to become hopelessly tangled in mid-air. Dave McCullough estimated that about 250,000 of these were made.

Carnival Glass: The application of a sprayed on vapor of metallic salt onto the hot glass marble was pioneered at Champion in 1984. It was an immediate success due to its striking color. Carnival marbles have been produced subsequently by Mid-Atlantic, Vacor, and JABO.

Cat's Eyes: Champion did not make cat's eye marbles while Dave McCullough was there; however, many cat's eye marbles have been found at the site. Some were made by Champion, others by either Marble King or Heaton Agate. Many cat's eye types from all over that were once stored in "The Pit" are still to be found scattered around the factory site.

Flats or Gems: In 1983 the little, irregularly shaped glass gems or flats were produced by Champion for the first time. They have remained a staple of the company every since. In the early 2000s, the marble orders were scarce, but sales for gems/flats continued.

Furnace Scrapings: In early 1995, there was considerable excitement in the marble world regarding what was then being called a "recent Champion Agate furnace scraping marble." It was told at the time that these marbles resulted from glass scraped from the side of the glass tanks as they were being dismantled for replacement. According to information that collector/dealer David Chamberlain had received, about 8,000 marbles were made and of these about 1,500 were of high quality and were selling at that time for $20 each. The remaining marbles were misformed, fractured or otherwise imperfect. Those sold for an amazing $5 each at the time. In 1999 Dave McCullough revealed that those marbles were in fact made from recycled cathedral glass brought to Champion from Wissmach Glass, a flat glass manufacturer in Paden City, West Virginia. This recent story, and one that the truth won out on, should serve as a monumental reminder of the oral exaggerations and mythical stories that spring up around unknown marbles to create explanations and help sell them. The marble world is and has long been plagued by such stories, bearing no connection to truth or anything that happened; but, they simply sounded good. Collectors have long been too fast to accept these and repeat them as true without questioning their believability, source or plausibility. Let us learn from Furnace Scraping!

Pearls: Iridescent white opaque (a type of carnival marble) that first appeared at Champion in 1985. These marbles were used in costume jewelry and for other applications.

Tops: Circa 1970 Champion Agate produced an unknown number of what have been dubbed "Tops." These were probably made by allowing gobs of glass to enter the rollers that were actually too large for the roller and this resulted in nipples forming at the ends of the initial sheared gob. It is not known how many were made or for what purpose. No prices have been established. It was recently learned that the tops were made by a Champion employee named Jones. He made them just to be doing it!

Wirepull marbles: These Champion items were a product of the 1980s and named by marble collector/author Dennis Webb after he first saw them. For some reason, unknown to us, Webb mistakenly attributed these to Jackson Marble Company. These marbles, in sizes usually ranging from 9/16ths to 5/8ths, came in a clear base with one color striping or red, orange, yellow, white or blue. Less common purple and green striped examples do exist. A very few larger sizes are known as well. A limited number of two color hybrids, including purple/white, orange/yellow, yellow/white, blue/white, and red/yellow have been documented. Green base glass with white striping and red base glass with white striping are just two varieties of these hybrids. The Wirepull marbles were made when the extruder apparatus, a part of the glass furnace, normally used to make a cat's eye marble, was modified to leave only a 1/8" hole in it. This allowed the extruder that normally injected the color to make a controlled cat's eye marble to move randomly and inject color within the marble resembled tangled wire.

Pee-Wees: Champion pee-wees were mostly made in the 1960s – and reportedly not in large numbers. Champion's top size marble was approximately 3/4ths of an inch. A few are found slightly larger.

CHAMPION AGATE
Packaging

Champion Agate packaging and the contents thereof represent a major challenge to the historian and collector for several reasons. For production in recent years, the Champion employees have stated that it has been a long time since they used their own labels on their products. They often utilized packaging materials and supplies provided by and naming only their customers, the sellers in the marketplace of the Champion products.

An additional challenge is that original Champion labels have been used and misused by jobbers and dealers putting marbles from anywhere into the marked Champion package and Champion has done the same thing by putting other's products into their bags (i.e., the Bicentennial bags). For years Champion brokered marbles that were other company overruns as well as marbles from companies that had gone out of business such as Master Glass, Jackson, and others. See the text about The Pit.

The Champion known packages are:

Bicentennial Special Pack: This is truly a beautiful and imaginatively conceived bag. Celebrating the 200th birthday of the United States, Champion Agate included marbles from Champion, C. E. Bogard and Sons, Heaton Agate, Jackson, Marble King, Master Glass, Peltier, and Ravenswood. This collection, all in one bag, represented marbles made over a period of many years by several U.S. marble makers. Dave McCullough related that most of the Champion Agate Bicentennial Special Packs that are seen for sale today do not contain the marbles originally intended for them. When "The Pit" at Champion was cleaned out, many boxes of the bags were found and sold empty. The tops of the bags were pre-sealed and marbles were inserted in via the bottom and heat sealed by post-market dealers. Charles Stutsman, a dealer/collector from Indiana, bought many and filled them with odds and ends that he bought from Champion and elsewhere that were not original to the bags. Even the stunning red, white, and blue marble, often called the Bicentennial Special, was just a fancy Old Fashioned from the 1980s and not 1976. In fact, any of the bags with Old Fashioned or Whirlwind marbles are not those originally packaged by Champion but are bags filled at a later date.

Poly bags: Most collectible Champion Agate bags found are poly (clear plastic) with stapled paper headers. These bags of various counts are known to contain Champion marbles and marbles made by other companies. Most will be red or white, or yellow paper with printing of red or black ink "Made in the U.S.A. Champion Agates, Champion Agate Company, Inc. Pennsboro, W. Va." Known poly bag counts include:

4: contains shooters (usually transparent marbles)
5: shooters or mixed larger and small marbles
20: mixed size marbles
15: mixed size marbles
21: mixed size marbles

25: mixed size marbles
40: mixed sizes but mostly 5/8" marbles
60: may contain some pee wee, 9/16" or 5/8" marbles.

Some poly bags contain Chinese checker marbles, although they are not identified as such.

Old Mesh Bag: These survive in very limited numbers. The original yellow mesh bag contains twenty-five marbles of 5/8" size and probably date to the 1940-50s.

Modern Mesh Bags: Similar to the modern nylon mesh bags used by JABO, Inc. and Vacor, the Champion mesh bags usually contain glass gems or iridescent or plain clearies. These packages were often intended for the craft, floral arranging or other decorative use markets. Often these have a store label identifying the retailer and not mentioning Champion as the manufacturer.

Plastic Jars: Champion plastic jars came in two sizes, 21 oz. and 24 oz. These bear no labeling, indicating they were made by Champion and often are simply marked glass marbles or glass gems and with the weight. Some jars will be labeled for a specific retailer such as "Michaels – The Arts and Crafts Store."

Be aware that there are marble packages and boxes that use the word Champion but have nothing to do with the Champion Agate Company.

CHAMPION AGATE
Employees

A list, far from complete, of those known to have been employed at Champion:

Frank Broadwater 1949 - 51; M. Broadwater; Ronnie Brookover; Harry W. Collins; William H. Collins; Troy Cunningham; Sue Davis; Andrew Doak; David Fullen; Scott Fullen; Robert Harris; Frank Henderson 1950s; Palmer Hill 1940s; Ronald Hurst; Carroll Jackson 1940s; Lehman Jackson; Roger Jones; Rosalea Jones; Helen Kelley 1950s; Lawrence Kendall; Richard Kinney; Clarence Layfield 1940s; William Lamm; Linda Lamp; Rose Lamp 1950s; Keith Lingler; Jerry Leggett; Lee Lowther; Rusty Lowther; Ronald L. McKinney; Donald H. Michels; Georgia J. Miller; Steve Playso; K. O. Ramsey; Millard F. Riggs, Sr.; John Shackelford 1990s; Pete Simmons 1949-51; Colten Smith; Glendall Smith; William Lee Smith; Jessie Underwood; Gale Whitehair.

Champion Agate storage building called "the pit" by employees and taking on almost mythical status in marble lore, status not necessarily merited. *Photo 1984 Dennis Webb Collection.* The original Champion factory would be to the left of the image and across the road that appears in the images lower left.

Champion Agate original factory Pennsboro, West Virginia, as it appeared in 2004 when used as storage and office space. *D. Simmons photo.*

Champion Agate pit, an inside view.

Champion Agate original factory, Pennsboro, West Virginia, as it appeared in 1994.

Champion Agate closer view of the "new" building. Note the one operating furnace inside. *D. Simmons photo.*

A view of Glass Factory Hollow, Pennsboro, West Virginia, giving the relative placement of the various marble related structures. L to R: is the rounded metal Champion "new building," behind the large tree with a black roof is the early Alley Agate/Pennsboro Glass building, and on the right – showing a varied roof line and surrounded by piles of colorful glass cullet – is the "old" or original Champion building. The black line crossing the image is a power line. *Spring 2005 photo D. Six.*

Champion Agate pit, also inside the legendary place. Photo 1985.

Champion Agate's "new building" Pennsboro, West Virginia, where production was relocated. This view is shot with the photographers back to the "Old factory" and indicates their close proximity. Note the small orange glowing furnaces operating inside. The foreground is scrap or cullet glass stacked in front of the old factory site awaiting melting. 1998 photo.

Champion Agate storage and shipping facility west of Pennsboro, West Virginia, near Ellenboro on Old U.S. 50. *Photo taken 1999 courtesy Marble Magnates.*

Champion Agate cullet cart containing the scrap glass awaiting re-melting and being formed into marbles. *Photo 1994. Dennis Webb Collection.*

Champion Agate packaging facility interior. *Photo taken 1994 courtesy Marble Magnates.*

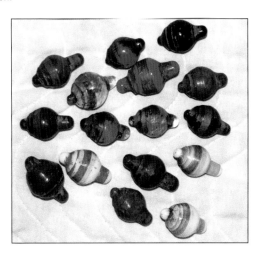

Champion Agate tops. 1972. These result from time to time in the marble industry when too much glass gets on the rollers to be rolled round, etc. These tops were made intentionally by Champion. *D. Chamberlain photo.*

Champion Agate cullet being hand shoveled and then moved via wheel barrow to the furnace where it is dumped, awaiting hand shovel feeding into the furnace. John Shackelford at work, May 1994.

Champion Agate 1930-40s mesh bag with early Champion Agate header. *Courtesy Marble Magnates.* $50-80.

Champion Agate 60 count Chinese Checker poly bag and header. $25.

Champion Agate 25 count poly bag. $15.

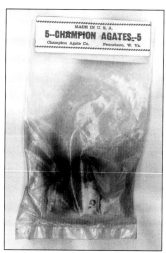

Champion Agates, Champion Agate Co. Pennsboro, W. Va., poly bag of five shooters. *D. Six collection.* $10-15.

Champion Agate sample bag with mailing label attached. *Courtesy National Marble Museum.* No value determined.

Champion Agate 12 count poly bag. $15.

Champion Agate "Bicentennial Special Pack." Released in 1976, this large, printed poly bag contains marbles from at least seven different companies as originally packaged. $50. A selection of after market bags were filled at a later date by Charles Stutsman using a different mix of marbles but the same, original bags. $10-15.

Champion Agate poly bags, either variety of header. As shown, $5-12.

Champion Agate so-called "Furnace" or "Furnace Scraping" marbles. *Collection of D. Simmons.*

Champion Agate mesh bag circa 1990-2000s using West Union address. $10-15.

Champion Agate Co. paperweight's base. An uncommon marble promotional item is this solid cobalt blue with iridescent paperweight. "Champion Agate Co. Call 659-286 Pennsboro W.Va." is raised in the glass. 2 1/2" in diameter. In an odd bit of marketing, the inscription is on the base/bottom and not visible when the otherwise spherical paperweight is in use. Made by Welch Glass, a one-man company in nearby West Union, West Virginia, circa 1960s. Only one known to date. *D. Six collection.* No value determined.

Champion Agate Old Fashioneds. *Collection and photo D. Chamberlain.*

Champion Agate marbles made in Spring of 2005. *D. Chamberlain photo.*

CHRISTENSEN AGATE

Payne, Ohio
1925 - 1927
Cambridge, Ohio
1927 - 1933

Christensen Agate examples of diverse production.

Christensen Agate Collection and *photo D. Gardner*.

This very significant, but short-lived company had its beginning in 1925 in the small Northwest Ohio town of Payne. Little is known of this early operation or of the marbles produced there. The need for significant efforts to research the earliest years is apparent as little has been reported or is known at this time.

In 1927, Christensen Agate moved to a small brick building at the end of Bennett Avenue in Cambridge, Ohio. There were monetary incentives from the city to do so. It was at this location, in close proximity to the Cambridge Glass Company, that Christensen Agate made its most well-known marbles.

The Christensen Agate company was organized by a group of Ohio business persons and a marble machine builder. The founders of the company were investor-businessmen W.I. Jones, H.H. Culper, Owen M. Roderick, Robert C. Ryder, and Beaulah P. Hartman in addition to Howard M. Jenkins. Jenkins was from Pittsburgh, Pennsylvania, and was the marble machine builder. He was also the company president. Jenkin's first patent for a marble machine (#1,488,817) was issued April 1, 1924. He later patented an improved model (#1,596,879), while then a resident of Clarksburg, West Virginia.

Important to the success of Christensen Agate was the hiring of the German-born and trained glass chemist, Arnold Fiedler. Mr. Fiedler, who had worked at Cambridge Glass (and at Akro Agate after Christensen Agate closed) utilized methods of combining glass that, before this time, were unknown in the marble industry. Because of his expertise in glass-making, Christensen Agate marbles are distinctive in the compatibility of their glass colors. Different colors of glass would neither run or blend, but would maintain crisp, clean lines between colors. Fiedler developed many bright and exotic colors for their marbles that to this day remain the most spectacular and colorful machine-made marbles ever produced.

Christensen Agate met its end in 1933, during one of the darkest years of the Great Depression. Several reasons may be attributed for its demise. The technologically superior West Virginia marble companies could out produce Christensen Agate with vast quantities of marbles and thus undersell them. Secondly, it is possible that making marbles was not the major nor most lucrative of the several company owner's businesses and the marble company was an early venture to be closed when times became lean.

Christensen Agate was in business for a total of eight years but actually produced marbles for a period of perhaps five or six years. Today, because of the limited production capability of this factory, estimated by Dennis Webb's source at about 30,000 marbles a day,

Christensen Agate marbles are considered scarce to rare, especially when one considers that after a period of over seventy years – through loss and breakage, many of these marbles have simply vanished. There is little wonder that identified Christensen Agate marbles often command a premium today.

CHRISTENSEN AGATE
Marbles Produced

A significant collection of Christensen Agate marbles is owned by the Guernsey County (Ohio) Road Department. Viewing it will bring one to believe that Christensen Agate produced some of the brightest and most strikingly colorful of all machine-made marbles, and also some of some of the dullest and least recognizable. Virtually all of the marble companies made some fairly plain marbles that, if seen in a fair-sized grouping with the well-known marbles, would hardly be noticed at all and would have little or no value to most collectors and dealers.

Dyed Clay Marbles: Some Gropper and Sons packaging of Christensen Agate marbles contain dyed clay marbles along with recognizable glass ones from the factory. It is uncertain, at this time, at least, who made the clay marbles. Dennis Webb reported (Greenburg's 1988) saying that he heard that when Christensen Agate closed down in 1933, there were many boxes of these marbles remaining at the site.

A study of scrap glass found at the Christensen Agate site, years before the building was demolished and the site was more or less accessible, reveals much. The findings of marble researchers include the following scrap glass at the site: glass from the nearby Cambridge Glass Company; Vitrolite – the heavy industrial glass from Parkersburg, West Virginia; flat colored cathedral glass; and other solid colors including yellow, blue, green, clear, red (several shades), lavender, and orange. Marbles and marble scraps have also found at the site. From the most dominant color combinations to the least, in the order of their dominance in what was discovered, the combinations included: red/white, blue/red, blue/white, red/green, red/yellow, blue/yellow, and yellow/green.

The found marbles and marble parts by type and volume, from most to least include common marbles, were virtually unrecognizable as Christensen Agate. Then, in decreasing numbers, two color opaque swirls and translucent and transparent swirls; slags, flame, guineas, and cobras (cyclones) were also recovered.

In slightly technical terms, Christensen Agate produced predominately single stream marbles (coming out of the tank orifice in one single stream). That is to say the different colored glasses were mixed together, and being of different consistencies, stayed separate and did not blend easily as is seen in marbles from many other companies. The color lines are usually clean and sharp and not, as is often seen in other companies marbles, turning into a third color hybrid. This sharp division of color in Christensen Agate marbles is a feature credited to the genius of German-born Arnold Fiedler, who also worked at Cambridge Glass and Akro Agate. Fielder is credited with developing some of the brilliant colors used by these companies.

Christensen Agate did not produce many small 3/8" to 1/2" marbles, nor did they make many marbles over 3/4". The largest Guinea known is 3/4". No Christensen Agate marbles in the 7/8" to 1" category or larger are known.

Flames: It is now generally conceded that Christensen Agate was not the only company to make the style of marble known as flames. Alley and Ravenswood also certainly produced flames. The most well known and costly are the Christensen Agate flames. Flame patterns occur when the mixed glass forms finger-like points on the surface of the marble. To be considered a true flame, there must be at least four points. Some collectors and dealers say five are preferred. A few flames have numerous points, almost too many to be counted. On some flames the points go half way around the marble and meet flame tips from the other side. Two color flames are typical but three color are most sought after and the bigger the better.

Slags: As one of the early machine-made marble companies, Christensen Agate produced its own version of the popular slag marble. These marbles may have one or two seams and the white striping glass may be toward the interior or near the marble surface. Some of these slags have the so-called "9" pattern seen on M.F. Christensen, and on some Akro Agate and Peltier marbles of this type. They do not have the distinctive feathery lines of the Peltiers. The Christensen Agate slags are in colors of blue, aqua, brown, clear, green, purple, red, orange, yellow, and the very rare peach (the latter is unique to this company).

Stripes and Swirls: Christensen Agate striped marbles come in two opacities – opaque and transparent. Usually in each, the striped color floats on top of the base color and is oftentimes bright in contrast and tends to stand out in a group of marbles. Christensen Agate swirls are also opaque and transparent based and may have two, three, and rarely four color swirls. Some swirls appear to be hand-gathered and would have been among the earliest produced by the firm.

Other named Christensen Agate marbles:

American Agate: Another company-named marble. These swirls have either an opaque or opalescent white base – these are mixed with either a bright electric red or orange swirling.

Bloodie: This was a company name and boxes marked "World's Best Bloodies" do exist. This is an opaque white-based marble with translucent brown and red swirls.

Diaper Fold: This marble has a single seam into which the swirled colors seem to disappear. Hence the name diaper fold.

Guniea: Probably the most recognized Christensen Agate marble is the Guinea. These factory-named marbles are found in rare boxes labeled "World's Best Guineas." The story goes that this unique marble was named because its spots and coloring resembled the guinea hens that hung around the factory area. (Greenberg's 1988) A few guineas have an opaque base but most will have a transparent base. Clear, amber, and cobalt blue are the usual colors, although green and red examples are reported to exist. All of the colors start at one or two poles, which act as eyes into the marble. Some guineas have as few as two or three colors with large areas of clear glass. A variation of the Guinea is commonly called Cobra, or sometimes Cyclone. These extremely uncommon marbles have recently become popular and the prices asked and money given appear to be higher than for regular guineas. In these marbles, all the colors are on the interior. Less common still is the Guinea-Cobra or Guinea-Cyclone in which the colored areas will be both on the surface and in the interior of the marble – in short, the perfect hybrid. As with true Guineas, the latter variations have been recently reproduced and extreme caution should be exercised in the purchase of any of these marbles. Collectors must be careful of both reproductions and factory reject halves that have been fused together. Know your dealer!

Layered Sand: Everett Grist once described those solid opaque swirls as resembling colored sand layered in a jar. And so they do. Several collectors have suggested that they appear to be the most sophisticated machine-made marbles ever made.

Moons: Another factory named marble is the moon. Moons appear in original packaging as "World's Best Moons." These translucent opalescent marbles are strikingly beautiful when shown in front of light, where they appear orange-ish. In regular light they appear bluish. Akro Agate moons do not appear bluish. Marble King has also produced a type of moon which, along with the orange-ish tint, and appears cloudy on the interior.

There are other swirl marbles made by Christensen Agate that have been identified by collectors and named – not by the factory, but by dealers and collectors themselves.

Turkey: Flames and Layered Sand swirls are exceptions to the idea of a random swirl. So too is the swirl known as the Turkey. The actual pattern does resemble the head of a turkey and some even appear to have eyes.

Other names for Christensen Agate marbles have been around for some time, even before Dennis Webb reported them as early as 1988. These include:

Blue Bells – Light blue on opaque white.
Blue Laces – Light blue on transparent amber base.
Jennys – The red Jenny was reportedly named after an employee named Jennings.

CHRISTENSEN AGATE
Packaging

Premium marbles produced by the Christensen Agate Company are some of the most prized machine-made marbles and finding these marbles in their original packaging is indeed a bonus.

Company packaging includes stock boxes in at least seven sizes from peewees through size 6. Marble collector, Hansel de Sousa, has beautiful examples of these uncommon boxes. Many of these boxes have plain lid tops but the end flaps usually state the number of marbles inside, the size, and the words "Most Perfectly Formed Marbles," and "Manufactured by The Christensen Agate Co., Cambridge, O." Most boxes from this company contain 100, 50 or 25 marbles. A few smaller count boxes are known to exist. The larger count boxes generally contain slags, two and three color flames, and swirls. Some of these boxes are imprinted with the words "Favorite."

The smaller boxes (25 count) are some of the most sought after in the marble world. They are mostly size 0 and 1 marbles and include the following marble types: "World's Best Moons," "American Agates," "World's Best Bloodies," "World's Best Guineas," "World's Best Toy Marbles," and "Assorted Agates." Some contain slag marbles.

Several jobber companies distributed Christensen Agate marbles. The M. Gropper and Sons Company, little doubt this being the same firm that sold Peltier marbles, used a 225 4th Ave., New York City address for their Christensen Agate sales instead of the Ottawa, Illinois, address Gropper used for their Peltier marbles.

The Gropper boxes are difficult to find and, although Gropper claimed to be the "sole distributor" for Christensen Agate, such a claim is not strictly true. The J.E. Albright Company of Ravenna, Ohio, is known to have also packaged and sold Christensen Agate marbles.

The Gropper Company sold stock boxes of 100, 50, and 25 marbles, including slags, "World's Best Guineas," and two and three color swirls. Many of these boxes are labeled "Favorite" and/or "Marble Assortment." Gropper also sold gift sets in colorful boxes with detailed graphics showing marbles and children's faces. The boxes contain 44 marbles and a bag. The marbles are assorted two and three color swirls.

Smaller Gropper boxes do exist, but are extremely uncommon. One such box, containing six two-color swirls, has three cut-outs and beautiful graphics of a large marble on one side and children at play on the other. Another box, also with three cut-outs and children at play with marbles, contains four assorted swirls and ten dyed clay marbles.

In 2002, a case of twelve never-before-seen Christensen/Gropper boxes was found in California. Thanks to the efforts of marble collector/

dealer Floyd Brown, of Exeter, California, these rare boxes were made available to the public. One was immediately sold at auction for over $2,000. These boxes, first seen in Stanley Block's big *Marble Mania* book, contain ten Christensen Agate slag marbles and fifteen dyed clay marbles. This box is green with imposing graphics and is labeled "Favorite Marble Assortment."

The other company that distributed Christensen Agate marbles, the J.E. Albright Company, sold mostly stock boxes of slags and small boxes of dyed clay marbles.

A word or two about the dyed clay marbles mentioned is needed. Dennis Webb (Greenburg's 1988) reported then when Christensen Agate closed its doors in 1933, many cases of clay marbles were still in their warehouse. It is believed that these marbles were not produced by Christensen Agate, but their origin remains unknown with some suggesting that they were indeed Christensen products.

Mesh bags and other types of packaging are unknown at this time to the authors or those we interviewed.

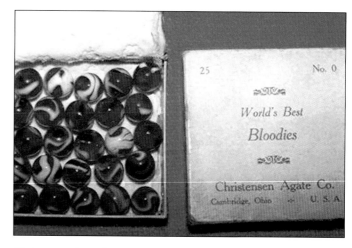

Christensen Agate box of 25 No. 0 Bloodies. *H. de Sousa Collection.* Scarce. No value determined.

Christensen Agate factory, Cambridge, Ohio, as it appeared in 1996. It was used as a shop for the Guernsey County Road Department before being demolished in 2000. *Photo by Marble Magnates.*

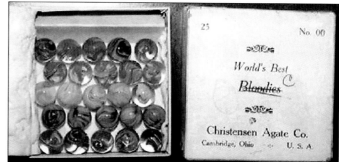

Christensen Agate 25 count box containing No. 00 "World's Best Bloodies" marked out to read "C" which was shorthand for clearies. *H. de Sousa Collection.* Scarce. No value determined.

Christensen Agate box with imprinted lid No. 0 Bloodies. Not quite full. *H. de Sousa Collection.* Scarce. No value determined.

Christensen Agate 25 count box, "World's Best Guineas." *H. de Sousa Collection.* Scarce. No value determined.

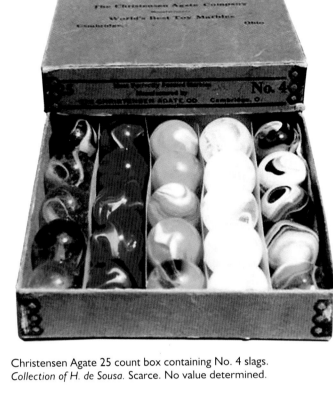

Christensen Agate 25 count box containing No. 4 slags. *Collection of H. de Sousa.* Scarce. No value determined.

Christensen Agate Gropper jobber's box of 100 count No 00 slags. *H. de Sousa Collection.* Scarce. No value determined.

Christensen Agate Gropper jobber's box of 50 count No. 2 agates. Lid shown, contents to follow. *H. de Sousa Collection.* Scarce. No value determined.

Christensen Agate 50 count box, lid shown previously.

Christensen Agate World's Best Toy Marble box containing 50 No. 2 marbles. *H. de Sousa Collection.* Scarce. No value determined.

Christensen Agate gift box with graphic lid, bag, and 20 marbles. *H. de Sousa Collection.* Scarce. No value determined.

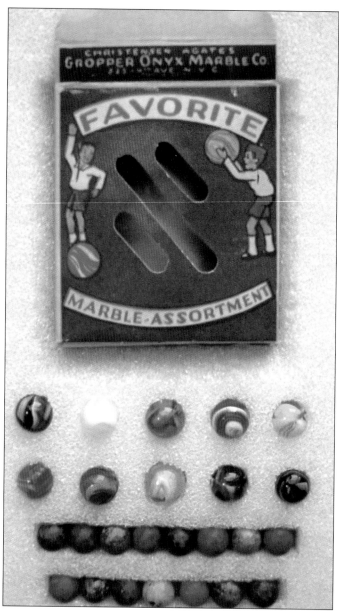

Christensen Agate Gropper jobber's box containing glass slags and clay marbles. Shown is the front of the box. Twelve of these packages are known to exist. $2,000-4,000.

Christensen Agate Gropper jobber's box with lid. Containing two sizes of marbles and bag. *H. de Sousa Collection.* Scarce. No value determined.

Christensen Agate Gropper jobber's box shown above. Here is the illustration on the reverse.

Christensen Agate Gropper jobber's box containing both glass and clay marbles. Front of box shown. *H. de Sousa Collection.* Scarce. No value determined.

Christensen Agate "American Agates." *D. Chamberlain photo.*

Christensen Agate typical end flap for hard-to-find stock boxes. Contains 25 No. 4 marbles.

Christensen Agate Gropper jobber's box, showing the reverse.

Christensen Agate Gropper jobber's box. Reverse and glass marbles.

Christensen Agate ad for marbles and packaging. Includes some of the packages shown previously. *Courtesy H. de Sousa.*

Christensen Agate Gropper jobber's box. *H. de Sousa Collection.* Scarce. No value determined.

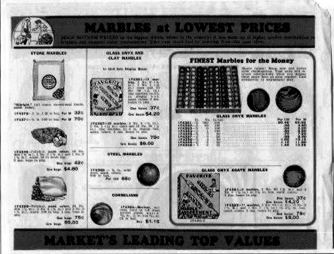

DAVIS MARBLE COMPANY

Pennsboro, West Virginia
1947 - 1948

Davis Marble Works production. *D. Chamberlain photo.*

Wilson Davis returned home from military service in 1946 to his family's farm just four miles south of Pennsboro. He entered into business in partnership with his father, Burnell Davis, to produce marbles. Wilson Davis, reflecting recently on his thoughts before going into the marble business, told us: "I had dreams; you wouldn't believe the dreams I had. It was common knowledge in Pennsboro that a marble machine would make $25.00 clean – I mean a day, if it was running full time, making 16 five gallon buckets in twenty-four hours. It was good money back then. That was the reason they all wanted to get in on it; Jackson, Heaton, Hanlon, Playrite, all of us." The appearance of success for several other Ritchie County marble companies at this time inspired father and son to give their attention to the seemingly open market.

The father and son then cut their own wood and constructed a 36 x 48 foot structure on a cement slab in an unused field. They then looked into acquiring a marble machine. Wilson Davis sought help first from the machinist, George Murphy, brother to one of Champion Agate's shareholders, who had made machines for Champion. Murphy turned down the commission. This was a time when several local marble companies were starting up, and Champion did not need any further competition.

Davis then went to Lawrence Alley, who was at that time doing well at his nearby St. Marys, West Virginia, factory. Alley was cordial, but had no machines for sale, and informed him that the cost of having a new machine made was about $2,500.00. Alley also told him that he had once sold a machine to Corning Glass in New York, who had wanted to do some experimenting, and it was this machine that Davis ended up purchasing from Corning for $800.00. During the Christmas holidays of 1946, Wilson Davis, Cline Riggs, and Jake Timmons drove a flatbed truck to Brooklyn, New York, to bring back the marble machine.

Jake Timmons built the glass tank, they obtained a striping pot, and production began in the spring of 1947. They found they could produce 6 five gallon buckets of marbles in eight hours, and had few problems with the process. Two or three women were hired to package the marbles, first in net bags, and soon switching to cardboard boxes to save money.

Using glass from such sources as, among other things, Coca Cola bottles and red and beige Vitrolite scraps, Davis made some very nice two-color marbles, typically opaque white striped on a transparent base of green, brown, crystal, blue, yellow, or peach. Some marbles were also produced with the striping in a color other than white, such as some with a crystal base and opaque purple striping, and some with translucent white with opaque red striping.

It was just as the Davis company was gaining momentum in production that they noticed that the price of marbles locally had already begun to fall. There were several other recently opened factories in the same county, including Cairo Novelty Works, Jackson Marble Company, and Playrite. The abundance of producers had flooded the market with marbles.

Marble jobbers had contracts and pressured buyers not to buy except from already established manufacturers. It was during this period that the West Virginia marble companies gathered at several meetings in Parkersburg and Clarksburg to discuss production, prices, and market shares in the face of increased competition, domestic and foreign as well. All of the newer companies were represented and most of the older ones, and yet nothing was accomplished that could be helpful to struggling companies like Davis. The few large concerns held 90 percent of the market and didn't need to cooperate, and the small companies could get no cooperation for any decent share of the market Wilson Davis recalled for the authors.

Becoming more anxious to sell their product, Davis placed a small advertisement in the *New York Times*. There were lots of replies, the best from a small toy manufacturer who wanted marbles to give away as premiums, their main lines being dolls and other larger items. Of the approximately fourteen million marbles Davis produced, ninety percent went to this firm in a sale that was not profitable. These marbles were packed in small red boxes without the Davis company name on them, and were shipped directly from the factory to Puerto Rico.

During the year that the Davis machine was running, the price of cullet glass more than doubled, with crystal jumping from $8.00 to $18.00 a ton, and ruby red from $20.00 to $60.00. Natural gas prices were also rising. These cost increases added to the tremendous competition in the market. With the difficulty in finding buyers who would deal with a small upstart company, and the price of marbles continuing to drop, it began to become clear that the timing was just not good for Burnett and Wilson Davis to establish themselves in the marble business. Reluctantly, they ceased operations, yet kept the marble machine around for years before selling it, thinking they might want to get back into it someday if conditions became more favorable.

Wilson Davis recalls they made their last run of marbles in the spring of 1948. In 1980, thirty-three years after ceasing operations, a tornado destroyed the building, now being used as a barn, which had been built to house the marble operation.

Davis Marbles Produced

Opaque.
Striped Opaque.
Striped Translucent.
Striped Transparent.
Transparent.

Davis Marble
Identification Tips

Davis marbles do not appear to be uniform in size or color. The vast majority found are transparent swirls with more or less muddy white striping. These are very much like the marbles from Jackson and Playrite. The base glass, in inconsistent colors, is mostly root beer, peach, green, blue, and clear. One notable marble is a nice clear with yellow striping. Other than clear, the base glass colors are not uniform with ranges from very light to fairly dark transparent. The translucent swirls are much the same. There are some interesting variations in that a few marbles were found to have gray, purple, or light green opaque striping.

The striped opaque marbles are mostly gray or brown base with blue striping. A fairly rare opaque marble, many of which were found broken, is a creamy white opaque base with bright red opaque striping.

The source for glass used at Davis was Vitrolite in colors of cream, brick, red, peach, and tan. Coca Cola bottles and brown transparent glass, possibly beer bottles, were also used. No scraps of sheet glass or "stained" glass were found at the Davis site.

Davis marbles range in size including 9/16", 19/32", 5/8", 11/16", 23/32", and 3/4 of an inch. Very few were found under 1/2", those were mostly clearies.

There seems to be a correlation between size and color. Almost all peach/flesh colored marbles are 9/16" as are most with emerald green. The marbles with yellow striping on a clear base seem to vary in size more than other colors, from 9/16" to 3/4".

The blue base translucent and transparent swirls seem to be mostly 9/16" to 5/8". Tan, brown, and green base marbles range from 19/32" to 5/8".

Davis Marble Packaging

Davis marbles were first packaged in mesh bags with paper headers. To save money, they switched to small, rather plain red boxes that were not even identified as to maker. Finally, most of the marbles were sold wholesale to a company who exported them to Puerto Rico. All of this is per the recollections of co-owner Wilson Davis. No samples of Davis packaging were available for photographing.

The Davis Marble Works factory was destroyed by a tornado in June 1980. It was used to store farm machinery at that time. *Photo courtesy of the Davis family.*

Davis Marble Works history being recorded at the West Virginia Marble Festival, Cairo, West Virginia, 1999. Wilson Davis (left), co-owner of the factory, explains to an attentive Michael Johnson and Susie Metzler. *Photo by D. Six.*

Davis Marble Works typical production. *D. Chamberlain photo.*

Davis Marble Works, Pennsboro, West Virginia. The factory building was utilized as a barn when this circa late 1960s photo was taken. *Photo courtesy of the Davis family.*

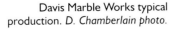

Davis Marble Works typical production. *D. Chamberlain photo.*

HEATON AGATE CO.

Cairo, West Virginia
1946 - 1971

Heaton Agate production. *D. Chamberlain photo.*

Heaton Agate production. *D. Chamberlain photo.*

An article from the *Pennsboro News* (W.Va.) dispels the marble circuit myths that Heaton Agate got its start in 1939 or produced cat eye marbles a good ten years before the Japanese entered the U.S. marble market. The article is from 1946, although the exact date is unknown:

Glass Plant is Building" and proceeds "The Heaton Agate Company has completed grading and begun construction on a cement block building that will house the machinery for making glass novelties and marbles for various construction and recreation purposes. This plant will be managed by Bill Heaton, successful theater owner of Pennsboro and Cairo, and Oris Hanlon, who recently moved here from Massillon, Ohio. Present plans are for full operation by 1 January. About twenty persons will be employed. The Heaton Agate Company is located in East Cairo, on the south side of the Baltimore and Ohio Railroad.

David Hanlon, son of Oris, recalls his father and uncle, Bill Heaton, were partners in the earliest days of Heaton Agate. Due to some personal disagreement which is today unknown, 1946 saw the creation of two separate marble companies in the small town of Cairo: Cairo Novelty and Heaton Agate.

In a 1986 interview recorded by Dennis Webb with Roger Howdyshell of Marble King, Inc., Howdyshell reported, "Bill (Heaton) came into marbles like a Johnny-come-lately, but he did some good things. He was intelligent enough and he would come over and talk to me and find out what he wanted to know. He would then talk to Fisher (of Vitro Agate) and find out what he wanted to know."

Heaton produced Chinese checker marbles from about 1949 in colors of blue, light blue, white, yellow, green, purple, and black and also a pretty faun color in 9/16" size.

Jack Bogard, a member of the family that would later purchase the Heaton company, reported that Bill Heaton only used one machine at a time in Cairo because of regular shortages of natural gas in town.

Robert Paugh, a Heaton Agate worker in 1947-48, remembers making cat eye marbles and, more specifically, a very early and not too successful version. He also stated that the furnace was set up to run two color marbles for play. He said that three color examples that can be

found were probably blends or between runs. Paugh has some marbles that they made out of beer bottles. One of his jobs at Heaton was to break the bottles before the glass was put into the tank so they wouldn't explode. Pay at the factory was 50 cents an hour in the era of 1948 – 1950.

The authors were told by various company employees called their 5/8" size marbles "game shooters" and their 3/4" size "shooters." Marble sizes ranged from 3/8" to about 1". Heaton Agate is known to have traded marbles with Vitro Agate, Marble King, and possibly Master Glass as well.

Elizabeth and Nina Sandy, sisters who both worked at Heaton Agate, told the authors that Bill Heaton actually worked at the plant and described him as a very demanding boss.

In a 1999 interview, Ralph Kester Six, a lifelong resident of Ritchie County, gave some insight into Bill Heaton, the man. Six had a small trucking business and hauled glass of all colors for Heaton until 1956. He hauled from the marble factory in St. Mary's and Bridgeport to Heaton's factory in nearby Cairo. Six was responsible for unloading the scrap glass, shoveling by hand, at the Heaton site. He never knew Bill Heaton to smile – everything was business. Six would also deliver marbles from Heaton to Marble King in St. Marys and recalls these were bulk boxes. When there he would back to the loading dock but recalled he was not allowed in the building or even onto the loading dock. The Marble King employees unloaded the boxes, he recalls not being allowed in or near the building. Six did not recall ever delivering marbles from St. Marys to Cairo.

By the late 1960s, Heaton seems to have been anticipating retirement. Before Bogards eventually bought out Heaton, the business was almost sold to Bob Michels, who thought he might go into the marble game himself. His mother told him, "You can't do that – you'd be in competition with your cousin" (at Champion Agate). He recalled that he then reasoned she had a point so he didn't buy. Heaton also offered to sell to Blaine Lemon, a former Vitro Agate plant manager, but as it was a long drive from his home near Parkersburg, West Virginia, combined with the extensive road work going on at that time in the construction of US Highway 50, Lemon declined.

In 1971, Heaton sold his company after operating it for twenty-five years and having made millions and millions of marbles. The company was to become C.E. Bogard and Sons.

William "Bill" Heaton passed away in 1987.

HEATON AGATE Marbles Produced

Cat Eyes: Heaton cat eyes are generally 5/8".
Opaque: Most opaque are 9/11" to 5/8".
Opaque Swirls.
Translucent Swirls.
Transparent Swirls.
Transparents: A few transparents have been found in sizes up to 15/16".

The greatest variety in sizes are in the opaque, translucent, and transparent swirls; the range is from 3/8" to about 15/16". Most, however, are in the vicinity of 5/8".

HEATON AGATE Identification Tips

One way to identify a Heaton Agate marble is to find it in its original packaging, but there remains the issue of companies acquiring stock from other marble companies, so this requires study. Other methods for Heaton marble identification have been from marbles in collections of members of the owner's family and former employees and their families. Some digging at the site prior to the present ownership, which takes a strong stand on prosecuting trespassing marble diggers, also has been helpful.

At least half of the two-color, random-pattern swirls are found to be white-based. These include red, orange, green, blue, and brown. All three levels of opacity are featured here. The striping colors are varied as well, ranging from fairly bright to rather washed out.

Many two-tone blue and two-tone green random swirls may also be attributed to Heaton Agate.

One of the most beautiful marbles from this factory is one that marble historian, David Tamulevich, has named "Robin's Egg". It has a light blue base with light white striping, a truly beautiful marble. Alley Agate in Pennsboro is known to have made one that is quite similar. Another beautiful two-color random swirl is a pinky/peach with red striping. It appears to be an uncommon marble.

There are a few three-color swirls, but they are uncommon. Known varieties include:

Opaque to translucent white with black and green striping.
Red, white and blue.
Red, orange on white base.
Red, brown on a white base.
Red, black on a white or tan base.
Green, oxblood on a white base.
Clear, green, on a white base.
Brown, clear on a white base.
Green, yellow on a white base.
Black, oxblood on a white base.
Brown, white on a blue base.

Although Heaton Agate is reported to have been set up to run only two-color marbles, three-color varieties do exist, though not in great numbers. One known four-color variety is an orange, clear, tan, and red.

Cat Eye: Several authors have suggested that Heaton Agate started the cat eye business in 1939, but the company did not produce any marbles until 1947. It is not presently known when Heaton began producing cat eye designs. Heaton Agate cat eye marbles are usually of the four vane variety, with the distinction of having the vanes not quite touching in the center. Heaton cat eyes, like those of Master Glass, are rather pale in color and are translucent to almost transparent. The Heaton cat eye colors found in original packages are various pale shades of white, yellow, green, red, and several distinct shades of blue – pale to medium.

Opaques: Heaton produced Chinese checker opaque types in sizes 9/16" to 5/8". These are generally indistinguishable from marbles of that type from many other factories. Known colors include white, black, blue, green, gray, faun, pink, yellow, and lavender.

Other marbles produced include industrial marbles for various purposes and other transparents of various colors in sizes ranging from 9/16" to almost 1".

HEATON AGATE Marble Packaging

Heaton Agate marbles were often sold in poly bags with headers that said "Big Shot." These bags contained either cat eyes or random swirls in various color combinations and numbers.

Opaques were usually sold in bags of 60 (10 of 6 different colors) for board games. Most 5/8" marbles were sold in bags of 14, 19, 20, 22, 30, 31, and 40.

Some bags may possibly be faked with reproduction labels and may contain Marble King shooters or other marbles. It should be kept in mind, however, that Heaton Agate and Marble King did trade marbles and Marble King patch marbles as well as cat eyes have been identified in collections of Heaton marbles.

Heaton marbles have been found in "Mr. Peanut" promotion bags, usually thought to have been distributed only by Marble King.

There is a yellow mesh bag containing thirty Heaton swirl marbles that has a red and black header that reads "30 Playtime Marbles." The origin of this bag and header is unknown.

Heaton Agate marbles appear in a jobbers box from Pressman. The box is 5" x 2-1/2" x 1" and has two cut outs on the front of a red, white, and blue box like a French flag. In red print it reads, "Big Shot," in white. There is a picture of marbles and in blue it reads " J. Pressman & Co. Inc. New York, N.Y., Made in U.S.A." The same box may be found with Alley marbles inside as jobbers were not concerned with consistency.

Heaton Agate Cardboard Box "Big Shot marbles" 3" x 4" x 3/4", red, yellow, and white with ten cut outs on top. Contains thirty-one Heaton Agates and says, "Manufactured by Heaton Agate Co., Pennsboro, W. Va." (Pennsboro being the Heaton's in-home office address).

Known Heaton employees include: Inez Batten, Troy Collins, Mary Lou Cornell, Bud Gilmore - a long time employee, Raymond Hinton, Robert Paugh, June McGinnis, Eleanor McGinnis Six, Pearl Reed, Elizabeth Sandy, Nina Sandy, Eva Jo Six, Anna Lee Swisher, Pat Webb, Jack Windom.

Heaton Agate factory, Cairo, West Virginia, as it appeared in 1999, after Heaton and later Bogard had ceased to produce at this site. *S. Metzler photo.*

Heaton Agate's Bill Heaton and wife Golda (Hanlon) Heaton.

Heaton Agate employees on the factory loading dock, Cairo, West Virginia. Left to right: Gilmore boy, Ines Batton, June McGinnis, and Anna Lee (last name unknown). Circa 1950s. *Six family collection.*

Heaton Agate 25 count box. $150.

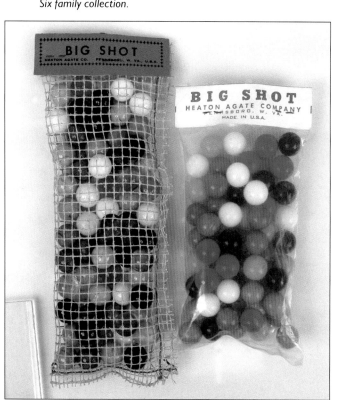

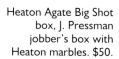

Heaton Agate Big Shot box, J. Pressman jobber's box with Heaton marbles. $50.

Heaton Agate bags, mesh with red header, $35-45, and later poly bag, $15-20.

Heaton Agate Big Shot poly bag Cat's Eye marbles. *J. Thompson photo.* $10-15.

Heaton Agate Swirls, note the Pennsboro, West Virginia, address used. Heaton lived in Pennsboro, but the factory was always in Cairo. *A. Rasmus Collection.* $30.

Heaton Agate poly bags: left: transparents, $10-15; right: opaques 60 count bag, $30.

Heaton Agate factory samples, includes misshaped and others. *D. Chamberlain photo.*

JABO, INC.

Reno, Ohio
1987 - operating at time of writing

JABO Inc. examples of production. Fall 2003 Classic pee wee marbles. *D. Chamberlain photo.*

JABO Inc. Classics. *D. Chamberlain photo.*

Long before the 1980s, making marbles had become a marginal business, and there were few people who knew this better than Jack Bogard. Throughout most of the 1970s and '80s, Jack owned or was a partner in Bogard & Sons and the Bogard Company, which had operated both in Cairo and on Nutter Farm Road, in Ritchie County, West Virginia.

Jack had gotten into the marble business in 1971 when his family purchased Heaton Agate in Cairo from Bill Heaton. Jack had worked driving trucks in the 1960s and among the loads he carried were marbles for Heaton. By 1969, Jack had grown tired of truck driving and began looking for a new profession. This was the same time that Bill Heaton was looking to retire.

The Bogard family went into the marble business with Jack and one brother, Jerry, doing most of the work. From the start, it became a real struggle to keep the business going. With the toy marble business nearly non-existent, the Bogard Company made mostly industrials; one color clear or opaque marbles were primarily used as agitators in aerosol paint cans. They had only two major accounts, Krylon and Plastikote, both of which had come along with the Heaton purchase.

Bill Heaton had told Jack that there was no way to make a living in marbles if you only made industrials, so the Bogard Company tried making cat eye and Chinese checker marbles in addition to the industrials. It was quickly learned, however, that it was even harder to sell these marbles than it was to sell the industrials, and within two years they dropped them entirely.

Over the next decade, and now close to running the business alone, Jack Bogard worked tirelessly to promote the use of industrial marbles. All this hard work did eventually pay off, though not right away. By 1984 the company was in serious financial straits. A friend suggested that he enlist the services of Joanne Argabrite, who ran a successful accounting business in Parkersburg, West Virginia.

Joanne grew up living both in Cairo and Parkersburg, each having marble factories. She knew very little about the marble industry until she met Jack Bogard. Over the next three years, as she worked to straighten out Jack's finances and pay off creditors, she learned a great deal about the marble business and became convinced that it could be a profitable business. She struck a deal with Jack that gave her part ownership in the company. In return, Joanne would run the finances of the business. Jack would continue to oversee the use and maintenance of the marble machines and all aspects related to actual marble production.

In 1987, Joanne created JABO, Inc. (the name is a combination of Joanne and Bogard) and leased a building along Route 7 in Reno, Ohio.

JABO, Inc. then purchased the Bogard equipment and auctioned off the Cairo property as a means to settle the Bogard Company debt. Jack immediately started up the operation in Reno, operating two marble-making machines, still producing only industrial marbles.

A major advantage to the Reno location was that the price of natural gas, used to run the furnaces, was approximately one-third of what it had been in Cairo. Still, at first, there was only enough business to run approximately eight or nine months out of the year.

Jack was often away due to family obligations and it soon became clear that if the company was to grow, it needed to bring in someone who not only had time to spend at the plant, but who would have a vested interest in JABO's success. Ideally this person would have expertise in working with glass and marbles and would have contacts that would help JABO expand its sales base.

In 1991, Jack suggested they talk with Dave McCullough, who at that time was General Manager of Champion Agate in Pennsboro, West Virginia, another marble manufacturer. Jack and Dave had known each other for many years and occasionally had had some business dealings. Jack heard that Dave was looking for a new situation where he could grow as a businessman and as a glass artist. After meeting with him, Jack and Joanne felt he possibly had what they were looking for, a combination of work ethic, commitment, respect, and contacts within the industry, as well as a working knowledge of glass, especially marbles. They offered McCullough a share in JABO, Inc., which he accepted and began working at JABO, Inc. on July 1, 1991.

It is interesting to note that while at Champion Agate, McCullough got hooked on making marbles and was made plant manager within six weeks of hire and given a simple directive: do what you want, but turn a profit. While at Champion, Dave was responsible for producing the Old Fashion and, later, the Whirlwinds, both of which resemble the machine-made marbles of the 1930s and '40s – particularly those of the Ravenswood Novelty Works. Often today these marbles are passed off as being older than they are by marble show, antique, and flea market dealers, as well as on Ebay and other auctions.

The move to bring Dave McCullough into the JABO family turned out to be a great one. Not only did Dave have the expertise that Jack and Joanne had hoped for, but he also had the time to put into overseeing the daily operations. In addition, many of the customers that Dave had developed and dealt with while at Champion wanted to keep working with him and chose to move their business to JABO. Consequently, JABO, Inc. quickly became a year round operation. The majority of their business was still in industrials, craft marbles, and gems, which still continue to be a large part of JABO's business today.

About three months after he started at JABO, Inc. (around October 1991), Dave made his first run of non-industrial marbles using a machine Jack had brought from Cairo. He produced a unique three-color marble of white, green, and red (with the red sometimes bleeding into a yellow). These were similar in style and produced in a manner similar to the Old Fashions from his Champion Agate days. He ran them for only twenty-four to thirty-six hours, producing between 150,000 and 200,000 marbles. By Dave's personal reckoning, most of this run ended up for sale at nearby flea markets. Dave had some trouble maintaining the temperature in the tank without burning out the colors he was working with, but the knowledge he gained gave him the ideas he needed to build the tanks for his later runs of the now-famous Classics.

In January 1992, JABO moved its manufacturing operation literally a few dozen yards down Highway 7 into a prefab building they had constructed the previous year. At that point, they were operating four machines. In addition, they constructed a sixty by eighty foot building for packaging and storage space. Three old railroad cabooses were brought in to serve as site offices. Corporate offices were in Parkersburg.

In the summer of 1992, Pete McMillan, a longtime marble dealer and collector from Michigan, was on a buying trip to the western states. Someone suggested that if he was interested in marbles, he should check out the marble factory in Anacortes, Washington. Pete had never heard of a factory there, so he made a trip to the Pacific Northwest and was surprised to find it was Vitro Agate, which had moved to Anacortes from Parkersburg, West Virginia, in 1989. Dick Ryan, one of the owners, had hoped to run the marble business with fewer people, using computers to monitor the machines and save on labor costs. Instead, he and his partner, Tim Sullivan, found glass too tricky and temperamental a material to work successfully in that fashion. In conversations with Dick Ryan, Pete found that although the orders were there to keep Vitro running, the effort and expense involved in doing so were getting in the way of their highly successful rope business. At the point Pete located them, Vitro was down to operating only two days a week, and had a large inventory of marbles in bulk, including many that had been made in Parkersburg and shipped to Anacortes during the move west.

Ryan remembered that at one time both Jack Bogard and Dave McCullough had expressed an interest in buying the Vitro operation when it was still in Parkersburg, and he asked Pete to relay a message to Dave that if he was still interested, the company was for sale. In May 2003, Jack Bogard, JABO President, stated that he too had been interested in purchasing Vitro Agate while it was still in Parkersburg.

After he returned to the Midwest, Pete McMillan stopped by JABO to see Dave and told him about Vitro and Dick Ryan's offer. McCullough immediately called Ryan, then discussed the purchase with Jack Bogard and Joanne Argabrite. They all agreed the purchase was worth pursuing. Joanne then called Dick Ryan and worked out the details and terms. It was a huge financial investment for JABO, Inc., and in particular for Joanne, but she had the vision and the faith to make it happen. When asked why they took that kind of financial risk, Dave said there were several reasons, the biggest being the gut feeling that JABO, Inc. could really stand to expand its operations and that there was a market out there for its products. Dave also knew the Vitro equipment was good, and he was particularly interested in the 1", 3/4", and the pee wee marble machines that Vitro owned.

Although not stated in any recorded conversations, it is known that Vitro Agate in Anacortes also had possession of the coveted marble machine owned by the House of Marbles in England that had been used by Vitro to make marbles in sizes greater than 1" for that overseas business. That machine ended up as not part of the sale to JABO. In his personal notebook dated December 3, 1991, Lewis L. Moore, former plant manager of Vitro Agate (Parkersburg) states, "B. Bavin (House of Marbles, England) and his bookkeeper was in this evening along with M. Hall (Mid-Atlantic Glass) and we went out to supper and talked for over three hours. Bavin will call Ryan (Vitro Agate, Anacortes) and get the 1-1/4" machine sent to Mid-Atlantic." That machine did make it to Mid-Atlantic Glass and was seen there as late as 1994, before it was sent to the House of Marbles Museum in England.

In an interview with the *Parkersburg News* in October 2003, Jack Bogard remarked, "I didn't want to see it (all the Vitro Agate equipment) go to Mexico."

In late 1992 and early 1993, Jack Bogard went to Anacortes to supervise the packing and shipping of their purchase. In all there were seventeen semi truck loads, which included eight to ten complete marble machines plus parts for a half dozen more. Tons of cullet glass were shipped and about 3/4 of a truckload of finished marbles – roughly 25,000 to 30,000 pounds, both Parkersburg and Anacortes. One inventory list, for Van #13, which was loaded and sent on May 6, 1993, included 48,058 pounds of cullet, chemicals, soda ash, and office equipment.

By 1993, JABO, Inc., had acquired the use of the Vitro Agate name and the packaging labels now read: "Vitro Agate, Division of JABO, Inc."

During the next few years, JABO, Inc. continued to expand their entire operation to include not only Classics and industrials, but also decorative gems and flats, plus Chinese checker marbles as well.

One significant move came in 1995 when JABO purchased a 390 x 40 foot building on a fourteen acre tract near Williamstown, West Virginia. The goal was to use four marble machines and sixteen employees to produce a half million industrial marbles a day. The main reason for this expansion was to increase both production and the space in which to store inventory. The company had been reluctant to take additional orders without the ability to meet the demand. The sign, which stood near the road marking the entrance to this facility, carried the old Vitro Agate logo and announced that they had been in business since 1931. The Williamstown industrial marble site was run by Jack Bogard until September 28, 2003, when it was suddenly shut down and the marble machinery was moved to Reno, Ohio. It was also about this time that Jack Bogard decided to semi-retire, maintaining a role as consultant to JABO.

During another period of expansion, in Reno, Ohio, during 1998-99, a modern, very large storage building was erected. In addition, the three railroad cabooses were replaced by a spacious mobile home that is used as the site office. The company headquarters and address remain in Parkersburg.

Today, JABO, Inc. recycles leftover or broken glass from regional plants including Fenton Art Glass in nearby Williamstown. As Ms. Argabrite once remarked: "It's piles and piles of glass. We just throw it in the heater, heat it up, and make marbles." It may not be such a simple task as that; the industrial marbles must maintain a certain durability and even the multicolor marbles for play must use different kinds of glass that are compatible.

Joanne Argabrite, Jack Bogard, and Dave McCullough have built JABO, Inc. into a formidable business which now sells ninety-five percent of the industrial marbles used in the U.S., Canada, Puerto Rico, and Europe. The "Classics" are produced usually twice a year; Spring and Fall, but on a much smaller scale. A large part of the company's business is done on the Internet at www.jabovitro.com.

In 2003, JABO, Inc. reported that its fifty-five fulltime employees produce between 2.5 million and 3 million marbles a day, most of which are industrials.

Recently, Joanne Argabrite summed up what in her opinion is the reason for JABO's success. "My personal feelings are that we are successful because we have three people with diverse skills that come together as a team and it gives us the edge that a one person operation cannot achieve without stretching themselves so thin that something gets set aside."

JABO, Inc. has been and continues to be a major sponsor and supporter of the West Virginia Marble Festival held in Cairo (Ritchie County), West Virginia, each May and donates marbles, shirts, caps, and jackets for marble tournament winners. Likewise, with the inception of the annual Marble Festival in Sistersville and the newly-formed West Virginia Marble Collectors Club shows in Parkersburg, JABO has been there as an active supporter of these events. JABO also is a corporate sponsor of the National Marble Museum. JABO continues to support the National Marble Tournament held each year in Wildwood, New Jersey.

Much of the information in this chapter is courtesy of David Tamulevich, who generously allowed us the use of his interview notes.

JABO Marbles Produced

With the possible exception of Mid-Atlantic Glass, with its limited production styles and colors that are well-documented, no other U.S. marble manufacturer has had its for-play marble output so closely scrutinized as has JABO. There are days when the Spring or Fall "Classics" are being produced that buyers are lined up at the door for a chance to pick through the newly formed marbles. In this section we will concentrate solely on the JABO Spring and Fall "Classics" and other limited and special run marbles.

The first run of "Classics" produced by Dave McCullough was made about September 1991, approximately three months after McCullough joined JABO. It was a very unique three-color swirl of red, white, and green (with the red sometimes bleeding into a yellow). JABO made only about 150,000 - 200,000 marbles and most ended up at flea markets.

JABO "Classics" have been pretty much an experimental sideline for Dave McCullough and JABO. These marbles have usually been made when a window of time and the right glass are available at the same time. Dave rarely keeps notes on how he produces a certain variety of marbles, and seldom attempts to duplicate that variety a second time. The process and experimentation are the prime motivations for him. He is not interested in duplicating a variety of marble produced by a company in the past. His goal is to see what happens when he mixes different glass and chemicals in various ways and at different temperatures, hopefully resulting in a unique marble.

As a general rule of thumb, if all is working well with the machine being used, JABO makes a run for about four days, which produces about a million marbles of several varieties. There is an additional twenty-four hours in which hybrid marbles are formed before the machine is fully into its next set of colors.

McCullough and JABO are strict about the sizing of marbles they market with most "Classics" being 5/8". A smaller number of 1" marbles are made. In addition, and generally twice a year, 3/4" marbles are run for Ford Motor Company, some of which are made available to the public. Ford takes around 10,000 to 15,000 pounds of them (approximately 600,000 to 900,000 marbles). Sixty 3/4" marbles equal one pound. As Ford uses them for industrial purposes and does not care about the color, it has been a great opportunity for Dave to experiment. Rarely have other 3/4" runs been made. Other sizes are uncommon and have accidentally slipped into circulation. JABO does have Vitro's pee wee machine which Jack Bogard reconditioned and Classic pee wee marbles were shared by McCullough in the May 2005 West Virginia Marble festival in Cairo, West Virginia. Previously some experimental marbles were run on it. In October 1999, McCullough ran a very limited run of red and white "Classics" (approximately 150 pounds), very few of which reached the public. The first run of pee wee "Classics" for general consumption were produced along with the regular "Classics" in the fall of 2002.

The process and methods of JABO lead to many different color combinations, especially in hybrid varieties, marbles that happen between two planned runs where extra colors of glass will create three and sometimes four or more colors in a single marble. It has been estimated that at least eighty different varieties of "Classics" were produced prior to the summer of 1998. It is quite likely that many more than that were actually produced.

One note about marbles that fluoresce. Prior to government restrictions first laid down in the 1960s, marbles from many older companies used dangerous chemicals such as uranium oxide, arsenic, and others. Since then, many restrictions limit the chemical content of modern marbles. For one thing, they are not as hard and chip or flake more easily than older marbles. Since 1993, many marbles from various runs of "Classics" do glow under a black light. Other recent black light marbles include several runs of "Old Fashions" that McCullough made at Champion Agate in 1984-85; a limited number of Vitro Agate "Classics" produced in Anacortes; and the Marble King line of "Wee Glo" marbles first produced in 1998 but not officially marketed to the public until the year 2000.

There are several ways in which JABO marbles may be identified. One is by a V pattern of one of the colors similar to the one found on some Vitro Agate Anacortes marbles and which is found on many Vitro Agate Parkersburg marbles. It is thought that the same machine was used in all three locations to produce such similar marble designs. Another characteristic is an S or reversed S pattern in a color. In May 1999, Dave modified the machine that came close to, but did not completely eliminate these patterns from the marbles.

There will probably be dozens of varieties of "Classics" produced that will not be pictured here – early runs, or spur-of-the-moment runs, or numerous hybrids that we have missed. Dave McCullough once remarked that as he watched a run coming down the rollers "an unexpected color would suddenly appear, and then disappear after perhaps twenty pounds of marbles. It is in the nature of the glass to surprise you, and one of the joys of randomly swirled marbles such as these is finding combinations (of colors) that you've never seen before."

Dating some of these marbles can be difficult as it is a common practice to mix new batches with the remains of prior runs. Although it is not too common, as most batches of "Classics" are sold out, some mixing has occurred.

In terms of monetary value of individual marbles, it is hard to say. It mostly depends on the number of colors present, how eye-catching the design, and how rare it seems to be. One inch "Classics" have sold for as much as $100.00 each, though in general $1.00 to $5.00 or even $10.00 seems to be the current range. Dave McCullough said in a telephone conversation that one of his fall "Classics" for 2003 sold on the Internet for $40.00 and that was in less than two weeks of it being made.

There is a growing interest among both marble collectors and dealers in JABO "Classics" because of their uniqueness and the limited numbers produced. Their value should rise steadily. This is especially true of factory bagged marbles and of the larger sizes, there being fewer available. Considering, however, the price of certain Akro Agate, Christensen Agate, and Peltier marbles, which can shock especially the novice collector, JABO "Classics" usually produced in numbers of less than a million are a fun investment.

In terms of condition, JABO marbles, especially the 1" size, are often found with nicks and dings. The reason for this is that the company sells the vast majority of "Classics" in bulk as they come from the machines, without additional sorting and grading, so manufacturing and handling flaws are mixed in with more perfect marbles. The result of this method being that upwards of ten to fifteen percent of any given bulk box is of diminished value. With the rapidly growing demand for more "Classics", JABO is considering making them more a priority and a primary line for the company, and along with that, upgrading and limiting what is released to the public.

As an interesting sidelight to the JABO "Classics" story, marble collector and dealer Pete McMillan (of McMillan and Husband) has made his version of "Classics" at the JABO plant using glass that he purchased from Fenton. Many of these marbles are collectible when properly identified. Some of McMillan's marbles have been imprinted as Y2K marbles. Examples of these Y2K's were given one year in the free bags distributed at the West Virginia Marble Festival in Cairo, West Virginia.

Names of marbles: Naming marbles is not an exact or consistent science and most marble names are contrived by dealers and collectors, but Dave McCullough has, from time to time, sat down with friends to name interesting marbles. Sometimes names stick while others are quickly forgotten.

Chinese Checker marbles from JABO come in standard size and colors. One notable exception is the 7/8" ones produced in 1993. It was the only time this size marble was produced in the one color opaque style. These marbles were used in Dave McCullough's first stenciling experiment. Six designs were done by his wife, Bonnie, those being a mouse, a teddy bear with necktie, a bumblebee, a rabbit, a bird, and a juggling clown. Dave has also worked with George Williams of the Glass Swan in Jane Lew, West Virginia, to silkscreen a Gene Autry, a Hopalong Cassidy, Annie, Moose, and Popeye. Valentine marbles (usually on a ruby marble) with words like true love, Be My Valentine, and Sweetheart were also made. A Merry Christmas screened marble was also produced.

Mica Marbles: In April 1997, David Tamulevich took some mica chips to the Reno plant and gave McCullough the idea of making the world's first machine-made mica marbles. They were produced experimentally and only about two pounds were made. Dave McCullough calls them "D.T. Specials."

Two Presidential Sets have been made. Dave McCullough has made two varieties of Presidential marbles in boxed sets between 1996 and 1997. He has updated them to include George W. Bush after the election in 2000. After producing these beautiful sets, Dave remarked, "The first time someone puts them in a book, I will deny any knowledge of them." These presidential marbles come silk-screened on 1" red, white, and blue Marble King marbles.

In 2004, in the fall classics run, machine operator Bill McFall doubled up on a few 1" marbles to create a very few oversize classics which are 1-1/4".

JABO Packaging

JABO, Inc. marbles for play, the "Classics," come from the factory in bulk cartons, mesh bags, poly-bags, and plastic jars. Cartons are cardboard boxes containing fifty pound and twenty-five pound weight. The mesh and poly-bags were originally packaged with headers similar to the one used by Vitro Agate in Anacortes. The major difference being that the JABO headers, while maintaining the red and white lettering on gray background, stated that this company was "Vitro Agate, Division of JABO, Inc." These packages were marketed in 5/8" size counts of 25, 45 + 1, 50, and 75. Also made were packages of eight one inch shooters. These headers were in use until the end of 1999 when they were replaced by the new JABO V label in colors of red, white, and blue.

This new header design was actually given an early introduction to the public at the Third Annual West Virginia Marble Festival in Cairo on May 1, 1999, when Dave McCullough brought four hundred specially made up bags using the new headers as giveaways to those who attended the festival. These special mesh bags (of the 25 + 1 count) were in four different marble color groups of one hundred bags each: blue/yellow; orange/yellow; black/yellow; and blue/black. These marbles were from the Spring "Classic" run. The shooters were silk-screened "Y2K2000".

There are other contemporary JABO packages, not from the JABO factory.

In 1999, Peter Warnelas, a retired marketing expert, came across some JABO marbles and became infatuated with them. He not only found them beautiful, but felt there was a potentially large market if they were packaged and marketed properly. With that in mind, and after consultation with Dave McCullough, he has come up with his own logo design and packaging. In May 1999, he began offering them to the public using marbles from the 1999 Spring "Classic" run.

See the marble resources section in the back of this book for a note on some privately packaged JABO marbles in attractive containers by Mike Warnelis. Another marble package first seen in 1999 using JABO marbles has a header that reads David Crown Enterprises, a West Virginia souvenir marketing firm. They are sold as new marbles and no attempt is made to fool the marble-buying public into thinking they are old. A bag labeled "Bogarts" (a play on the name Bogard) also contains JABO marbles.

A special marble bag using JABO marbles was put together by the organizers of the Sistersville (West Virginia) Marble Festival which were sold at their September 2001 event to benefit the victims of the 9/11 attacks. Other specialized packaging that may contain JABO marbles includes the promotional bags put out by West Virginia marble festivals: Cairo, Sistersville, and Parkersburg. The beautiful cloth bags were made by the Comstock History Store of Virginia City, Nevada.

David Tamulevich, marble researcher, has noted that in the last few years many bags of marbles have appeared at flea markets, antique shops, and marble shows that are reproductions of bags that were originally produced as promotional items in the 1920s, '30s, '40s, '50s, and even '60s. Many of these bags have newly rusted staples and faked rust stains on the headers to deceive buyers into thinking they are much older than they really are. He states that he has personally seen over thirty varieties of fake bags advertising anything from soft drinks to gasoline companies that contain JABO marbles.

Al Rasmus, a leading and highly-respected authority on marble bags agrees that "JABO's are becoming more prevalent; I'd say at least a third, and maybe a little higher, of the reproduction bags now contain JABO Classics."

JABO, Inc., in the face of stiff foreign competition in traditional marble markets, has become innovative only recently in capturing a new niche in sales of its main product. JABO, Inc., in the year or so prior to this writing, has begun to produce printed marbles featuring company and state logos and other specialty licensed products. JABO employee, Skip Drain, works with license firms in reproducing logos and characters to their exact likeness. Four imprinted sets made their public debut at the September 2003 Sistersville Marble Festival: the 6 marble Betty Boop set; the 6 marble Garfield set; the 3 marble Garfield 25th birthday set; and the Ohio and West Virginia state marbles, as well as West Virginia and Ohio collegiate logo marbles.

JABO, INC. employees known include Eugene Brown; Carl McQuillian, Jr.; Jo Drain; Skip Drain; Walt McKee; Ronald Ewers; Harley Alkire; Robert Mease; Bonnie Blovir; Bill McCall (who made oversize marbles); and David Day.

JABO Inc. factory, Reno, Ohio, as it appeared in the spring of 2004. *D. Simmons photo.*

JABO Inc. sign along Ohio Route 7 in front of JABO, erected 2004-05.

JABO Inc., inside the factory, production marbles awaiting packaging and shipping. *D. Chamberlain photo.*

JABO Inc. Special Classics in after market hinged, divided, locking plastic case. Marketed by Mike Warnelis. $30-40.

JABO Inc. employee, Dave Day, works at the hot end of a marble furnace. Due to the extreme heat, marble factories often are largely open to the outside for ventilation. Photo 2005.

JABO Inc. 1997 Presidential set produced for Dave McCullough. Limited edition, signed in wooden box. $500.

JABO Inc. Classics after market packaging of cardboard box and clear plastic lid with graphic "JABO" imprint. Marketed by Mike Warnelis. *Photo Steve Sauer.* $20-25.

JABO Inc. poly bag with header reading "VITRO AGATE, A division of JABO, Inc." This was the last label to include the name Vitro Agate. Contains 50 count JABO Classics. $15.

JABO Inc. poly mesh bag, circa 2001. The header reading "25 + 1" count was for play marbles and shooter. This printed header was first introduced in May 1999 at the West Virginia Marble Festival. This is the package as given away to all participants at the West Virginia Marble Festival, Cairo, West Virginia, compliments of JABO. $3-10, depending on contents.

JABO V header on a 25 + 1 new mesh bag as given to the public at the West Virginia Marble Festival including a printed YSK 2000 shooter! $10-15.

JABO Inc. reverse of poly mesh bag above.

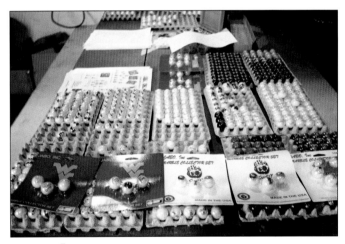

JABO Inc. display of packaged and printed marbles. 2005.

JABO Inc JABO V header on a poly bag. Circa 2002. $5-10.

JABO Inc. company catalog circa 2004 illustrating the available company packaging options. *Used by permission of JABO, Inc.*

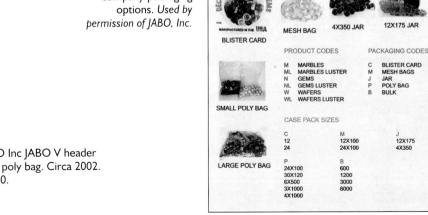

JABO Inc. a bin of Spring Classics inside the factory May 2005.

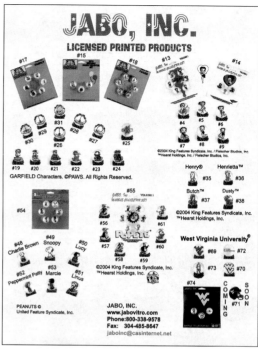

JABO Inc. Licensed Printed Marbles appearing in the company catalog circa 2004. *Used by permission of JABO, Inc.*

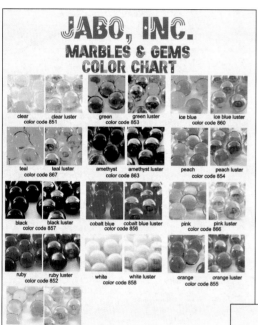

JABO Inc. company catalog circa 2004 illustrating the usual production colors available in marbles and gems. *Used by permission of JABO, Inc.*

JABO, Inc. Armed Forces collection. *J. Thompson photo.* $15-20.

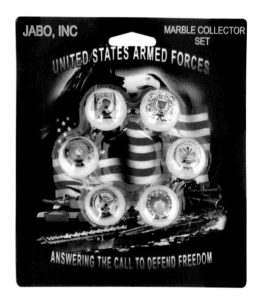

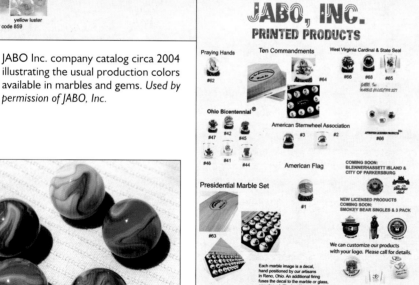

JABO Inc. company catalog of printed marbles, a part of the product line that was receiving considerable marketing effort in the few years immediately preceding the printing of this book. *Used by permission of JABO, Inc.*

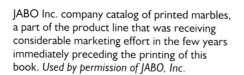

JABO Inc. Fall 2003 Classics. *D. Chamberlain Photo.*

JACKSON MARBLE COMPANY

Pennsboro, West Virginia
1945 - 1946

Jackson Marble production examples. *D. Chamberlain photo.*

Jackson Marble production examples. *D. Chamberlain photo.*

The Jackson Marble Company was another of several small companies that started up after World War II in Ritchie County, West Virginia. It is generally known locally that Carroll Jackson, formerly a marble machine operator at Champion Agate, started his business at the east end of Pennsboro around 1945 and made marbles for about one year.

Jim Davis, the retired Pennsboro, West Virginia, contemporary marble maker and resident glass historian, related to us the story that Mr. Jackson was a very business-minded man who, before he even got started, had made inquiries of buyers of marbles. They encouraged him to get into the business, saying, "You get started and make them and we'll buy." It took about a year to get set up and going. Then, as it turned out, all the folks who said they would buy … didn't.

Jim Davis and several other glass personalities related to author Dennis Webb some years ago that the total Jackson marble output was no more than about two boxcar loads, or about six million marbles. At best this is an estimate but gives us some sense of the extremely limited production.

Jackson had just one marble machine, made by experienced local marble machinist, George Murphy. Carroll Jackson's son, Norman, remembers one winter, when he was age five or six, being curled up under the hot machine to keep warm and falling asleep. Jackson's older son, Lehman, merely remembers shooting many marbles into the nearby hill with his slingshot at about age nine or ten. Family recollections are few as the children were quite young at the time.

At one point in 1947 or 1948, Jackson drove a truck borrowed from George Murphy loaded with bagged Jackson marbles to Baltimore to sell, but the trip was unsuccessful and he didn't sell any. Mr. Murphy then took the truck to several filling stations and sold the marbles. He was paid $14.00 in commission by Jackson.

Jackson bagged his marbles in red or yellow mesh bags with their own red labels stating, "JACKSON'S MARBLES." He issued two sizes of bags, a smaller, approximately twenty-five count, and a larger, approximately forty count bag. Many of these bags were left over when Jackson closed down, and were sold empty to the nearby Playrite Novelty Company, who apparently packaged many of their own marbles in the Jackson bags and used Jackson headers on those bags.

Carroll Jackson died in 1987, and there is very little documented record of his marble enterprise and not much recalled in family and community memories. There does exist a good sampling of marbles made during the company's short life. Beautiful two and three and sometimes four color swirls, in many opaque, transparent, and translucent colors.

The building that housed the company burned down around 1972, having been previously sold to George Murphy, along with some old marble stock that Murphy sold off over time.

Jackson Marbles Produced

Opaques.
Striped Opaques.
Striped Translucents.
Striped Transparents.
Transparents.

The sizes for most Jackson marbles are 5/8", although a few have been found in 9/16" and as small as 3/8". There are a number found in 11/16" and a few in 3/4". The largest known size is 13/16".

The source for their glass includes nearby Vitrolite for blue, red, and light green. Several pieces of red automotive lenses have been found at the site. Brown transparent glass, possibly beer bottles, has been found.

Jackson Marble Identification Tips

This short-lived company produced marbles in styles and colors similar to those from several other Ritchie County, West Virginia, companies, including Cairo Novelty, Playrite, and Davis. This is evidenced by the fact that many of the marble machines used in these firms were made by the same men and that scrap glass and cullet were purchased from the same or similar sources. At least ten years of unauthorized digging at the Jackson site has produced a great, definitive array of two and three color swirls and fantastic four color marbles that have made their way onto the market. The striping, of white, red, yellow or blue is usually thick and rather lazy-looking. A few seem to have an almost corkscrew effect.

The three and four color swirls are generally opaque while most of the transparent and translucent swirls are two color only. Several of the two color swirls as well as the three and four color swirls appear to be unique to this company and when properly identified should be quite collectible.

The spectacular four color swirl is red, black, brown, and light tan. Three color swirls include a beautiful opaque red and blue on a milky white base. Another even more striking marble is a nice opaque red and green on a clear base.

Among the unique two color swirls are a translucent red in a clear base and a feathery white on a black or dark purple base. There is an opaque solid marble of one color that can be white, black, tan or blue. A number of crystal, purple, blue, and green transparent marbles have been uncovered. Sizes vary from 3/8" to 3/4" and it can be supposed, since a few have wisps of white striping, they may be the beginning or end of runs.

JACKSON Packaging

Jackson marbles were packaged in two sizes of mesh bags in two colors with red paper headers with black writing saying "Jackson's Marbles Made in Pennsboro, W. Va., U.S.A." The mesh bags came in twenty-five and forty count and the bag colors were red and yellow. Although both bags are fairly rare, the yellow are harder to find.

It is to be noted that when Jackson went out of business, both bags and labels were sold to the Playrite Company, thus giving rise to confusion as to the similarity of marbles produced by those companies.

Jackson Marble's Carroll Jackson, photographed circa 1940s.

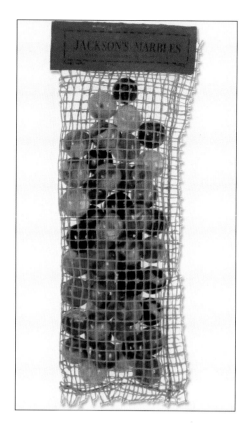

Jackson Marble mesh bag. 40 marbles. *J. Thompson photo.* $200-250.

Jackson Marble factory site as it appeared in 1996. No images of the factory have been located by the authors after diligent inquiries to the family, community, etc.

Jackson Marble mesh bags. 25 count swirl marbles. $100 each.

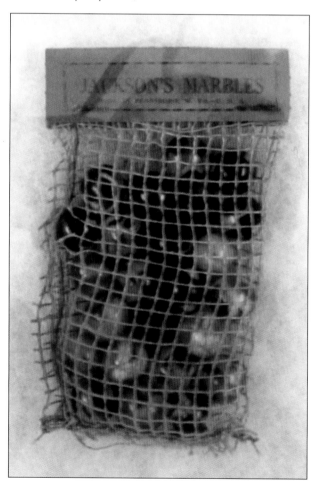

Jackson Marble label on bag containing 25 Playrite Novelty marbles, not Jackson marbles as the label indicates. *J. Thompson photo.* $100-125.

Jackson Marble examples of marbles produced, the dominant Jackson marbles are Random Swirls of the two and three color variety with a slight predominance for two colored types.. *D. Chamberlain photo.*

Jackson Marble examples of marbles produced. *D. Chamberlain photo.*

KOKOMO OPALESCENT GLASS COMPANY, INC.

Kokomo, Indiana
Circa 1939 - circa 1942

Kokomo Opalescent examples of marble production. *D. Chamberlain photo.*

Kokomo Opalescent examples of marble production. *C. Kobata photo. K. Humphrey Collection.*

The Kokomo Opalescent Glass Company was established in 1888 and continues its operations today at 1310 South Market Street, Kokomo, Indiana. The chief product of this company is rolled glass, which is used in lamps, church windows, and art works, including architecture, that features flat glass.

The company, as with the city, derives its name from the Miami Tribe Chief Ma-ko-ko-mo. In the late 1930s, company officials faced a decision about how to dispose of some defective plate glass. It was decided to use the rejected glass to produce marbles. It was thought that any marbles made would be of high enough quality to match industry standards.

Kokomo glass has always been made from recipe, not recycled from prior uses and is made using fine quartz sand from the same sand pits in Ottawa, Illinois, that are used by Peltier Glass.

Marbles were made directly from the rejected glass and no remixing of colors was done to achieve a particular color for marbles. They used only one marble machine, which was capable of rolling out several different sizes. Rollers of various diameters were kept on nearby racks.

An informational sheet printed by a local collector and reading as if it were an original company publication reads, "From 1939 until 1942 we manufactured marbles on a machine that we purchased from Peltier Glass of Ottawa, Illinois. Never realizing a satisfactory profit from the marble operation, we sold the machine back to Peltier in 1942." An addendum says "1943, 1944, 1945?"

The American Glass Factory Review's *Glass Factory Year Book* of 1940 has this information in the Kokomo entry for that year: H.E. Wright, president; D.F. Elliot, secretary; R. C. Trees, treasurer and executive manager. Products mentioned are American antique and opalescent sheet glass. Production capabilities are 3 day tanks and 1 6-pot furnace. Interestingly there is no mention of marbles or glass spheres in their listing for 1940 or any other year when marble production for Kokomo would have been ongoing. The importance of marbles to the overall company may be hinted at in this omission?

Ken Humphrey, a Kokomo businessman, relates a humorous incident at the factory. "I know a man who made marbles at the plant in the summer of 1940. He was only sixteen years old and they left him alone at the plant one night running the marble machine – no one else in the entire plant or office. The machine went crazy and he had glass going everywhere. He ran down the street a few blocks where he knew a more seasoned worker lived. Not being sure of the exact address, he started knocking on doors until he found the man who was quickly able to restore order." The sixteen year old fellow with the summer job when the marble machine went off was Bob Miller – later in life he went on to become a multimillionaire in the furniture business.

Kokomo Marbles Produced

From information shared by local historian and collector, Ken Humphrey, we learn that solid colors produced were baby blue and lemon yellow. He reports no other solid colors have been positively identified. Patches and ribboned marbles were made with an opaque white and transparent white base glass. Patches and stripes are of one color, those being: orange, burgundy, red, yellow, brown, green, blue, turquoise, and olive green. Many of these marbles are identical to late Peltier marbles. Kokomo did produce one distinctive marble. The base glass is a steel gray, which fluoresces. Two of four colors are on the marble. Yellow and brown are just ordinary looking colors. The blue and especially the red are super opaque, deep and bright.

The late Wallace C. Huffman of the Elwood Haynes Museum in Kokomo noted upon examination of his Kokomo collection "a wide variety of colors but a limited number of designs." Haynes provided descriptions for Kokomo marbles of:

Opaque Black.
Patched and Ribboned.
Patched Opaques: Green on white, red on white, and brown on white.
Patched Transparents: White and green on a clear body and blue on dark blue body.
Ribboned Opaques: Orange on white, light blue on white, yellow on white, and brown on white.
Ribboned Translucents: Light blue on white, orange on clear crystal (this orange is a particularly deep, rich color, unlike the reddish-yellow seen in many marbles). Several of the above designs contain seedy glass.
Ribboned Transparents: White on dark blue.
Transparents: Red and white on light green and red and white on light blue.

Author's comment: We have compared known Peltier marbles with known Kokomo marbles. The similarities are astounding. There is no doubt of several possible explanations for this, including source of raw materials and the marble machine itself.

The Kokomo marbles we have studied are from three reliable sources: Ken Humphrey, a marble collector from Kokomo, Indiana; Mark Reidelsperger, from Muncie, Indiana; and The Wallace C. Huffman Collection, Kokomo, Indiana. We have little doubt that there are many Kokomo marbles out there in the world in Peltier collections.

Kokomo Packaging

Marbles produced by the Kokomo Opalescent Glass Company were sold only by that company and not to other producers. It is not known if their marbles were sold to independent jobbers. The only packaging we have seen or know of consists of the following:

A mesh bag with a paper label containing 30 marbles. $300.00
A mesh bag with a paper label containing 62 marbles. $600.00
A colored box with a marble display of 4" x 5". It was purchased empty and it is not known how many marbles it originally contained. Estimated value: $1200.00

There is a box of Kokomo marbles in the Elwood Haynes Museum in Kokomo, Indiana.

Kokomo Opalescent production examples. *C. Kobata photo. K. Humphrey Collection.*

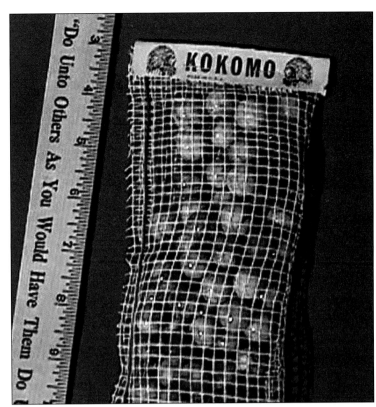

Kokomo Opalescent "Kokomo" with Indian Chief mesh bag. 62 count bag. As shown, $600. Smaller 30 count bag, $350. *K. Humphrey photo.*

Kokomo Opalescent factory, Komomo, Indiana. *From Kokomo Opalescent Glass company archives.*

Kokomo Opalescent "Kokomo Marbles" box lid. *H. de Sosa Collection.* Scarce. No value determined.

Kokomo Opalescent "Kokomo Marbles" box interior, for box shown previously.

LIBBEY OWENS FORD

Vienna, West Virginia
Circa 1940 - 1970s

While the Libbey Owens Ford (LOF) factory in Vienna, West Virginia, did not produce toy marbles or marbles for play it was a prolific producer of marbles for its own internal use. The factory manufactured millions and millions of marbles for later re-malting to produce fiber glass. The reason marbles were made was due to the ease in handling and shipping them as raw glass. They move easily along conveyor or other mechanical systems and can be dumped, poured, shoveled, and moved with ease.

In an interesting twist, the Vienna LOF site was at one time the Vitroltie Division of the parent company. It occupied the same site that Vitrolite Co. and the original Vitro Agate had occupied decades earlier!

One reason these rough looking marbles appear in West Virginia and the region at marble shows and antique shops is that they were transported from Parkersburg via the Baltimore & Ohio railroad and the cars in which they were transported literally "leaked" marbles along the railroad. These were in turn picked up by children and the curious. Employees of LOF likely carried examples home and thus into the community as well. The authors have seen quart jars of them offered for sale often. The marbles are green-ish in appearance and very rough surfaced, having numerous flaws. The flaws were not a concern for the producers as they were never intended for any purpose other than to be re-melted. The rough surface gives them what some deem an "old" look and confusion can result for beginning collectors and the general public. It is to add the LOF story to the larger marble history and give it context that they are added here and not to suggest they are play, toy or collectable marbles.

Exact dates for marble production are not know. Trade directories report "glass fiber" production as early as 1955. Ex-employees told us that some years back the production in Vienna ceased and the machines were shipped to other factories within the corporation.

Libbey Owen Ford (LOF) marble tank at the Vienna/ Parkersburg operation includes three visible marble machines. Glass can be seen flowing into the cutter box but no marbles appear to be rolling down the chutes. This is because they moved too fast to be caught on film! Unknown photograph. Circa 1950s.

MARBLE KING, INC.

St. Marys, West Virginia
1949 - 1958
Paden City, West Virginia
1958 - operating at this time

Marble King production examples. Paden City, West Virginia. *D. Chamberlain photo.*

Lawrence E. Alley sold his successful marble-making business, ALLEY GLASS MANUFACTURING Company, to Berry Pink and his partners in 1949. The incorporation documents were dated June 24, 1949, and recorded in the Office of the County Clerk of Pleasants County, West Virginia, on November 30, 1949. That documents reads, in part:

"The undersigned agree to become a corporation by the name of MARBLE KING, INC. The principle office or place of business of said corporation will be located in the City of St. Marys, West Virginia. The objects for which this corporation is formed are as follows: To manufacture, produce and make glass in all forms, including marbles, glassware, ornaments, novelties, toys, containers, cut glass, glass products, and products in which or in connection with which, glass is or may be used. The amount of capital stock with which it will commence business is $15,300 of 100 shares of no par value. The names and addresses of the incorporators and the number of shares of stock subscribed for by each are as follows:

Berry Pink, 49 Shares, 350 5th Ave. Empire State Building, New York, NY

Lucius H. Coleman, 1 Share, 351 5th Ave. Empire State Building, New York, NY

Adele Rubin, 1 Share, 350 5th Ave. Empire State Building, New York, NY

Given under my hand and the Great Seal of the said State, at the City of Charleston, this 14th day of June, 1949. D. Pitt O'Brien, Secretary of State."

These shares sold or accounted for at the time of filing for incorporation account for 51 percent of the total stock created in the new company. The authors have been told repeatedly, by numerous people, that a fourth owner was Sellers Peltier, son of the owner of another glass and marble company, Peltier Glass Company of Ottawa, Illinois. While we do not know exactly when in the early organization of Marble

King Sellers Peltier takes an ownership, it seems he is orally credited with owning 49 percent of Marble King in that early period. See Roger Howydshell's interview of May 15, 1986, below.

One of the first things that the new owner Berry Pink did was to hire Roger Howdyshell as plant manager to handle the day-to-day operations in West Virginia while he, Pink, managed the promotions and sales efforts from his Empire State Building office in New York City, New York.

Current Marble King owner, Berry Fox, and others over time have repeatedly told the authors that during the first few months Marble King sold leftover Alley marbles and marbles made by Peltier Glass at their Ottawa, Illinois, facility while beginning to organize their own production and factory. These diverse marbles were at times mixed and packaged either with promotional labels or the new Marble King label.

Primarily Marble King used the Alley marble machines and built new ones reflecting the style of marbles the new company wanted to produce.

Marble author and researcher Dennis Webb conducted interviews that were taped and later transcribed. From a July 21, 1983, interview with Roger Howdyshell, Webb asked about the rumored source of Marble King marble machines:

D. W.: "You bought all the Akro Agate machines?"

R. H.: "We bought just the marble machines. Only we never did get them. They had the right of refusal. We bought the Master Glass machines when Israel decided to sell out."

D. W.: "People want to know what happened to the Akro machines."

R. H.: "They were junk. Bob Dean used to work for the old Akro Agate Company. Dean was the manager at that time and when they sold the Akro Agate Company out in the early 1950s, we bought all their equipment. We actually contracted to buy it and never paid and never took the equipment."

Akro experts Roger and Claudia Hardy report to the authors that the Akro marble machines were actually sold for scrap metal.

The incursion of the Japanese cat eye design in 1950-51 dealt an almost fatal blow to the domestic marble industry. The immense success of this Japanese marble resulted in a loss of interest by American children in almost all other marble designs. U. S. makers, led by Marble King and Vitro Agate, attempted to curb the flow of these cheap imports by appeals to Congress for import duties. A commonly repeated marble lore story is that of 1950s era Japanese freighters used marbles as ballast in their holds for the trip across the ocean. The story concludes with the flooding of the U.S. marble market when the marbles were unloaded in the U. S. as toys. This story is detailed elsewhere in this text.

There was enough panic to cause at least one meeting of U. S. makers to be held in Washington, D.C. to establish a concerted effort to stop the imports. Roger Howdyshell of Marble King appeared before a Senate Sub-Committee to testify. This attempt to curb toy marble imports appears to be, historically speaking, the first time American manufacturers joined in this manner to save any domestic industry from foreign competition.

In two separate interviews with Dennis Webb, Roger Howdyshell told of Marble King's first crisis – the inexpensive foreign imports. From the May 15, 1986, interview:

D. W.: "What actually happened?"

R. H.: "I appeared for the marble industry before Senator Neely's sub-committee in Washington and presented a paper on marbles and the impact of the marbles being imported from Japan. I think the year I made the presentation was 1955. Mr. Fisher's son, Art Fisher Jr., was in the government – in the Adjutant General's Office – although I gave the information (to the sub-committee), he prepared the paper for me."

From the July 21, 1983, interview:

D. W.: "Didn't you also go to Japan?"

R. H.: "This is what happened. We could get no helpful legislation out of Congress so we at Marble King took matters into our own hands. You see, the cat eye marble was actually named by the Japanese. Those marbles first hit us in 1950-51. I don't know the exact date."

In a May 15, 1986, interview Roger Howdyshell recalled, "In 1955, Mr. Pink, Don Peltier, and myself went to Japan with the intention of buying a plant and setting up an operation over there to make cat eyes to be shipped to Marble King and let West Virginia package them. I don't know what happened (over there), but I was not in on the negotiations. I was there because they wanted me there, and Don had gone because his dad owned 49 percent of Marble King. So Mr. Pink took us along, but we were not in on the final negotiations. What happened, I do not know. But I do know that from the information we had gotten we were able to come back and do our own cat eyes in St. Marys. We did all of our experimental work in the rear – although we had furnaces out front. We also had two day tanks out in the back where no one could get to it and couldn't see. This is where Mr. (Howard) Hildrith comes into the picture. He was then running Vitro Agate and he was to come up to find out how we made the cat eyes. Of course, no one could see as it was closed in. He was to spy on us on how we were making it (the cat eye) and see if he could get into the plant. All this happened in 1955, the year my daughter was born. We got started in cat's eyes in June 1955. I don't know when Vitro got in – whether it was late '55 or early '56."

This production of cat's eye design by Marble King during its St. Marys, West Virginia, era allowed the company to survive. The Marble King cat's eye has not changed significantly over the years and more closely resembles its Japanese ancestor than do other U.S. made cat eye designs that followed.

Marble King had a contract with General Foods to provide marbles for premiums. In recalling it Howdyshell said, "We negotiated (in 1955) with Post Cereal Division of General Foods to produce marbles for their Post Toasties. At first we did not pack the marbles – we made them and shipped them bulk to Indiana. They were packed in a tube of six or eight. We have since packed the tubes for them, but for the first big order we did not. In that year we were running seven or eight machines – we couldn't keep up. There was a lot of things – the bottle hanger orders and the new bags taking 225 marbles. It was in 1955 that we came up with the cloth bag that was made in Japan. With General Foods, the first order we got was one hundred million marbles. That's a lot of marbles. We signed a contract for delivery. We got into a jam and boy, they were just coming down my throat and, of course, Vitro got part of it after that. We made ours first then they (Vitro) made some. We made most of the order. We didn't get into trouble until the latter part of 1956 – we just couldn't make enough. Mr. Pink wouldn't divert from his chain stores to give to Post Cereal. It was his bread and butter. But on the other hand, he had signed a contract. I had signed a contract for the company. I was the one who was left hanging and in the spring of '56 General Foods had to go to Vitro, and of course they had to pay more." (transcript of Webb interview with Howydshell, May 15, 1986)

At this time the *Glass Factory Yearbook* of 1955 lists "Marble King Inc., St. Marys, W.Va. Berry Pink, president and treasurer; R.W. Howdyshell, vice president, general manager and purchasing agent. Berry Pink Industries Empire State Building, New York, NY, purchasing agents. Glass marbles. 7 continuous tanks, 3 day tanks."

Operations continued in St. Marys, West Virginia, until the factory was destroyed by fire on January 6, 1958. A newspaper article from St. Marys Jan. 7, 1958, states, "A fire which broke out at 4:15 a.m. yesterday in the Marble King, Inc. plant at St. Marys, destroyed the plant and did what manager Roger Howdyshell said was over $100,000 worth of damage with the plant a total loss. Actual loss will have to await a check, Howdyshell said, as he reported the fire destroyed all company records."

"Five plant employees were working when an explosion of undetermined origin occurred at the rear of the plant with the blaze following. Members of the St. Marys Volunteer Fire Department and other plant employees called out by the blaze engaged in fighting the flames. For a time the blaze was said to have threatened the Quaker State refining plant on adjacent property with all off duty refinery personnel, numbering approximately eighty men, called out to protect that property. Most of the (Marble King) plant machinery was new and ultramodern, Howdyshell reported. At peak, forty-five persons were employed."

Robert "Coon" Pryor, Jr., retired Quaker State Oil Co. employee, in a 1999 interview with author Susie Metzler stated: "I helped put out the great fire. All the Quaker State workers knew the marble plant was lost but worked like demons to keep the fire from spreading to the refinery." He reported that, like many others, he saved and kept marbles and packaged marbles. One Quaker State worker actually saved and kept boxes of toy glass dishes that were still there.

Roger Howdyshell, discussing the 1958 fire in St. Mary's with Webb in a recorded interview the 15th of May 1986 states "We burned out in 1958 and everything was just destroyed. We had a wooden frame building and the fire started in the rear where we were doing the experimenting. There was a tank back there running glass and there was a butane line over from the (Quaker State) refinery on the outside of our building. We don't know what exploded – whether the gas line exploded or the butane blew out over an old gas line. We had insurance, but we didn't have enough. I had nothing to do with the insurance policy. He (Berry Pink) had this all out of New York. But I don't know what his thinking was – we had only $50,000 of insurance and we lost a quarter of a million dollars. The rollers from the marble machines we saved from the fire, but the rest of the machines were completely destroyed."

Webb asked, "So you did resume operations?" Howdyshell replied, "Within 30 days; yes. We leased this (Paden City) building. Mr. Charlie Ray, who had a large interest in the old pottery factory, called me and asked me if I would be interested in settling in Paden City. There was no property around, we were negotiating one in Sistersville. Mr. Pink had such fond memories of Sistersville when he was in the town, the people, that he wanted to go back there. It didn't make any difference to me but the building we were looking at was not really suitable and they asked such an outlandish price for it you would have thought we were millionaires. Then I talked about this building and, of course, it is more what we wanted."

"We were running marbles here in Paden City in thirty days. We built five tanks and had eight machines rebuilt in that length of time. We rebuilt our plant here (Paden City), we leased the building. We leased 25,000 square feet and we built our tanks here in Paden City and we built the machines down in St. Marys and brought them up here. Then within forty-five to sixty days we had our packing room built and within sixty days we were shipping. During the downtime, Marble King lost some of their business to Vitro Agate."

During the May 15, 1986, interview, Roger Howdyshell revealed some information that was prior to that time little known in the marble world:

R. H.: "During 1957 and even after the fire in '58, Marble King negotiated with Art Fisher to buy Vitro Agate. The price wasn't that bad and had it been me and I had the finances, I would have bought it if he would have actually sold. After the fire, we didn't have any production and there was immediate production we could have had. We would be buying out a competitor and as far as I was concerned, even if it was one quarter of a million or three million dollars, it was worth it, but Berry just wouldn't come to terms. Pink and Fisher never had a real liking for each other."

The time in St. Marys, 1949 - 1957, proved fruitful for Marble King. Their marble-making innovations combined with an array of popular and colorful marbles contributed to the company's success. The continuing influence of Berry Pink, his public relations skills, and marble contest sponsorship were, in some ways, responsible for keeping marbles on the public scene.

According to an eyewitness account by Chester Bills, a long-time resident of St. Marys, given the authors on May 3, 1999, this rapid return to business was aided by the ability of Marble King to return to the partially damaged glass-making plant at the back of the burned out building. The smoke stacks were still standing and the furnace equipment still functioned. They just covered the area over with sheet metal and kept making glass Bills recalled. The finished glass for the marbles was then transported to Paden City until the entire operation could be carried on in Paden City. No finished marbles were made in St. Marys after the fire, only glass for use in Paden City.

Marble King enjoyed fairly good times in Paden City during the 1960s. It was time when the smaller companies that had been competition were out of business and Marble King cat's eye marbles with considerable success. A significant development came in 1963 when Roger Howdyshell, Duncan V. (Don) Peltier, and Cornell Medley bought Marble King, Inc. and Berry Pink Industries.

In 1965, Berry Pink Industries was dissolved and became Berry Pink Industries Division of Marble King, Incorporated. For a time in 1967, marbles produced by Marble King were sold by Peltier Glass Company.

On July 1, 1983, Roger Howdyshell, plant manager since 1949 and for some time a partial owner, became sole owner of the company. For many years since, Marble King has continued the Berry Pink tradition of sponsoring and contributing to the annual National Marble Tournament in Wildwood, New Jersey.

On Friday, September 19, 1980, Rick Steelhammer interviewed Roger Howdyshell. This interview is reprinted with permission of the *Charleston Gazette* (West Virginia). It is titled, "For the first time since the incursion of the Japanese cat-eye, a new threat from abroad has been rumbling south of the border." "In terms of marble manufacturing, Mexico has everything," Howdyshell said. "They've got all the raw materials, they've got plenty of cheap natural gas, and the labor there is cheaper." He added that Mexican marbles are allowed into the U.S. marketplace without tax. The Mexican marbles threaten domestic trade and are already hurting overseas accounts. Large chain stores can purchase the Latino orbs for less than what Howdyshell can afford to sell. "Even though we have quality, we can't offer price," Howdyshell said.

The Paden City manufacturer has enlisted the aid of comic book heroes Spiderman™ and the Incredible Hulk™ to join in his Mexican campaign. He packages a set of blue marbles, which match Spiderman's tights, under an authorized Spiderman label, and packages of green marbles, which compliment Hulk's green tones, under a label that bears Hulk's authorized cartoon image. "It's a gimmick," said Howdyshell. But he noted that packaging is one of the few means of improvising in the marble game. "There's not much you can do with a sphere besides change its colors," he said.

Much of Marble King's finished product comes from West Virginia produced materials. Howdyshell uses trimmings from nearby glass factories, can use recycled glass, and his company makes its own virgin glass using fine sand mixed near Berkeley Springs.

The Dennis Webb/Roger Howdyshell interview of July 21, 1983, contained the following:

D. W.: "Have you made marbles for other marble companies and have other companies sold your marbles?"

R. H.: "Oh, yes, we have."

D. W.: "I mean marble swapping."

R. H.: "Yes, Vitro and I have never had a relationship like that. We are real competitors. We compete in all the fields against each other. I have made marbles for Michels up at Champion, also for Bogard and vice versa. We are competitors in certain lines like with Champion in the game marbles and also competitors with Bogard in the industrial marbles."

D. W.: "Are you veneering* all of your marbles now?"

R. H.: "No, we are not veneering any."

D. W.: "When did you stop veneering?"

R. H.: "Well, we started veneering marbles back in '56 or '57. That was just before we had a fire. Then we came up here (Paden City) and we did it again and I would say the last time we veneered was in 1965."

*Veneering was pioneered at roughly the same time in the 1950s by both Marble King and Vitro Agate. Veneering is the process of covering a less expensive white or clear glass with a thin surface layer of colored glass to provide some visual appeal. The veneered color(s) often cover only part of the surface, patch like, to contrast with the cheaper under color of glass. Veneering produced a less expensive colored marble.

Roger Howdyshell's successful reign as "Marble King" ended when he passed away on April 18, 1991. His wife, Jean, became president the following day. His daughter, Beri Fox, served as business manager. The 1991 National Marbles Tournament was sponsored by Marble King in Roger Howdyshell's name. Beri Fox (nee Howdyshell), named for Berry Pink, was appointed to fill her father's position on the tournament's executive committee. She fields her own tournament team called "Marble Kings." Beri Fox continues to be active, not only in the company, but in promoting marbles as a game and tournaments as well.

An article in the *Paden City News Register* on September 1, 1996, reported the following: "Marble King produces 1,000,000 marbles a day. Thirty-eight workers are employed. Sales are exceeding one million dollars a year and are expanding into a worldwide market. England, France, Austria and Canada are among the customers. Chinese checker marbles are currently being sold by the millions in Germany. Their glass is picked up from Fenton Glass Co. in Williamstown. Physical education programs are now teaching children to play marbles at the elementary level. Marble King is featured in a (book)… *How Things Are Made*. Marble King has been featured in a P.B.S. special called "Made in West Virginia"."

Since (Roger Howdyshell's) passing in 1991 Marble King has renovated its offices and nearly doubled its workforce. It is still locally owned and operated and its employees come from Wetzel and Tyler counties, West Virginia.

Beri Howdyshell Fox said, "We've been real lucky with the workforce here. Everybody has kind of pulled together since my dad died." Fox said Marble King has never taken a hard look at expanding its product line beyond the marble. "We're always developing new styles and new kinds of colors, so we're trying to stay focused on the marble."

"Sand, feldspar, soda ash and pigment to add color are the raw materials needed to make marbles, but Marble King is environmentally friendly. Between 85 and 90 percent of its marbles are made from recycled glass," Fox said. Marble King buys defective or throwaway glass from places like Fenton Art Glass Co. and Gaffert Cullet Co. in Williamstown, Dalzell Viking Glass in New Martinsville, and Wissmach Glass in Paden City. Glass is also purchased from area recycling centers. "After we get the recycled glass on site, it is separated by color: clear, pink, blue, amber or whatever," Fox said. "When recycled glass is melted, it comes out the same color as before. We have very little waste."

Depending on its size, a marble needs from twenty-four to forty-eight hours to cool completely. New colors are invented by experiment or accident when production changes from one color to the next. "When we get toward the end of a run, we will sometimes play with the machines to produce neat colors," Fox said. "Sometimes some of our best colors are the result of mistakes."

Marble King marbles have their place in Hollywood, starring in such movies as *The Goonies*, *Hook*, *Dennis the Menace*, and *Home Alone*. Steven Spielberg, producer of *The Goonies*, flew the Howdyshells to California for a premier showing of that movie.

An article appeared in *Glory Hole*, the newsletter of the West Virginia Museum of American Glass. It was Newsletter #12, dated Spring/Summer 2000 which reads: "West Virginia Governor, Cecil Underwood, recognized marble manufacturer, Marble King of Paden City, for its leadership and success in the state's exporting efforts. Jean Howdyshell, President, and her daughter, Beri Fox, Business Manager, were also honored by the U.S. Department of Commerce. Press releases at the time stated that Marble King employs seventy-nine workers who manufacture, package, and ship marbles twenty-four hours a day, seven days a week. Marbles are exported to the United Kingdom, Ireland, Belgium, France, the Czech Republic, Germany, Australia, Hong Kong, Canada, Mexico, and Poland. The company now exports entire container loads – between 30,000 - 40,000 pounds of marbles. Sadly, it was reported that Jean L. Howdyshell, President of Marble King, Inc., passed away August 20, 2003."

Among her many lifetime honors, Mrs. Howdyshell was featured in *Entrepreneur Magazine* as West Virginia's recipient of the Entrepreneur Award in 1995. She was also on the Board of Directors of the West Virginia Manufacturers Association and the Society for Glass and Science Practices. Mrs. Howdyshell was a sponsor of the National Marbles Tournament.

Her daughter, Beri Jean Fox, now runs the entire Marble King, Inc. operation.

MARBLE KING
Marbles Produced

Cat Eye: Usually four very well-defined X vanes that are joined in the center like the Japanese variety. These generally come in sizes 5/8", 3/4", and 1 inch. In 1978 Marble King produced a cat eye in a large 1-1/4" size. These marbles are rare. Occasionally a Marble King cat eye can be found that is 1/2" and as small as 3/8". These are also rare. The regular colors for Marble King cat eyes are red, blue, white, green, and yellow.

A few have been found in orange. One uncommon type of Marble King cat eye is known as the "St. Marys" cat eye. Many of these marbles were produced when the factory was in that city. However, excavations at private property dumpsites in Paden City have revealed many of these same two-color "St. Marys" designs. These cat eye marbles are identical to the one-color type in style, but the vanes are of two colors. This means that one vane is intersected by a vane of another color. The color combinations include yellow/blue; red/blue; green/white; yellow/white; blue/orange. Hybrids are known to exist.

Other cat eyes from Marble King in Paden City have two colors on each vane – similar to some Vitro Agate cat eyes. These color combinations include a beautiful peach/yellow; yellow/green; green/white; dark peach/light peach; dark lavender/light lavender; red/green. Also seen are regular four-vane cat eyes with an iridescent spray on the surface.

Opaque Solids or Chinese Checker types: Found in several sizes, usually 9/16" or 5/8", and are in the standard colors of red, yellow, green, black, blue, and white. All but white and black may be found in original packages in several shades.

Transparent and Industrial Marbles: These marbles are usually indistinguishable from similar marbles produced by other companies. Marble King did, however, package some very attractive transparent marbles and packaged them either as Marine Crystals or Marine Puries.

Marble King "RAINBOW" design: These marbles (in their older variety) are often called patch and ribbon and are readily identified by the ribbon of colored glass around the equator and a colored patch at one pole. Most of these marbles are white-based with the patch and ribbon designs in colors of red, blue, green, and occasionally brown or black and even more rare are the yellow. Sometimes the green variety contains aventurine and are now called Grasshoppers. Two-color Rainbows (no white) have been given interesting names – some by the company, others by the children who played with them, and some by present-day collectors and dealers. The most well-known varieties include:

Bumblebee: yellow/black.
Graybee: yellow/gray.
   Oftentimes on these two types, the black or gray is washed out and appears as a kind of purple.
Black Widow: red/black This is a company name – although some call it a Wasp.
Cub Scout: Scout: yellow/blue.
Girl Scout or John Deere: yellow/green. The Girl Scout is rarely found to have thin lines of oxblood glass highlighting the ribbon. A beautiful hybrid of the Cub Scout and Girl Scout occasionally appears and we have called it "Hermaphrascout".
Tiger: orange/black.
Rubybee: red/yellow.
Spiderman: red/blue.
Hercules: blue/black.
Green Hornet: green/black.
Watermelon: red/green.
Dragonfly: blue/green.

Many hybrids of these two-color Rainbows exist in which a third or even a fourth color have been blended – as between runs – to make stunning and highly collectible marbles.

Some interesting Cub Scout, Black Widow, and Bumblebee varieties have been found that have a transparent base and occur as follows:

Blueboy: transparent blue base and yellow.
Beeboy: transparent purple base and yellow.
Blue Widow: transparent blue/black/red.

There are many other color combinations of the blended hybrids that have been given names like Robin, Copperhead, Irish, Peacock, West Virginian, Jillian, and Cookies and Cream. This nomenclature helps to give these marbles a common identify and to incidentally increase potential value. Many of these marbles have come from Marble King dump sites on private property in the areas around St. Marys and Paden City. Many of these marbles, perfectly formed, were possibly off-size, off-color, experimental, or just accidents that were rejected and never intended for sale or distribution but have survived and hold appeal for collectors.

Double Ribbons generally come in white base with two ribbons in these color combinations and in sizes of 5/8" and sometimes 1".
Red/brown
Yellow/brown
Red/green
Blue/red
Blue/brown
Brown/green
Red/yellow

There are a few multi-color variations: 1 brown ribbon/half blue/half green and 1 blue ribbon/half red/half brown are known.

The three-color patch and ribbons also occur on a white base and it may be considered four-color if the white is counted. Generally, however, these are called Tri-color Rainbows. The patches are almost always yellow, orange, sometimes reddish-brown or blue. The ribbons are usually half blue/half green. Of course, there are variations. Among these are the blue patch/half yellow/half brown ribbon and the blue patch/half green/half orange ribbon. The sizes are generally 5/8" and sometimes 15/16" or 1". Translucent marbles of this type have been identified as well.

As with marbles from any company, the brightest colors with well-defined patches and ribbons and the absence of blow-out holes (holes made by escaping air bubbles) are the most desirable.

Marble King has introduced new versions of some of the popular patch and ribbon designs, with the variation in that there is a patch on either pole separated by a ribbon of another color. This is most noticeable in the "new" Cub Scout. These have been seen in poly bags with reproduced labels and sold to inexperienced collectors as the older, more valuable variety. It is thought that Marble King never sold all one type or color of patch and ribbon types in one bag. Other new types include two blue patch/black ribbon; two black patch/green ribbon.

Since the mid-1970s, Marble King has produced a new generation of Rainbow designs, which include the following:

White base/red patch on each pole
White base/red patch on pole/green patch on pole
White base/orange pole/green pole
White base/brown pole/green pole
White base/red pole/blue pole
White base/two yellow poles
White base/two blue poles
White base/yellow pole/red pole
White base/yellow pole/brown pole
Green base or ribbon/red patch at each pole
Muddy black/white patch and ribbon
Muddy blue patch and ribbons

During the late 1990s, Marble King maintained for several years a "marble garden" in front of their office in which visitors were allowed to pick through and take samples. Sadly some visitors took this generosity to the extreme limit and brought in five gallon buckets at night and cleaned the garden out. While it was there, "the marble garden" yielded some never-before seen Marble King designs such as the muddy green and muddy yellow strange opaque with dark hi-light lines of patch and ribbon. Another type not seen anywhere else is the Marble King "Moonie", which is reminiscent of the type made by Akro Agate in the 1930s.

Wee Glow Marbles: In 1999, Marble King took out a registered trademark on a fluorescent marble they call Wee Glo. These marbles are pleasant enough in regular light but take on a fascinating glow under a black light. This type appears to be the first by a company to register such a trademark, especially since fluorescent marbles have been produced by nearly all the marble companies for a great many years.

Marble King marbles have been used as the commemorative marbles by the Sistersville Marble Festival. These are one inch, solid colored, iridescent marbles silk screened with a logo and other annual themes.

In 2003, Marble King started producing a four-vane, four-color cat eye. Most that have been seen to date have vanes that are orange, yellow, green, and blue.

MARBLE KING Marbles Produced

Cat Eyes.
Industrial and Craft Marbles and Gems.
Opaque Patched and Ribboned.
Opaque Swirls.
Opaques.
Patched Opaques.
Patched Translucents.
Promotional Marbles.
Translucent Ribbons.
Transparent Patched.
Transparents.
Wee Glo Marbles.

Marble King
Identification Tips

Patched opaques (called rainbows) are produced in sizes 5/8", 3/4", and 7/8" at the time of publication. The color combinations are green/white, red/white, blue/white, black/white, and red/yellow/white.

Shortly after the move to Paden City (1958), Marble King produced a four-vane, four-color cat eye in 1959 - 1960 only. The colors were red, dark blue, dark green, and yellow. They were expensive to make and not popular. They were made in 5/8" and 1" sizes. The design has been recently revived but in 1" and 1-1/4" sizes.

As of 2005 Marble King is the only U.S. maker to produce cat eyes with two or four different colors of blades in each marble. They are in the 5/8" size. Their standard Japanese-style cat eye marbles more closely resemble their Japanese ancestor than all others produced in this country. The colors are red, green, white, blue, and yellow. The sizes are: 9/16", 5/8", 3/4", 7/8", 1", and 1-1/4".

Flats, called "sparklet gems" by Marble King, and decorative marbles are produced in three body finishes: iridescent, frosted, and standard, and are in thirty-two color combinations.

MARBLE KING Packaging

In its fifty-six year history, Marble King, Inc. has become among the most prolific packagers of marbles. The only competition for top honors would be the Vitro Agate Company. Several generations earlier, the Akro Agate Company opened the door with a number of innovative packaging ideas.

Starting in 1949, and continuing for a time, Marble King used mesh bags to package marbles made by Peltier Glass, Heaton Agate, as well as leftover Alley stock. It did not take long for Marble King to enter the polyvinyl bag market (in the very early 1950s) with its own bag headers, which were usually an attractive red and white. The company also produced special advertising packages for soda, salt, peanut, and other companies.

St. Marys, West Virginia, resident and antique dealer, Chester Bills, has reported that for several years during the early 1950s, Marble King marketed a stocking-shaped marble bag for the holiday season.

Marble King was never known for fancy gift boxes of marbles and the best known box is actually the "Chinko-Checko-Marblo" Chinese checker box put out by Berry Pink Industries. This box may actually pre-date Marble King and the marbles could have been made by any number of makers. Berry Pink's association with the founding of Marble King did not start until 1949.

Berry Pink Industries produced a Chinese checker game box complete with playing board and sixty opaque one-color marbles in six colors. It was marketed as "Chinko-Checko-Marblo."

A box, as advertised in the 1954 Marble King packaging line, and again put out by Berry Pink Industries, is the "Big Value Assortment" which contains one hundred marbles.

Berry Pink Industries issued a box called "Champion Marbles." It is not known if all the marbles in this box were made by Marble King or by another maker.

The large Marble King cloth bag distributed by Berry Pink Industries in 1955 was made in Japan and Roger Howdyshell, former owner of Marble King, has stated that this bag contained two hundred twenty-five assorted marbles including cat eyes, rainbows, moonies, marine crystals, and large shooters. There is a copy-cat bag, also made in Japan, that is of poorer quality and valued considerably less.

The earliest identifiable Marble King bags are mesh and while Marble King was still retooling to produce their own unique styles of marbles, they marketed in twenty and thirty count mesh bags Alley and Heaton swirls and assorted Peltier marbles. Sixty count Marble King Chinese checker marbles may also be found in mesh bags.

Three, four, five, or six count "shooters" or "Bowlers" are also found in mesh bags.

Early Marble King poly bags are found to hold Alley swirls or mixed Peltier marbles in counts of fourteen, nineteen, twenty, or forty.

Over the years, Marble King marketed many poly bags with various styled stapled-on paper headers. Most headers were red and white, or red, white, and black. Some packages of Marine Crystals had green and white headers.

The many marble counts featured in Marble King packaging included virtually every type of marble produced by this company. The various counts include: 8, 10, 12, 14, 19, 20, 22, 25, 30, 36, 40, 45, 50, 60, 70, 85, 96, and 100. All of these have stapled or paper headers and a few include a sample tag or an informational tag relating to ordering marbles.

The eight count bags usually contain eight 7/8" shooters and the twelve count bags usually contain twelve 3/4" marbles. One inch shooters and bowlers are often found in poly bags of 3, 4, 5, 6, and 8 counts. The sixty count poly bags have six different colors of ten each, one-color opaque Chinese checker marbles.

Many thirty-six and ninety-six count bags contain Marine Crystals. An uncommon bag would be a ninety-six count pee wee cat's eye bag. Many one hundred count bags will contain Marble King, Rainbows, or Peltier Banana cat's eyes.

An interesting aside to the Marble King packaging story is that illegal excavating outside the Marble King grounds in Paden City has uncovered the decaying remains of hundreds of Peltier poly marble bags.

During the late 1950s, Marble King (with a little help from Vitro Agate) supplied boxed cereal companies with wrapped marble premiums as giveaways. The Marble King examples contain seven marbles.

Drawstring bags: Since the 1950s, Marble King has distributed plastic marble bags with draw-strings. The larger bag contains one hundred and forty marbles and the smaller one holds seventy. It is interesting to note that over the years the boys' outfits, as shown in the bright graphics, slowly evolve to fit the times. These bags are called "Tournament Assortment".

Blister Packs: Marble King put out standard blister packs of marbles. One contains five shooters and another holds fifty 5/8" marbles. One blister pack entitled "Secret of a Marble Champ" includes fifty marbles, a "Tournament Assortment", a genuine marble pouch, and an instruction booklet entitled "The Game of Marbles" by Shirley "Windy" Allen, a National Champion from Fairdale, West Virginia. There are three other blister packs. One, with a red cardboard backing, includes a mesh bag and forty cat's eye marbles. This pack is entitled: "Marble King says 'Knuckle Down' with American Marbles." A second blister pack features the Incredible Hulk with mesh bag and forty marbles. The third blister pack features another hero, Spiderman, with blue cardboard backing, mesh bag, and forty mixed red and blue marbles.

With the blister packs there are Hulk and Spiderman "go-withs," a one hundred count nylon mesh bag and smaller poly bags with superhero cardboard headers. These contain either twenty 5/8" marbles or six 1" shooters. These marbles may be Rainbows or Cat's Eyes.

Marble King also produced a drawstring bag featuring both the Incredible Hulk and Spiderman. It contains one hundred and forty marbles.

Modern Nylon Mesh Bags: These come in fifty and one hundred count and may contain either Rainbows or Cat's Eyes. Marble King does its own packaging and shipping out of two fairly large buildings at the factory site.

In a 50 lb. standard bulk pack the contents are:

1" marbles, 1000 pieces per 50 lbs.
7/8" marbles, 1500 pieces per 50 lbs.
3/4" marbles, 2500 pieces per 50 lbs.
5/8" marbles, 4000 pieces per 50 lbs.

A collectable marble item, not produced by Marble King, is the Marble King truck. This truck is produced in cooperation with the marble company by Eastwood Automobilia of Malvern, Pennsylvania. It features a bright red, yellow, and white 1957 International Full Rack Stake Truck. The Marble King logo and Paden City address are on the sides. The box that the truck comes in says the copyright is "1995 by First Gear, Inc. Manufacturer of Diecast Metal Replicas. Made in China." Included is a soft cloth drawstring bag containing twenty double patch 5/8" marbles and one 1" white shooter containing the Marble King logo.

Promotional marbles include:

In 1974 "The Big Blue Marble." Made for International Telephone and Telegraph's sponsorship of the National Marble Tournament.
"Marble King" advertising marbles.
West Virginia "Wild and Wonderful West Virginia" and "Almost Heaven West Virginia."
Individual marbles for Pepsi Cola and Coca Cola as well as bottle hangers. 14 or 6 count.
Mr. Peanut mesh-bag packages. 14 count.
General Mills package premiums in cellophane tubes.
Esso Oil Co. loose premiums.
Sunshine Rippled Wheat (mesh) 11 count.
Worcester Salt Marbles (mesh) 14 count + 1 shooter.

Poly promotional bags include a Bordon 14 count bag; Nestlé's Quik 14 count bag; Dolly Madison Dairy 14 count bag; Triple Cola (bottle hanger) 14 count bag; Tower Root Beer (with 14 Alley Swirls); Royal Crown Cola 15 count bag; Nehi Beverage 14 count bag; Nesbitt's Soda 14 count bag; Bonded Gas 12 count bag.

In the interview of May 15, 1986, Dennis Webb talked with Roger Howdyshell on promotional items/bottle hangers.

D. W.: "Marble King put together promotional items including bottle hangers using rainbow marbles."
R. H.: "We did it for all the major bottling companies at one time before we burned out. Marble King ran a special packing room with two men at a shift, twenty-four hours a day – for Cotts, Pepsi Cola, R.C. Cola, Coca Cola, and others and that is when the six-packs came out and they were really popular and the bottle hangers were made just for these packs. Special packaging was also made for Mr. Peanut and others."

Many packages and promotional marbles were made over the years as Marble King, promoted heavily by Berry Pink and his successors, flooded the marble market with all manner of products. Some of those are: Epko Film Service 14 count; Dean's Milk and Ice Cream 14 count; Photo Ad 14 count; Hood Dairy 25 count; Keasbey and Mattison 14 count; Eckert Packing Company 14 count: Sucher Packing Company 14 count; A Treat Soda 15 count, which is found also in a mesh bag of 15 count; Fidelity Bank 14 count; Cedar Point on Lake Erie 10 count; Tony's City Service 14 count; Isadettes 6 count; J. H. Brokhoff, Inc. 19 count; Jiff Peanut Butter 14 count; Colt Beverage 14 count; Mission 14 count; and Dumont Picture Tubes 14 count.

Marble King factory site aerial view of marble factory adjacent to oil refinery, St. Marys, West Virginia. The marble factory is in the right lower corner of the image. Photo pre-1958 and fire. For additional view of building, see Alley chapter. *Photo courtesy Chester Bills*, date and photographer unknown.

Marble King factory entrance and company logo. *1996 photo by Marble Magnates.*

Marble King factory in Paden City, West Virginia, as it appeared in 1996. *Photo by Marble Magnates.*

Marble King successor to the crown was Roger Howdyshell, who carried on the Berry Pink patronage of marble tournaments. In this 1969 photo, compliments of Marble King, Howdyshell presents a Marble King scholarship to Glen Sigmon of Boone County, West Virginia.

Marble King's current leadership comes from Beri Fox shown here in a 1993 photo by Michael Keller. *Used by permission, courtesy Goldenseal Magazine.*

Marble King's Berry "Marble King" Pink and unidentified companion. The caption might read, "It takes concentration." Pink played a major role from his New York office in establishing West Virginia as a power in the marble world. *1940 photo compliments of Marble King.*

Marble King owner Jean Howdyshell followed her husband in leading the company and poses here in a 1993 photo beside the factory entrance and the logo. If the two men preceding here were the "Marble King," then Jean Howdyshell surely earned the title of Marble Queen. *Photograph by Michael Keller, used courtesy Goldenseal Magazine.*

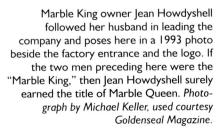

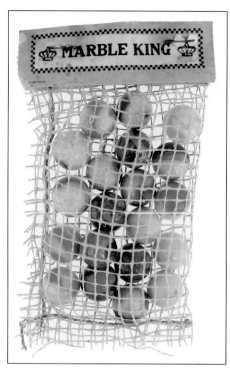

Marble King mesh bag, St. Marys, West Virginia. Containing Alley Agate Co. marbles left on site when acquired by Marble King. *J. Thompson photo.* $25-30.

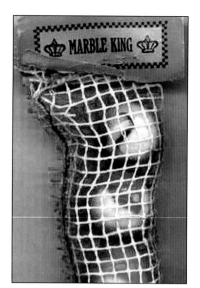

Marble King mesh bag with 1" shooters. *A. Rasmus Collection.* $40.

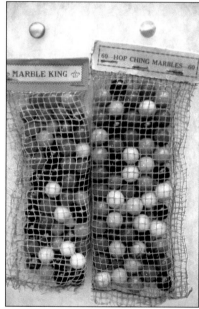

Marble King mesh bags of solid color opaque game marbles. Left: Marble King header; right: Hop Ching, 60 count. *Collection of Marble Magnates.* Either, $30-50.

Marble King bags with advertising headers, left poly bag, $15-20, and right mesh bag, $20-25.

Marble King labeled early mesh bag, but containing Peltier marbles. See text. $20-40. *Jeremy Thompson photo.*

Marble King poly bag with bottle hanger advertisement for Royal Crown Cola. *Marble Magnates collection.* $35.

Marble King poly bag with bottle hanger advertisement for Coca Cola. *Marble Magnates collection.* $15.

Marble King three variations of 60 count opaque game marble packages. *Marble Magnates collection.* $20 each.

Marble King 1950s advertising poly bag with header. "Dean's Milk & Ice Cream." 15 count patch and ribbon marbles. *Al Rasmus Collection.* $25-30.

Marble King poly bag of five 1" Big Boy Cat's Eye shooters. The bag contains the harder to find blue and yellow cat's eye shooters. *Marble Magnates collection.* $20.

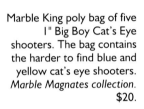

Marble King "Shooters Rainbow Marbles" 15 count poly bag and header. $15.

Marble King marbles in poly bags recovered from the site after the 1958 St. Marys factory fire. Collected at the time by Robert J. "Coon" Pryor, employee at the adjacent Quaker State refinery who helped in putting out the fire. *Pleasants County, West Virginia, Historical Society collection, gift from Pryor.*

Marble King poly bag of 100 count Rainbow and patch marbles saved from the 1958 fire. *Collection of Marble Magnates.* $100.

Marble King poly bag 40 count Rainbow Marbles, including shooter. *J. Thompson photo.* $20-25.

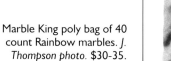

Marble King poly bag of 40 count Rainbow marbles. *J. Thompson photo.* $30-35.

Marble King poly bag of 36 count Marine Puries. *Marble Magnates Collection. J. Thompson photo.* $10-15.

Marble King St. Marys bag containing marbles made by Peltier Glass Co. *J. Thompson photo.* $30-40.

Marble King poly bag of 96 count peewee Cat's Eye marbles. *J. Thompson photo.* $60-80.

Marble King blister pack with patch marbles. *A. Rasmus Collection.* $25.

Marble King Rainbows in 25 count poly bag with less common black and red header. *J. Thompson photo.* $15-25.

Marble King poly bag and header with 6 count 1" shooters. *D. Six collection.* $5-10.

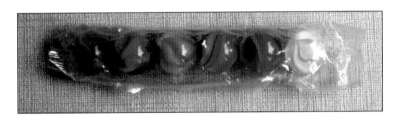

Marble King plastic sleeve for cereal premium containing six Cat's Eye marbles. *Dennis Webb Collection photo.* $25.

Marble King poly bag and header with 8 count 1" shooters. *Marble Magnates Collection.* $5-10.

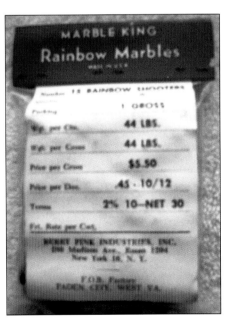

Marble King Rainbow poly bag with Berry Pink Industries weight and price information and New York address. *Marble Magnates collection.* $30-40.

Marble King poly bag and header with 15 count Cat's Eye marbles. $8-15.

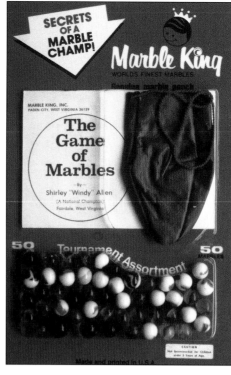

Marble King blister pack, all patch marbles. *A. Rasmus Collection.* $15-20.

Marble King "Secrets of a Marble Champ!" blister pack with 50 marbles and bag. Includes booklet as in previous photo. Note variance of bag and marbles, no cat's eyes in this selection. *Dennis Webb Photo Collection.* Value see above.

Marble King blister pack with patch and cat's eye marbles. *Dennis Webb Photo Collection.* $15-20.

Marble King, earlier version than shown in previous photo of Tournament Assortment in poly bag. *Marble Magnates Collection.* $10 empty bag; $20-25 with original marbles.

Marble King printed poly bag Tournament Assortment of 75 count. *Gift from Beri Fox to authors in 1994.* Contents of bag shown around bag. $20.

Marble King "Secrets of a Marble Champ!" blister pack with 50 marbles and bag. Includes booklet by 1951 National Marbles Champion Shirley "Windy" Allen. *A. Rasmus Collection.* $50.

Marble King cloth Tournament Assortment bag from Berry Pink Industries. *Marble Magnates collection.* Empty, $30; $50 with original marbles.

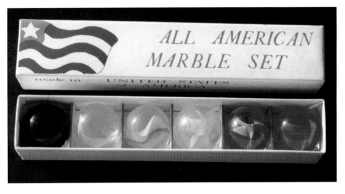

Marble King set of over 1" cat's eye marbles distributed by McMillan and Husband. *D. Chamberlain Collection.* $100-125.

Marble King 1954 catalog sheet. *Image courtesy G. Sourlis.*

Marble King 1954 catalog sheet with fine print reading "F.O.B. factory St. Marys, West Va." Note the Berry Pink New York address and the "Marble King" character. *Image courtesy G. Sourlis.*

Marble King licensed Eastwood Automobilia in 1995 for the production of a 1957 International R-190 Full Rack Stake Truck. The truck, produced in China, comes with the Marble King logo and a bag of marbles that included a Marble King logo shooter. If all intact and good condition, $100.

Marble King catalog sheet featuring Spiderman packages, copyrighted 1979. *Used with Permission, Marble King.*

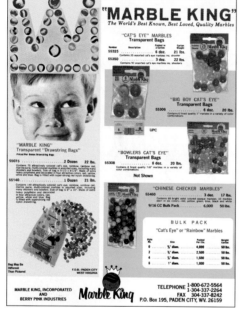

Marble King contemporary catalog sheet. *Used with Permission, Marble King.*

Marble King catalog sheet featuring The Incredible Hulk, copyrighted 1979. *Used with Permission, Marble King.*

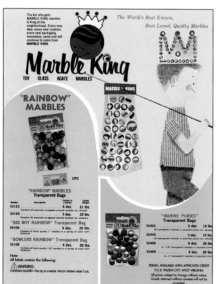

Marble King contemporary catalog sheet. *Used with Permission, Marble King.*

Marble King contemporary catalog sheet used with permission by Marble King. Note the original booklet that came with the similar package has now become the printed back of the package. *Used with Permission, Marble King.*

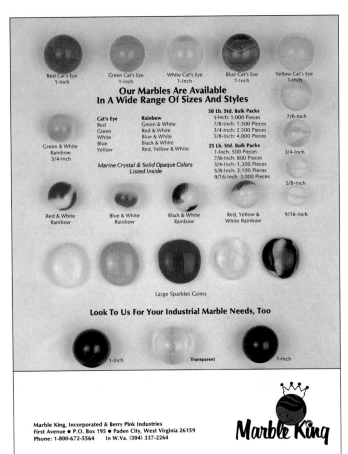

Marble King contemporary catalog sheet showing sizes, some cat's eye marbles and other data. *Used by Permission of Marble King, Inc.*

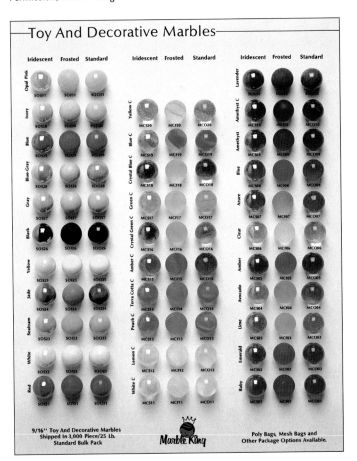

Marble King four color 1" St. Marys-style cat's eye marble. *Collection of D. Chamberlain.*

Marble King contemporary catalog sheet showing color names, etc. *Used by Permission of Marble King, Inc.*

MASTER GLASS COMPANY

Bridgeport, West Virginia
1941 - 1947

Master Glass production examples. Master Glass is not recognized for producing outstanding cat eye marbles, but these examples prove there are exceptions. *D. Chamberlain collection.* $20-25 each.

Master Glass production examples of their general lines. *D. Chamberlain collection.*

The Master Glass Company began business on August 1, 1941, in Bridgeport, West Virginia, in a glass factory previously occupied by the Bridgeport Chimney Lamp Company. It was located between the B & O Railroad line and Simpson Creek in Bridgeport, although the mailing address for Master Glass was in nearby Clarksburg. Master Glass was a reorganized version of the Master Marble Company from the Grasselli District of Clarksburg, but now solely owned by Master Marble stockholder Clinton F. Israel. Israel had bought out all other partners and moved to the 1.4 acre Bridgeport site with on-hand stock and equipment. The marble machines were those designed and built in 1930 for Master Marble by John F. Early who, like Israel, was a former Akro Agate employee. Master Glass continued to package their marbles as "Master Marbles" and "Master Made Marbles," the same brand name that had been used by the Master Marble Company, thus creating confusion today in identifying the origin of some packaged marbles.

As tall as a two story building but with only one story, the large factory was mostly a tin shell on a skeletal wood frame, although some parts were brick and wood. Across the creek from the factory proper was a small building used as an office with storage space for a large stock of pasteboard boxes and sales and advertising items. This two story building held the offices upstairs and on the ground floor included a garage for Mr. Israel's car. Under the structure was living quarters for a night watchman, all this as told the authors by John Barnes.

The company owned a railroad siding that came up along the creek for loading boxcars with marbles and other products for shipment. Master Glass owned the spur and rented the switch from the B & O Railroad. During peak production years, three marble machines were running. In later years, only two were in use. Except for Sundays and rare shutdown days, the factory was producing twenty-four hours a day. In the late 1950s and early 1960s, their natural gas bill often reached $900.00 per month. At that period there were usually five or six employees on duty at a time, the entire staff being about twenty-five people. The machines of Master Glass ran more slowly than ma-

chines of some factories, and produced a maximum of 90 marbles a minute in 5/8" size, and 60 a minute in 1" size. The temperature in their melting tanks was generally 2800 degrees Fahrenheit. Brightly colored marbles in hundreds of containers, usually old metal laundry baskets, filled the floor space in the largest room.

The Glass Factory Directory edition of 1946 lists Master Glass Co., Inc., Clarksburg, West Virginia, Clinton F. Israel, president and general manager. Production facilities were listed as 5 day tanks and the product line was given as "Glass toy marbles, lenses, industrial glass balls, pressed ware, private mould work, signal and automotive ware. Small pressed ware." By 1955 and 1957 the trade journal entries list only Israel as an officer and again notes 5 day tanks. By the 1957 listing a slightly shortened product list included "glass toy marbles, lenses, industrial glass marbles, pressed ware and small pressed ware."

Master Glass sold "glass balls" in thousand marble units for commercial purposes. Master Glass, in its day, was the biggest supplier of these industrial use marbles. According to a small local history, the uses included smoothing copper plates in the lithography industry, as ball bearings in Lazy Susans, and in filters and condensers. They were also used in highway signs as reflectors, in the bottoms of ponds in fish hatcheries during spawning season, and in mausoleums to help move heavy coffins. (*Bridgeport The Town and It's People* by Avis Caynor)

Master Glass produced marbles in seven sizes, ranging from 9/16" to 1". It is reported, but not verified, that they made some very small peewee's, 3/8" and smaller for a time thinking they might be able to drill holes in them for beads. They never did complete the project. (Authors interview of 16 May 1996 with John R. Barnes, husband of long time employee Martha Barnes and a frequent visitor to factory.)

Another unverified but intriguing legend told us in our 1996 interview with John Barnes is that Mr. Israel had a huge marble machine that he didn't use. It had rollers and mechanisms for making marbles as big as 2-1/2" and as small as 1". Just before the outbreak of the Second World War, when the sale of strategic materials was banned to the Axis Powers, he sold it to a man who wanted to ship it to friends in Germany. The marble machine, ship and all, ended up at the bottom of the Mediterranean Sea, victims of an Italian gunboat. We offer no opinions on the authenticity of this story but find it, in truth or legend, intriguing indeed!

When the Akro Agate Company closed in 1951, Master Glass purchased a large stock of Akro marbles, packaging materials and glass formulas, as well as the right to use the Akro Agate logo and trademark. It is reported that for some time Master Glass sold this old stock together with some of its own marbles in boxes marked Akro Agate. A very few examples exist of Chinese checker sets labeled "Chinese Akro Agate Checkers – manufactured by Master Glass Co."

Curiously, Clinton F. Israel and partners Walter Shrader and M. Pauline Dennison, reincorporated the defunct Akro Agate Company. It was chartered as Akro Agate, Incorporated. The date was September 21, 1955, with a capital stock of $10,000.00. The charter states that business was to be conducted at Harvey Street, Clarksburg, West Virginia, which was, in fact, the old factory site of Akro Agate. It was a standard incorporation document stating that the corporation intended to produce all manner of glassware. This corporation was dissolved on May 13, 1957, with no known record of it ever having produced any glass.

An undated Master Glass flier, perhaps of the 1960s, advertises: "Master Marble Akro Agates, in Packages and in Bulk." This same flier also lists "Brand Names: Clearies, Glassies, Opal, Game, and Cat's Eye." Around that time period the company's best sellers were ten marbles in a package for five cents, twenty for ten cents, twenty-five for fifteen cents, sixty for twenty-five cents.

In addition to marbles, the Bridgeport company's letterhead claims that Master Glass manufactured automotive lenses and pressed ware. To date no attributed examples of this pressed ware are known to the authors or to the West Virginia Museum of American Glass.

Pauline Dennison, a longtime employee who started with Master Marble Company as a bookkeeper, became a minority stockholder in the last years. Other known company employees included former Akro employee Dominic Oliverio and Martha Barnes. Barnes began working for Master Glass in 1948 at an hourly wage of 45 cents. A loyal worker, she remained with the company until the end and was the only employee still with Mr. Israel when they locked the door on the final day in 1974.

By the early 1970s, Israel had neither hired any new staff nor acquired any new equipment for decades. The only repair work that had ever been done to the factory building was when the roof was replaced in 1949 after being damaged in a cyclone. Reports by employees and those close to them indicate that the employees, machines, and the factory building itself all seemed an overwhelming task to the also aging Israel. The City of Bridgeport had been eyeing the property for some time, wishing to tear down the decaying factory and use the prime real estate to provide recreational facilities to an upwardly mobile community. The City purchased the building and property for $80,000, and Master Glass ceased operations on June 1, 1974. Clinton F. Israel, active in Harrison County marble-making for fifty years, died on February 25, 1975, after a brief illness.

MASTER GLASS Marbles Types Produced

Cat Eyes.
Brushed Opaques.
Brushed Translucents.
Brushed Transparents.
Opaques.
Patched Transparents.
Sunbursts.
Transparents.
Translucents.

Master Glass marble sizes produced include 3/8" to 1". Traces of oxblood have been found in a few brushed patch marbles. There has been much speculation that the 1" marbles produced or sold by Ravenswood Novelty Works and marketed as "Paul Bunyons" were actually made at Master Glass, or even Akro Agate. We have found no evidence to support this view.

MASTER GLASS Marbles Identification Tips

As described in the chapter on Master Marble, the marbles produced by Master Glass appear rather on the pale side in color when compared to similar but earlier production from Master Marble and Akro. In regard to the Master Glass cat eye marbles, such a comparison to the two nearby large giants does not exist. Neither Master Marble nor Akro Agate produced a cat's eye, a marble type whose appearance comes about after their demise.

Much of the machinery used by all three of these companies was designed by John F. Early and/or his associates. That single source for the machinery would account for possible similarities in the products.

A method for determining differences, especially between Master Marble and Master Glass production, is that the colors used in Master Marble were by far more bold, intense, vibrant, and distinctive. Master Glass marbles tend to be duller, perhaps victims to less potent and/or less expensive colorants generally brought into use after the Second World War.

The majority of marbles that have been identified as Master Glass, either by being found in original packages or by archeological means, tend to be transparent clearies in various colors, brushed patch marbles in opaque, translucent or transparent base glass. A few Sunburst types have been found but the colors tend to be washed out. Some very attractive opaque marbles have been found, especially in orange, yellow, and blue that will stand beside those of other companies, in terms of brightness and quality. These opaques seem to be the exceptions to the "duller" rule.

The most easily identified Master Glass marble is their cat eye design, a marble made neither by Akro Agate nor Master Marble. Interestingly, there is a Master Glass Company advertisement that shows genuine Akro Agates, marbles made years earlier but marketed from old stock, being offered for sale on the same page as Master Glass cat eye marbles. These two marble types were a generation apart as well as worlds apart in quality and color intensity. The Master Glass cat eye marbles often have a rather irregular three-vane translucent to transparent look. Perfectly fashioned opaque examples can be found, being the exception and not the most commonly found type. Some Master Glass cat eyes have a banana look to them. The bulk of Master Glass cat eye marbles have vanes that are either off-center, wildly mutilated, or appear as almost unrecognizable blobs. The Master Glass cat's eye machinery was not exceptional in its performance.

The colors of Master Glass cat's eyes range from dull blues, whites, oranges, to pale green, yellows, and reds. There are, of course, uncommon exceptions and those are classified as hybrids and individually can be quite attractive. They have been found in combinations of red/yellow; green/white; purple/white; and red/white in a clear base. In these hybrids, the colors seem to be fairly bright and are as pretty as any other type of that design yet seen.

In general the cat eye marbles from Master Glass are the least attractive and thus least desirable to collectors of all contemporaries cat's eyes marbles

MASTER GLASS Packaging

It is believed that when the Master Marble Company was relocated and reconstituted as the Master Glass Company in 1941 that marbles, packaging material, and other assets were relocated as well. Subsequent packaging produced solely for Master Glass contained virtually the same logo, design, and color scheme as for the earlier company. Adding to the confusion today among collectors, is that both companies used a Clarksburg, West Virginia, address on packaging while neither company was located in that city.

It is known that Master Glass used the Number 5 box – the same as Master Marble; in blue and red with the exact same ten oval cutouts and logo. There appears to be two somewhat distinct series. Some collectors speculate that the newer one is of recent origin, the type of box sometimes called a fantasy or fake box. Others maintain that the box is merely a later reissue by the company with a few minor alterations. Regardless, the later issue is known to be readily available and may contain rather uninteresting brushed patch marbles. They have also been sold with JABO classics and Marble King patch marbles and/or cat's eyes.

Another interesting packaging twist is that when Akro Agate went out in 1951, Master Glass bought up a stock of Akro marbles, as well as packaging supplies, thus compounding confusion by putting both company's marbles in packages by Akro and Master Glass. To further complicate matters, Master Glass had Akro Agate boxes printed up with the Master Glass name on them. The boxes of this type that have been identified are boxes of 60 Chinese Checker marbles, the lids of which are either red and white or green and white. The writing is as follows: "60 game marbles No. 00" and "Chinese Akro Agate Checkers." At the bottom, the maker is identified as "Manufactured by the Master Glass Co., Clarksburg, W. Va. USA," these boxes are extremely uncommon and command a premium price.

The most common Master Glass packaging is the polyvinyl bag. This bag is different from those of other companies in that it does not have a center seam and does not have the usual fold-over and stapled header. Rather, the header is heat-sealed in the center with the bottom half sticking down into the bag. The usual marbles in these bags are cat eyes or clearies in the 5/8" size coming 10 or 20 to the bag. Five 1" clearies have also been found in such bags. In many bags it is difficult to see the marbles because the bags are cloudy from age or heat as the polyvinyl is breaking down.

The labels for these bags are usually light blue, light green, light yellow, peach, or white. All have black lettering. These headers usually read either "Master Marbles" or "Cat's Eye." The bottom part of the header reads, "Master Glass Co., Clarksburg, W. Va. Made in U.S.A."

Master Glass Co. furnace. Shown here is an unknown employee mixing or stirring hot liquid glass inside the furnace. Hot glass would flow from the tank on the other side/end and into the shearing mechanism, then dropping onto the marble rollers to attain shape. *Nov. 1955 photo courtesy Bob and Barbara Nichols, Bell Studios, Bridgeport, West Virginia.*

Master Glass Co. office in Bridgeport, West Virginia. *1970 Photo courtesy Bell Studio, Bridgeport, West Virginia.*

Master Glass Co.'s Clinton F. Israel and long-time company secretary, Pauline Dennison. Photo December 1948, photographer unknown. *Compliments J.R. Barnes Collection.*

Master Glass Co. factory in Bridgeport, West Virginia. *1970 Photo courtesy Bell Studio, Bridgeport, West Virginia.*

Master Glass Co. batch room. Here raw, dry chemicals were mixed with the sand to create the "batch" that was the raw materials heated to form the glass. *Nov. 1955 photo courtesy Bob and Barbara Nichols, Bell Studios, Bridgeport, West Virginia.*

Master Glass Co. bagging. The operator, possibly Martha Barnes, worked a foot pedal (see arm of same on side of bench) to allow marbles to roll down and into her awaiting bag. A box labeled Du Pont cellophane appears to have been the bag of choice at this time for Master Glass. *Nov. 1955 photo courtesy Bob and Barbara Nichols, Bell Studios, Bridgeport, West Virginia.*

Master Glass Co. marbles being sorted by size. Dumped into this "machine" they rolled until their size allowed them to drop through certain diameter openings into the awaiting buckets beneath. *Nov. 1955 photo courtesy Bob and Barbara Nichols, Bell Studios, Bridgeport, West Virginia.*

Left/Below:
Master Glass marble machine. Note the furnace or tank of hot liquid glass sits above and to the left of the apparent rollers. At Master, it appears the rollers/marble machine was lower into the buildings floor than the factory floor around the hot glass tanks themselves. This would be reasonable for access to both furnace/tank and marble making machinery as the hot glass must be above and flow down, into the rollers. This two level configuration was not the common arrangement in most marble factories. *Nov. 1955 photo courtesy Bob and Barbara Nichols, Bell Studios, Bridgeport, West Virginia.*

Master Glass close-up of the marble rollers showing the marbles dancing across the roller on their way to perfect roundness. An exceptional image showing how the rollers work to make round marbles. Note: these rollers are both shorter and greater in diameter than those found in most other West Virginia marble factories.

Right/Below:
Master Glass marbles inside the factory. A mound of marbles. Wooden barrels full, the floor covered. Some half century later this is a fantasyland for many collectors! *Nov. 1955 photo courtesy Bob and Barbara Nichols, Bell Studios, Bridgeport, West Virginia.*

Master Glass Co. labeling. Once sorted and bagged, the next station was this labeling desk. Here a printed paper label (see in his hand) was applied to the pre-filled poly bag. Note the flat of filled but unlabeled bags behind the operator and the foot pedal under this table that would operate the staling device to affix the label. The operator here is Clinton F. Israel himself. *Nov. 1955 photo courtesy Bob and Barbara Nichols, Bell Studios, Bridgeport, West Virginia.*

Master Glass marbles in boxes awaiting shipping. Note these boxes are marked for delivery and bound for S. Pons, Havana, Cuba. *Nov. 1955 photo courtesy Bob and Barbara Nichols, Bell Studios, Bridgeport, West Virginia.*

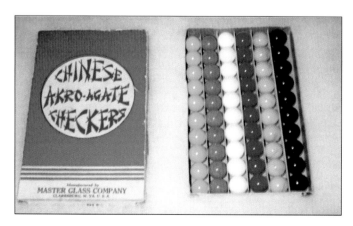

Master Glass imprinted box of "Akro Agate Chinese Checkers." *Author's collection.* The red box, $150.

Master Glass #5 cut away box. The most commonly found Master Glass box. Box with original marbles, $30; empty box as shown, $10.

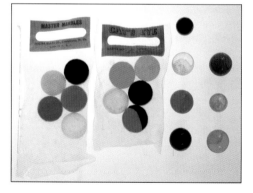

Master Glass poly bag. Many of these bags have fractured marbles in them, so close examination is suggested. $10-15.

Master Glass imprinted box still utilizing the allure of the Akro-Agate name. Green box is more difficult to find than the companion red box. *Author's collection.* $200.

Master Glass Co. poly bag. Cat's Eye marbles, 10 count. *J. Thompson photo.* $10-15.

Master Glass Co. promotional brochure cover with a wonderful image of a boy buried in marbles!

Master Glass Co., the continuance of the "boy in marbles" brochure, showing products and the Clarksburg mailing address.

Master Glass Co. poly bag. 1" glassies (label says Cat's Eye, but they are not!) *J. Thompson photo.* $10.

Master Glass promotional sheet (8 1/2 x 11"), folded for mailing. It includes the logo, some neat packaging, and company names for marble types.

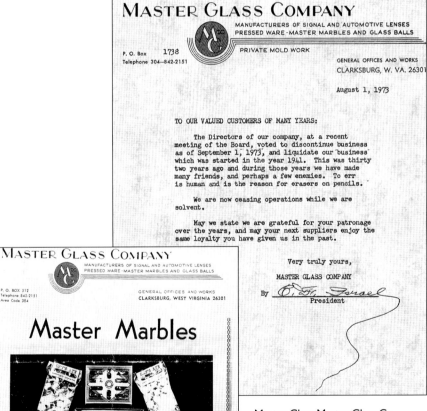

Master Glass Master Glass Co. letterhead bearing the date August 1, 1973. On the letterhead to the "Valued Customers Of Many years," from Clinton Israel as President of Master Glass, the letter announces their discontinuance of business as of September 1, 1973.

MASTER MARBLE COMPANY

Clarksburg, West Virginia
1930 - 1941

Master Marble production examples found at a secluded factory dump site by retired U.C.A.R employee Lawrence Cottrill in 1997.

Master Marble production examples found at a secluded factory dump site by retired U.C.A.R employee Lawrence Cottrill in 1997.

The Master Marble Company was organized in the Grasselli district of Clarksburg, West Virginia, by three longtime employees of Akro Agate: Clinton F. Israel, Claude C. Grimmett, and John E. Moulton. These three were joined just a short time later by John F. Early, also a former Akro employee. Perhaps a change in management style at Akro Agate led to these employee's unhappiness with the company and departure. Master Marble opened shop on May 20, 1930, and their first marbles were shipped on October 25 of that same year.

John F. Early was responsible for much of the design of Akro marble machines made earlier. The Master Marble machines he designed were thought by Akro management to be similar enough to the Akro machines to prompt Akro to bring several patent infringement lawsuits, all of which were won by Master Marble. In an attempt to obtain helpful information about the upstart company and perhaps still looking for evidence of patent infringements, an Akro employee was sent to covertly survey the Master Marble premises. Caught on Master Marble property, he was arrested and convicted of trespassing. The Akro Agate Company paid the fine to have him released from jail, according to J. Fred Early, John F. Early's son.

In addition to patent troubles, there were serious price wars in the early years of Master Marble, when giant Akro lowered its marble prices by thirty percent, hoping that the struggling new Master Marble could not compete. In spite of these early complications, Master Marble survived to become one of the great marble producers of the 1930s. Within two years, Master Marble was reportedly shipping marbles to every state in the Union, to Europe, to South America, and to Africa. About seventy-five workers were employed at that time per an undated magazine article interview with Clinton Israel.

A huge triumph for Master Marble was being awarded sole marble concessionaire for the Chicago World's Fair in 1933. For the Fair, Master produced special, very attractive packages to mark that event. The Master Marble exhibit, a house in the "Enchanted Island" portion of the exposition, was called "The House of Marbles." Its walls were layers of thick plate glass with five million marbles encased between them.

That same year, 1933, Master Marble was offering an impressively broad range of packaging choices, selling marbles not only under the brand name "Master Made Marbles," but also in mesh bags labeled "Ritzy Marbles." Their mesh bags that year came in both 13 and 30 count versions, and they also sold boxed sets in eleven different sizes ranging from a very small 6 count box that sold wholesale for $2.40 per gross,

to a 96 count box with a buckskin marble bag, $72.00 per gross. Some sets, slightly less expensive, included "leatherette" rather than buckskin bags. Eager to boast the originality of their designs, the company printed prominently on advertising fliers sent to retailers, "We originate but never imitate."

The sand used in Master Marble's glass was obtained from Berkley County, West Virginia, as was the case for many West Virginia glass producers. In a number of large furnaces, batch glass was melted, one distinct color to each furnace. This glass was ladled out of the large furnaces and transferred to smaller working furnaces where the colors were mixed to form multi-colored marbles.

Most marble collectors to date have associated the Master Marble Company with, besides game marbles and clearies, the soft-blended colors and pole-to-pole patterned marbles such as Sunbursts, Moss Agates, and brushed patches. Lawrence Cottrill, a former employee of the chemical plant that now owns the building and property that was once Master Marble, was able to recover some scraps of glass and partial marbles from the site, which he donated to the West Virginia Museum of American Glass in Weston, West Virginia. These fragments and scraps show us examples of vivid color combinations in random swirl patterns that do not remotely fall into the popular conception of Master Marble products.

In 1937, the *National Glass Budget Directory*, an annual trade directory, lists Master Marble Co. of Clarksburg with 5 day tanks, 4 machines. The officers at that time are C.C. Grimmett, president; Clinton F. Israel, secretary and treasurer; J.F. Early, vice president. The product line was cited as "glass toy marbles and glass balls of every description; special process, special machinery."

The 1940 *Glass Factory Yearbook* lists Master Marble Co., Inc. of Clarksburg, W. Va. Clinton F. Israel, president, treasurer, and general manager; J.F. Early, vice president; C.C. Grimmett, secretary. They had 5 day tanks and listed production as "Glass toy marbles, spherical lenses, industrial glass balls and glass balls of every description."

Master Marble operated in Grasselli for roughly eleven years, during which time they were very prolific. The packaged Master marbles produced in the 1940s remain prevalent toady and suggest the company production was significant. The company's end came as a result of a struggle for control with the four stockholders and a reorganization of ownership. Shortly before his death in 1998, J. Fred Early, son of Master Marble stockholder, machinist, and plant superintendent, John F. Early, wrote to the authors his memory of the dissolution of Master Marble. "In the summer of 1939, Clinton Israel and the majority of the Stockholders voted my father out as plant superintendent and his employment was terminated, although he still owned 20% of the stock. The Moulton and Grimmet Stock had been previously taken by the bank and sold to outsiders, friends of Clinton Israel. In April 1940, my father purchased a dairy farm in Medina County, Ohio, where he lived until his death in 1949, at the age of 73. He never forgave Clinton Israel for his part in (what he believed to be) stealing the Master Marble Company."

In 1941, Clinton F. Israel, certainly more of a savvy businessman than his partners, gained sole control of the company, acquired the company's stock and equipment, and set up the new Master Glass Company, which he relocated to nearby Bridgeport, West Virginia. The land and buildings were sold to the neighboring National Carbon Company on April 18, 1941. The former Master Marble building remains standing at the time of this writing on that property, under operation of U.C.A.R. Division of Union Carbide Corporation.

MASTER MARBLE Marbles Produced

Brushed Translucents.
Brushed Transparents.
Moss Agates.
Opaque Swirls.
Opaques.
Patched Opaques.
Patched Translucents.
Patched Transparents.
Translucents.
Transparents.

Advertised size range for Master Marbles are 00 to 6 or 9/16" to 1".

One price list for 1933 shows the following prices for "0" or 5/8" size marbles in quantities of 1000.
Sunburst $3.20
Comet $2.00
Meteor $3.40
Cloudy $2.50
Transparent $2.20

MASTER MARBLE Identification Tips

Marbles produced by the Master Marble Company used largely the same identical equipment later employed at the Master Glass Company. Another complication arises in identification of marbles that Master Marbles (and Master Glass marbles) were made on machinery designed by former Akro Agate employees creating similarities to Akro products as well.

A significant difference between Akro and Master Marble Co. is that Master used an older style cut-off system, which did not eliminate the cut-off marks at the poles. As a result, Master Marbles have a cut-off mark in the shape of a "U" or "V" along with tiny crimp marks and a feathering look at each pole.

A most obvious distinction between Master Marble and Master Glass marbles is that Master Marbles were produced earlier and the colors tended to be generally brighter, having used stronger, bolder coloring agents. Master Glass marbles, which were made up into the 1970s, often appear more washed out, less bold, and duller in color. Regrettably such statements of relative color, one being brighter or bolder than the other, have limited merit unless one can see and compare examples of both products.

Sunburst: The Master Marble Sunburst is very recognizable as a machine-made attempt to reproduce the older handmade onionskin marble. These marbles are found with varying degrees of a transparent base that may be only partly or almost completely filled with colored filaments of glass. These strands run from pole to pole and although most are three-color, there are known to be four-color varieties. These marbles are differentiated from Akro Agate "Sparklers" in that the Akro marbles have, as a rule, five colors and are more vibrant to the eye than the Master type.

Tiger Eye: This marble is basically a Sunburst where the filaments of colored glass occur in wide bands running from pole to pole. The colors in these marbles often consist of combinations of orange, white, black, green, blue, red, and yellow; with usually only three colors to a marble.

Meteor: This type consists of a wispy translucent patch on an opaque base. It is found in a variety of colors and occasionally contains traces of aventurine or thin lines of oxblood glass.

Comet: This variety is an opaque patch on an opaque base and, like the Meteor, comes in a variety of color combinations.

Cloudy: A Cloudy is a wispy translucent patch on a white base. It occurs in a variety of colors although brown and blue seem to appear most often. Some oxblood filaments have been seen in these marbles.

Brushed Patch: The Brushed Patch marbles may be seen with opaque translucent or transparent base glass ranging from clear to black amethyst and usually have white brushed patches. These are often indistinguishable from the same design made by Master Glass and Akro Agate.

Moss Agates: These marbles were produced by many manufacturers including Alley Agate, Vitro Agate, and Akro Agate. The one produced by Master Marbles seem to be almost identical to any of the others. A Moss Agate consists of a range of opacity in the milky white base from very translucent to mildly translucent with an opaque to translucent patch in one of a number of colors. Moss Agates made by Master Marble have been seen in the following standard colors: blue, green, yellow, red, and black.

MASTER MARBLE Packaging

The Master Marble Company distributed a variety of packaging, many of which are today uncommon and highly sought.

The most well-known and hardest to find Master Marble boxes are the 1933 Century of Progress Special Edition Sets produced specifically for the Chicago World's Fair. Dennis Webb reported that these boxes were sold only at the "House of Marbles" which was the Master Marble shop. Their exhibit appears to have been a last-minute addition to the 1933 Children's Playground on the Enchanted Island and was not there in 1934 as per numerous literature about the Fair the authors examined. One of these boxes had the Fair panorama on the outside cover; the second edition had the panorama on the inside cover. Both sets contained marbles and beautifully embossed marble bags. The larger box with the Fair panorama on the inside of the lid was 7" x 8-3/4" and contained 60 marbles plus the bag. The smaller box with the Fair panorama on the outside of the lid was 6" x 8-1/2" and contained 40 marbles plus the bag.

Stock and gift boxes of 50 and 100 marbles in sizes 9/16" to 3/4" are known. Some box lids are heavily embossed with the Master Marble logo or other decoration while others are plain with perhaps only writing on the edges of the lids. One stock box of 50 No. 2 "cloudys" has the words "Insist on Marbles Made by Masters" on the edge of the lid.

Many Master Marble gift sets have colorful sunbeam design lids. Some boxes have colored diamond designs on the lid with cutouts so the contents can be seen. One small box has a yellow lid with a star pattern design.

Other known Master Marble boxes include:

#5 box: This package is a smaller version of the #10 box and is more common than all the others. Although it contains Master Marble style marbles, there is speculation that it may have been only used at the later Master Glass Company. The box, when it is found to contain marbles, usually has brushed patch types (made by both Master Marble and Master Glass). This box exists in two slightly different styles. Whether or not the more recent incarnation is new and a fake/reproduction or an actual later period Master Glass restyling of the original Master Marble design is yet to be ascertained with certainty. Regardless, the newer style is so commonly available that at some marble shows, whole stacks of them may be found in a still folded, never used condition. A close examination of both boxes will reveal differences, especially in the area of the triple M logo and on the end flaps.

#6 box: This is a diminutive copy of the #13 box and contains six marbles of various styles.

#10 box: This has a large red diamond on the top surrounding the Master Marble logo with twenty cutouts making it a very fragile box. The rules for the game of Ringer are imprinted on the back. This box contains fifty-four brushed patch marbles. Most of these boxes have been found in poor condition.

#13 box: This small box has the sunbeam design surrounding the company logo. It has five cutouts on the top. Most of the box bottoms are plain, but there are some with advertising shoes, Popsicles, or even political candidates. There are thirteen marbles in this box. Many contain in random combination: Sunbursts, Meteors, Comets, Cloudys, or Brushed Patches.

#20 box: This box is labeled the "Official Marble Set" and is 5" x 3-1/4" x 1" and contains twenty 5/8" assorted marbles and a leatherette bag.

#60 Master Marble Game Sets: This box contains three #130 boxes with six different color opaque game marbles. Twenty marbles (ten of two different colors) are packed to a box. These smaller boxes have cutouts and cellophane covers.

#130 box: These boxes, as described above, were also sold separately and usually contain thirteen marbles of various styles.

Other display and gift sets that appear in Master Marble literature include:

#250 box with 25 marbles and leatherette bag.
#350 box with 37 marbles and leatherette bag.
#500 box with 34 marbles and buckskin bag.
#600 box with 52 marbles and buckskin bag.
#1000 box with 72 marbles and buckskin bag.
#1200 box with 96 marbles and buckskin bag.
#2000 box with 60 marbles and buckskin bag – this box is advertised as the "Deluxe College Box."

The least common box we have seen from Master Marble, with only three examples known at present, are from the collection of a longtime company secretary. It is a small sample box used as a mailer. It is made of stiff cardboard and measures 4" x 4" x 1-1/2" and, according to information on the inside of the lid, originally contained one #130 box with thirteen assorted #0 marbles retailing for 10 cents and a #60 box containing six assorted marbles retailing for 5 cents. The marbles in these boxes are listed as being assorted Comets, Clearies, Sunbursts, and Meteors.

An interesting side note to this particular box has recently surfaced thanks to veteran collector Hansel de Sousa. He showed us one of these boxes with a Master Glass return label from 1966. This could mean several things. Was the box actually Master Glass and/or leftover stock from Master Marble? At any rate, it is a rare box that has been around a long time.

All Master Marble bags we have seen are mesh with folded paper headers. The bags are red mesh. One type of bag shown in company advertisements shows "Ritzy Marbles" on the header. These came in four sizes of thirteen or eighteen marbles retailing for 5 cents and thirty or thirty-eight marbles retailing for 10 cents. The two larger sizes came packed with rule books for marble games.

We have seen a mesh bag containing twenty-five Master Marble Clearies and a beautiful little bag with a green header and white writing with twelve assorted opaque patch and translucent Sunbursts.

Almost all Master Marble packaging is identified with the company name and a Clarksburg, West Virginia, address.

Master Marble founders, left to right: Clinton F. Israel, John E. Moulton, John F. Early, and Claude C. Grimmett. *Photo courtesy Roger and Claudia Hardy.*

Master Marble factory as it appeared in 1932. Master occupied only the large building that begins in the center of the image and runs to the right and has all the windows. The physical building has changed little as of 2005. *Dennis Webb Photo collection.*

Master Marble House of Marbles at the 1933 Chicago "A Century of Progress" World's fair. Photo of the building on the fair grounds.

Master Marble as it appeared in 2004. This photo opportunity was allowed the authors by Dave Reep of U.C.A. R. – which presently owns the site.

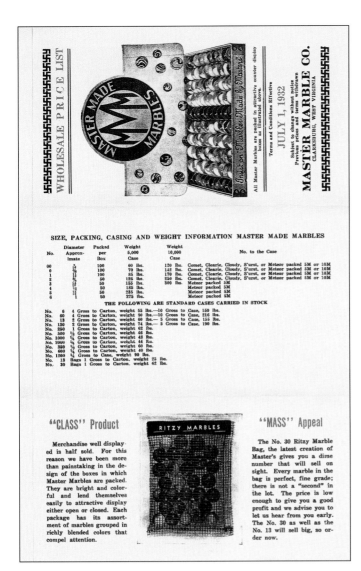

Master Marble 1930 price list.

Master Marble Co.'s House of Marbles souvenir postcard from the 1933 Chicago World's Fair. *Collection of H. de Sousa.* $80-125.

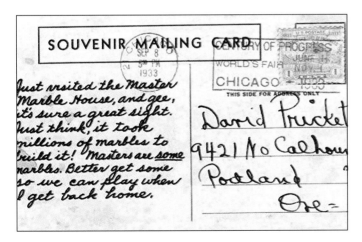

Master Marble 1933 World's Fair postcard show previously, the reverse containing the pre-written, imitating cursive script message with the "better get some" message. Great marketing!

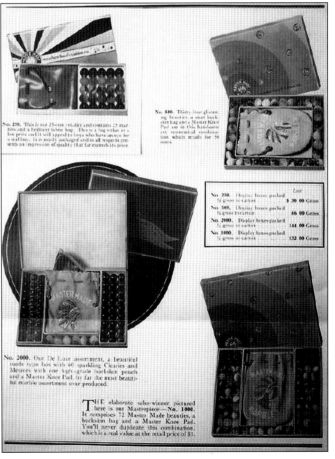

Master Marble advertising sheet. *H. de Sousa collection.*

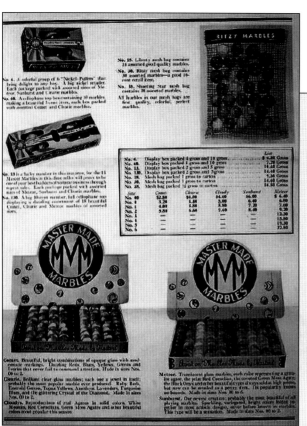

Master Marble advertising sheet. *H. de Sousa collection.*

Master Marble 1932 Wholesale Price list. Reverse.

Master Marble 1993 brochure, reverse side. Shows No. 20 Official Tournament set.

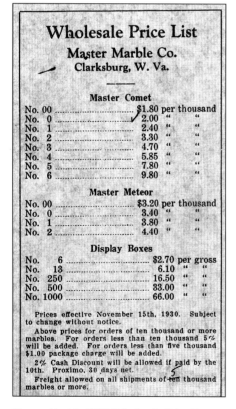

Master Marble 1932 Wholesale Price list, tri-fold to make a three panel brochure. Front side.

Master Marble marbles brochure dated 1933.

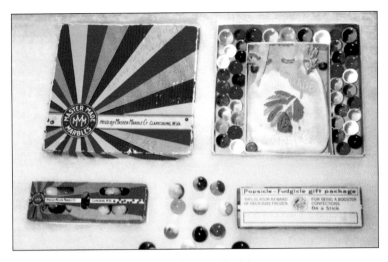

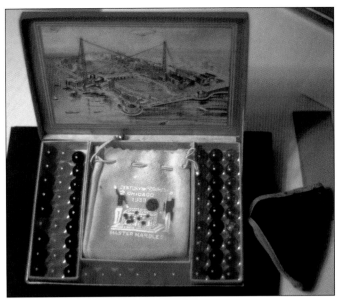

Master Marble top lid and box for "Sunbeam" gift box containing Indian Chief bag. $300. Bottom #12 advertising sleeve box top and bottom with contents, $100.

Master Marble Chicago World's Fair box, the largest size with view of the Fair inside lid, printed marble bag and original marbles. *Dennis Webb photo collection.* Scarce. No value determined.

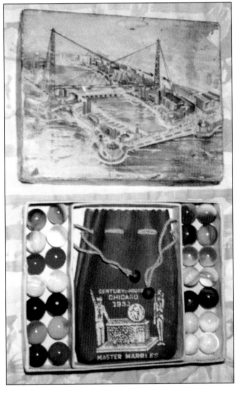

Master Marble highly graphic box lid design on gift box. Contains bag and original 20 marbles. *H. de Sousa collection.* $750.

Master Marble, the smallest of the 1933 Century of Progress boxes, containing original marbles and printed bag. Graphic of Fair site on lid. Approximately 5 x 6 in. $350.

Master Marble Chicago World's Fair middle size box. Fair aerial view on lid, imprinted two-tone bag and original marbles. *H. de Sousa collection.* $850.

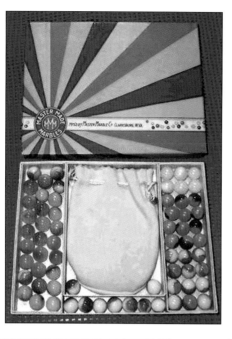

Master Marble "Sunbeam" gift box, name derived from graphic on lid. With bag and moss agates and patch marbles. *H. de Sousa collection.* $1,250.

Master Marble lone bag from gift box. Printed Indian Chief. $50-75.

Master Marble gift box with company logo lid, bag, original marbles, and marble shooter. *H. de Sousa collection.* $850.

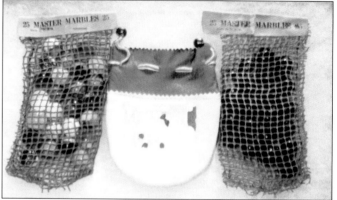

Master Marble mesh bags with Master Marbles header, $75-100 each; lone Century of Progress printed bag from gift set, $100-125.

Master Marble "Bull's Eye" gift box with bag, original marbles, and marble shooter. *H. de Sousa collection.* $1,500.

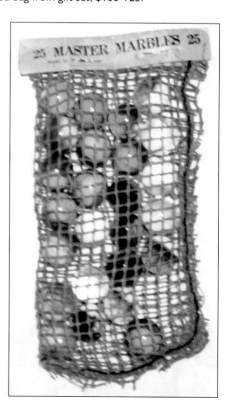

Master Marble mesh bag, 25 count header. Mixed variety of marbles. Also found with just one marble type in the bag. $75-100.

Master Marble uncommon mesh bag from the Century of Progress. *H. de Sousa collection.* $300 each.

Master Marble sample box. Showing lid. $350.

Master Marble, reverse of same bag shown from Century of Progress.

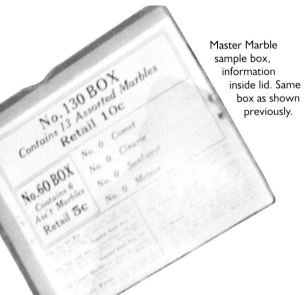

Master Marble sample box, information inside lid. Same box as shown previously.

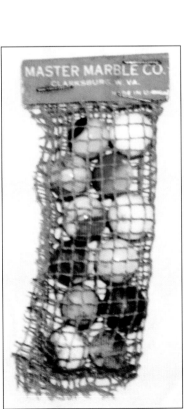

Master Marble Co. green header on mesh bag containing 12 marbles. $75-100.

Master Marble stock box of 50 No. 2. The end of the box reads it contains "Cloudy" marbles, but these do not match the known description. As shown, $500.

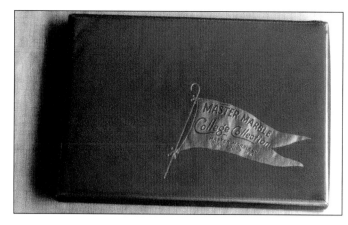

Master Marble College Collection box. *Dennis Webb photo collection.* No value determined.

Master Marble retail stock box of 100 count No. 0 moss agates. Lid shown, see following image. $300.

Master Marble lid for Century of Progress gift box. *H. de Sousa Collection.* See interior shot with other Fair boxes above.

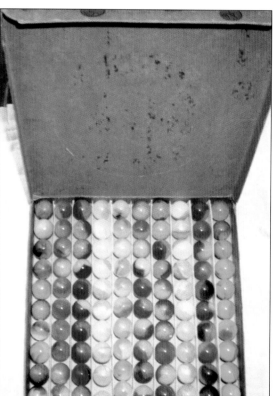

Master Marble moss agates inside the box, cover shown previously.

Larger stock boxes: left: "100 Wonder Glass Marbles" and logo box. Both are the only ones known of their kind at this time. *H. de Sousa collection.* Rare. $5,000 or market.

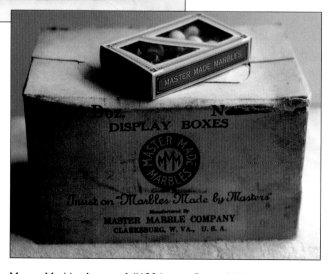

Master Marble. A case of #130 boxes. *Dennis Webb photo collection.* No value determined.

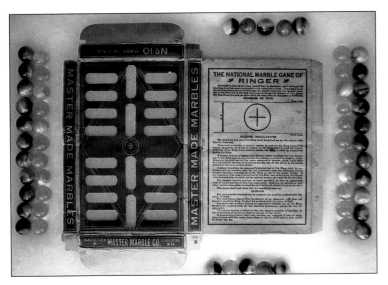

Master Marble large #10 box. This box was in fragile condition when found due to the large number of cut outs, leaving little actual box, and the weight of the number of marbles. The box here has been flattened to show the front and back and 54 original marbles. Box and contents, if intact and in reasonable condition, $200.

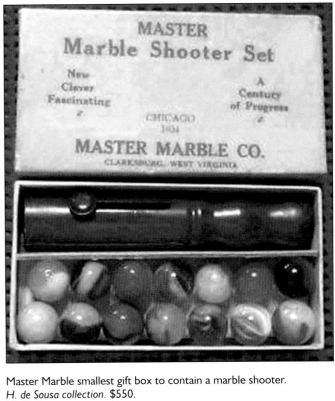

Master Marble smallest gift box to contain a marble shooter. *H. de Sousa collection.* $550.

Master Marble game set of 60 Chinese Checker marbles, three No. 130 boxes within larger box. $400.

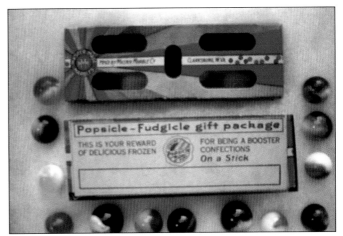

Master Marble #13 sleeve with advertising on one side panel and 13 original marbles. $80-100.

Master Marble top, small #6 cut out box. 1 1/2 x 2 1/2 in., $150; bottom cut out box #13, $100.

Master Marble production examples. *D. Chambelain photo.*

M.F. CHRISTENSEN & SON

Akron, Ohio
1905 - 1917

M.F. Christensen & Son examples of production recovered at factory site. *E. Schubert collection.*

As the American Toy Marble Museum tells the story, titled by them *M.F. Christensen and the Perfect Ball Machine*, the story of this firm goes as follows. The man behind M.F. Christensen & Son was Martin Frederick Christensen, a mechanical genius. He was the first to discover the scientific principles of sphere-making, which he patented to effectively monopolize an old industry and give birth to a number of new industries. These important scientific principles of manufacturing are still state-of-the-art over 100 years later, a part of everyday life today.

Christensen was a master of the drop forging trades who began his career working in the iron mills in New York State. In 1882, he moved to Akron, Ohio, to work for the Akron Knife Works (that's short-hand for The Whitman & Barnes Manufacturing Company,) where he produced blades for mower and reapers. In 1890, Christensen founded The Drop Hammer Forging Company. The company produced a vast number of hand tools, one of which was a garden hoe that he patented. It also produced a large amount of fancy iron fencing, some of which can still be seen standing in Akron. Christensen's mastery of the drop hammer forging and mechanical arts were recognized in 1893 at the World's Columbian Exposition held in Chicago. He was awarded a medal and a certificate by the Treasurer of the United States, issued by an act of Congress. In 1895 he changed the name of the company to The M.F. Christensen Company.

Balls of steel throughout the nineteenth century, known today as ball bearings, were made by hand. The process was relatively simple, but mind-boggling. A skilled steelworker would take a steel rod in one hand and with a metal file in his other hand would file away at the steel rod until he'd formed a sphere at the end of the rod. These ball bearings were accordingly extremely expensive. A bicycle that used ball bearings cost $100 in 1899. They also lacked uniformity, reducing their efficiency and they cracked easily requiring them to be replaced regularly. Needless to say, there weren't many machines that used ball bearings in 1899, and those that did use them, didn't work particularly well.

A story in the *Summit County Beacon* (Ohio) of January 20, 1900, is captioned: "LUCKY AKRON MAN. Sold Invention For Twenty-Five Thousand Dollars. MAKES STEEL BALLS. Machine Turns Them Out In Large Numbers. Will Work a Revolution In Manufacture." It further reads, "The story of how Martin F. Christensen, a mechanical engineer of Akron made $25,000 out of a single invention in three months reads like some strange things printed in the New York Sunday newspapers, but every word of it is true, and Mr. Christensen's bank book shows it. Last September the 3rd, he patented a machine for making steel balls for ball bearings, such as are used in bicycles. Thursday he sold four fifths of his invention for $25,000 and got the money ... The machine he built ... when it was perfected made steel balls at the rate of 65,000 a day and it took only a boy to attend it. The process is what machinists call a pretty one. Cubical pieces of steel, hot, each of which is to be made into a ball are fed into the top of the machine ... and drops it out the bottom of the machine a perfect sphere of steel. The fibers of the steel are not cut and are instead packed together more tightly than when cut from the rod into rough pieces to be fed into the mill. It is said that when the balls come from the machine they are perfectly polished and truly spherical."

Twenty-five thousand dollars was a lot of money in 1900 and that was before income taxes. However, the twenty percent interest in the patents that Christensen retained meant he realized about a penny on every ball bearing produced. And seeing that almost every major industrial advance made in the early twentieth century; like cars, airplanes, etc. used his ball bearings, one would not be surprised if Christensen retired early from the trades. He was fifty years old in 1900. However, on the day this article came out in the local press he was hard at work on a new invention that took further advantage of his scientific discovery – the physical properties required to mass-produce perfect spheres.

In Christensen's patent for the first practical steel ball bearing machine he wrote out the scientific principles of sphere making: cause a piece of plastic material (clay, molten steel, molten glass, soap, candy, etc.) to rotate with a constantly changing axis. This will render a sphere that is as close to mathematically perfect as is humanly possible to create. His next invention would apply these same principles to glass.

During the winter of 1900, Christensen found himself again working on a new invention related to the production of spheres. This time the spheres would be made out of glass instead of metal. Christensen was an expert while working with metals, but molten glass was an area in which he possessed no experience. For this he would need a glass master. Akron just happened to be the home of James Harvey Leighton, the only glassmaker in the United States who commercially produced handmade glass marbles. (See the early histories cited in the front of this book.) Christensen contacted James Harvey Leighton in hopes he could locate a suitable glass factory where he could test his new sphere-making machine. The details were hammered out and it was agreed to test the new machine in Navarre, Ohio, at Leighton's defunct marble works, The Navarre Glass Marble & Specialty Company.

Over the course of a week, Christensen tested his machine with positive results. It's probable that Leighton offered Christensen the use of the Navarre factory to produce marbles, perhaps to form a joint venture. Christensen surely declined the offer because the property and former company were tied up in the courts.

Christensen wasn't interested in manufacturing marbles, but in selling his new machine idea, just as he did the steel ball machine. It's believed that he took his wife on an extended trip to Europe to visit his sister and partake in the luxury of his newfound affluence gained from the sale of his steel ball making patent. Apparently he was in no hurry to market his invention. Eventually Christensen met back up with Leighton in Akron and they erected a glass foundry in Christensen's back yard. Mr. Christensen was ready to announce to the world the existence of his new machine with the hopes he could sell the patent to capitalists.

The Akron Beacon Journal of August 1, 1903, carried these headlines: "NEW GLASS MACHINE. Akron Man Has Very Valuable Invention. IT REPLACES HAND WORK. Turns Out Glass Marbles and Balls For Use on Casters. Offer Received From Capitalists Who Wish to Buy It."

The story reads at length as follows: "Martin F. Christensen of 457 East Exchange Street has completed an invention which will without doubt prove to be one of the greatest and most valuable inventions ever brought forth in this city. The new invention is a glass ball machine, which turns out at a rate of ten per minute, glass marbles and balls used in castors for tables, chairs, stools, beds and the like, and has been previously mentioned in the Beacon Journal.... The new invention is entirely original in form and principle, so that the inventor has been able to get almost a "ground patent," in his machine... The balls made vary from five eight of an inch to three inches in diameter. The smallest are used as marbles and the larger ones as balls for casters on tables and pianos ... The machines are set up in a set of three which one man can operate. These machines will turn out ten balls per minute, or 4800, working an eight-hour day. Mr. Christensen has three set of machines set up in his workshop at the rear of his residence. Here he mixes and manufactures his own glass with the assistance of an expert glassmaker and runs his own machines ... Capitalists After Invention. Inventors and scientific papers are very anxious to secure information of this new invention, but up to this time practically nothing has been given out. Negotiations are now on by a party of capitalists for the purchase of the invention and the deal will probably be closed soon. Capitalists recognize the value of the machine, because of the cheapness of the construction and operation. The balls are made of flint glass and are clear as a crystal. All balls made for castors have been made by hand molds, and in order to be sold cheap have been very imperfect, showing the marks of the mold. When it comes to making marbles no hand product can equal that of the machine. Imitation Agates Are Made. The marbles can be made in any color and no two exactly alike. When it is remembered that millions of marbles are sold in this country every spring, the value of the invention is apparent."

Although, Christensen flirted with the idea of selling his new invention to "capitalists," in the end he decided to instead operate his own company, which he called The M.F. Christensen & Son Company. He had one son, then in his mid-twenties, who was not easily employable in any regular trade and so instead of going into a partnership with Leighton he made a job for Charles F. Christensen. It must have been a popular thing to do that year, because Leighton did the same with his son Richard who had an interest in operating a job printing company, which they named The Leighton Printing Company.

And so was born The M. F. Christensen & Son Company. As soon as Christensen's new glass marbles hit the shelves of toy stores they caused a revolution. No one had ever seen anything like this before; beautiful glass marbles that were perfectly spherical and they were less expensive than comparable handmade glass marbles. The little boys went crazy for them and for the first time 'glassies' become a coveted item found in almost all marble bags. They were still a lot more expensive than common clay marbles, called "commies," but for a nickel it was well worth the price to get an American Cornelian as a shooter.

In Lauscha, Germany, home of the German marble industry, the glass marble makers expressed total amazement when they first viewed Christensen's marbles. They said wonderful things about the marbles and painted a very dark and depressing picture of their futures, realizing those marbles would put them out of business.

By 1910 marbles made by The M.F. Christensen & Son Company were being shipped to every continent in the world except Antarctica. With the profits Christensen built a beautiful new home for himself and his wife and built a nice house next door for his son Charles. That year he incorporated the company and largely turned its operation over to his son. Stock was also given to his daughter, Jessie, who played a significant role throughout the life of the company. It's not that Christensen

senior was finally retiring and sitting back to enjoy the good life. He was once again hard at work on a new invention, a machine that would once again revolutionize the manufacture of glass marbles.

Since 1900, the glass industry was experimenting with ways to automate factories and do away with the labor-intensive methods of handwork and feeding molten glass to molds and machinery to make the majority of all glass goods. While these experiments where largely unsuccessful, it was widely anticipated that an automatic gob-feeder was just over the horizon. With this in mind, Christensen invented a marble-making machine, today called a "marble auger" that could be automatically fed, thereby reducing his labor costs and dramatically increasing production.

Once he'd perfected his new machine, it could be fed by the traditional hand-gather method, but there was no real advantage to using it without an automatic gob-feeder. While there would be a savings in labor costs and increase production once combined with a gob-feeder, there was a serious trade-off with this machine; it had a higher reject rate and it could not produce a glass ball much larger than an inch in diameter. So the new invention would sit in a corner of the marble works covered up and waiting for technology to catch up with its potential. Little did he know, the invention of the first practical gob-feeder was still many years away; it wasn't patented until 1925 and wasn't used to make marbles until 1928.

Christensen's trusted bookkeeper was Horace C. Hill, the son of one of his best friends and neighbors. The marble-makers in the factory called Horace "Bucky Binder" due to the fact he took care of the books and he obviously had a bad case of buck teeth. Horace was so well regarded by Christensen that upon incorporating the company in 1910 he gave Horace shares in the company.

Hill got himself involved with a character in town, a man named Gilbert "Stubby" Marsh, who owned a children's shoe store, Wagoner & Mash, located in the heart of downtown Akron. Stubby was the son of a wealthy family, a fellow who thought himself somewhat of a playboy and who hung out with the sons and daughters of other wealthy Akronites. Somehow Hill and Stubby got together, decided to go into the marble business, and right from the start it might have appeared something was wrong. When legal documents were signed for The Akro Agate Company, Horace Hill didn't use his real name; he signed the documents Clinton H. Hill. An auspicious beginning.

On the surface Stubby was just another one of Christensen's customers, buying marbles wholesale and selling them in direct response through advertisements he took out in boys' magazines. Then one day Christensen discovered that Hill was altering the books and embezzling money. The extent of the thefts wouldn't be realized for a couple of years, but what Hill did was copy plans for Christensen's new marble-making machine, patented them as his own, and then set up a marbleworks in Clarksburg, West Virginia, as The Akro Agate Company for Stubby and himself. He also stole all the formulas that Leighton had given Christensen and he made copies of every supplier and customer. The latter would have been a list of every company that purchased glass marbles in the world; everything one needed to go into the marble business.

Of course, Christensen didn't realize the full extent of Hill's thefts until his customers sent notice that some firm in West Virginia was offering to sell marbles identical in looks to his and they were undercutting his prices. So the next time Hill came into town to visit his family, Christensen had him arrested on charges of embezzlement.

The story broke in the Akron Times, February 25, 1915, with a banner "HORACE C. HILL HELD FOR THEFT OF MONEY." It reads, "Horace C. Hill, former office man for the Christensen Marble Co. East Exchange Street, was bound over to the grand jury under $1,500 bond, yesterday afternoon, on a charge of embezzling $1,600 from the marble company. He was arrested at the hone of his mother, Mrs. Louise Hill, 361 Wooster Avenue, by Sheriff James Corey and Deputy George Ferguson. The offense occurred in 1912. Hill has been living in Clarksburg, W. Va."

The disposition of the terrible affair was also covered in the press. The Akron Times, March 27, 1915, reads, "Horace Hill, 32, Gets From One to Fifteen Years, Suspended, In Penitentiary for Embezzlement" and continues, "Horace Hill, 32, was sentence of from 1 to 15 years

Friday when he confessed to defalcations amounting to nearly $1,500. Hill was a cashier, bookkeeper, and chief office man of the M. F. Christensen & Son Company, marble manufacturers. His sentence was suspended on condition that he pay back the money. Hill told how he was able to obtain large sums of the company's money and still keep his books in perfect balance. In one month he says, he took $836.27. He said he would not make entries on the books when shipments were made and then watched the mail for checks in payment. Hill resigned his position and left Akron a year ago. Shortly after he left the loss was discovered, and he was indicted for embezzlement. He returned home recently to visit his widowed mother and was arrested."

One of the original incorporators of The Akro Agate Company made partial restitution to Christensen in Horace's name, but before full restitution was made Martin Frederick Christensen died.

Charles took over day to day operations of the company until December of 1917. There was an very harsh cold spell, the temperature plunged below zero and due to the rationing of gas cause by WWI, officials from the City of Akron requested that Charles turn off the gas furnaces in the marbleworks because homes in the neighborhood were without heat. Charles complied and that caused the molten glass in the huge furnace to solidify, rendering the furnace thereafter un-useable.

In the spring when gas was once again abundant, Charles felt he no longer needed to be in the trades, could easily retire, and so the furnaces were never again fired. It took a while to sell off the remaining inventory of marbles. According to the corporate records, The M. F. Christensen & Son Company sold their remaining stock of toy marbles on November 17, 1918, to (ironically) The Akro Agate Company for $689.00. This was possibly three or four railroad cars full of marbles.

Before the corporation could be closed, Charles died and Jessie Christensen took over full responsibilities, including seeing to it that Charles wife and daughter were taken care of throughout their lives. In the late 1920s, Jessie was able to help put straight the legal record as to

M.F. Christensen & Son image of factory from period company literature. *E. Schubert collection.*

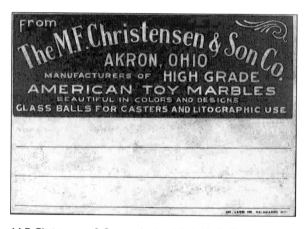

M.F. Christensen & Son packaging label. *H. de Sousa collection.* No value determined.

M.F. Christensen & Son factory in Akron, Ohio, as it appeared 2000.

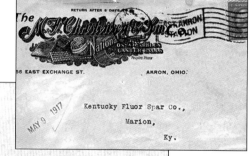

M.F. Christensen & Son fancy graphic on return address of envelope postmarked 1913. *H. de Sousa collection.* No value determined.

M.F. Christensen & Son return address from a period envelope and the marbles illustrated on the reverse of the same envelope. *E. Schubert collection.*

the creative ownership of the marble auger's inventor. In a federal lawsuit that Stubby Marsh brought against the Peltier Glass Company, Jessie provided Sellers Peltier with all the information he needed to defeat Stubby in court and with the courts ruling recognized Martin Frederick Christensen as the rightful inventor of the marble auger – the machine that's still in use today to make glass marbles.

The M.F. Christensen & Son Marbles Produced

The M.F. Christensen & Son Company only made and marketed eleven different types of marbles throughout the life of the company. The toy marbles were offered in ten different sizes.

Industrial Marbles, being clear glass.
Onyx Types of Green, amber, cobalt, and later purple and white.
Opaque Types of Persian, jade, Cornelian, black, and white.
Researched and drafted explicitly for this book by The American Toy Marble Museum, of Akron, Ohio, who heartily receive our thanks.

M.F. Christensen & Son box lid for 25 count No. 1 American Cornelian Marbles. *H. de Sousa collection.* Extremely uncommon. No value determined.

M.F. Christensen & Son box of 25 count No. 1 Persian Turquoise Marbles. *H. de Sousa collection.* Extremely uncommon. No value determined.

M.F. Christensen & Son stock box of 100 count No. 0 National Onyx Marbles. *H. de Sousa collection.* No value determined.

M.F. Christensen & Son box of Corelian marbles contents for lid shown previously.

MID-ATLANTIC OF WEST VIRGINIA, INC.

Ellenboro, West Virginia
1990 - 2004

Mid-Atlantic Glass marbles for play can be unexpectedly attractive. These are from a limited run, 2001. *D. Chamberlain photo.*

Mid-Atlantic Glass, unusual marbles from the 2001 September run, a limited production. *D. Chamberlain photo.*

Mid-Atlantic of West Virginia, Inc., began in 1937 as Mid-Atlantic Glass Co. It was located along the then two lane US Highway 50 and immediately adjacent to the Baltimore & Ohio Railroad. It is about thirty-six miles east of Parkersburg, West Virginia. In March of 1987 it was sold and reorganized as Mid-Atlantic of West Virginia, Inc. in May of 1987. The new company retained the same basic name, product line, and glass workers. The product line for decades was mouth blown, hand formed stemware and table glass with some production of florist, lighting, and other similar ware. Michael Hall and Ronald Spencer were two of the new owners and remained active in the company.

Mid-Atlantic broadened its sales line by selling gems (decorative flat marbles) purchased locally from a nearby marble factory. However, the customer demand could not be met by this means, so a nearby company building, about one hundred yards from the main glass plant, became the site for their marble-making ventures.

On or about November 2, 1990, the new production line of gems and marbles of 9/16" began. Glass colors for gems and marbles included dark blue, azure, clear crystal, pink, teal green, black, opaque white, and amethyst. Later, several new styles were added, including an iridescent pearl. Both gems and marbles were sometimes given an iridescent finish.

The marble machines at Mid-Atlantic were designed and built new specifically for Mid-Atlantic. The first three marble machines were new, high-speed duplex (two roller) models operated by experienced glassmen.

Observation of the marble-making process at Mid-Atlantic revealed that the machines round the marbles on the same principle as at other factories, using a double set of rollers, but at a seemingly greater speed of action. Our observation was that the Mid-Atlantic process incorporated more in-the-process cooling before the marbles drop off into a bucket than we have seen or know of at other manufacturers. At Champion the marbles rolled along a very gradual declining trough of about four feet in length. The mechanism that drops the cut-off gobs of molten glass down to the rollers appeared to us to be more efficient as the glass was already rolling down a hollow tube at the point of contact with the rollers. The whole process has the appearance of being a good deal more modern than the companies that use much older machines, although the basic process remains the same.

In September 1992, Mid-Atlantic acquired from Vitro Agate the well-traveled machine for making large marbles (up to 1-1/2") originally built for and owned by the House of Marbles in England. This machine

had started out in Parkersburg, West Virginia, was taken to Anacortes, Washington, and then moved back to West Virginia. It has been said that only Lewis L. Moore, former plant manager of Vitro Agate (Parkersburg) was ever able to produce acceptable marbles on the temperamental machine. In 1994, this machine was shipped again – this time to the House of Marbles Museum in England.

The Mid-Atlantic factory was always a noticeably clean, environmentally correct, and safe operation. The cullet and scrap glass piles were neat and orderly; the glass was clean and near at hand. Recycled glass from the main factory was often included as a base for their marbles.

Dennis Webb's 1995 marble book described how Lewis L. Moore had been hired as a consultant to Mid-Atlantic and that it was anticipated that the company would "soon be making colorful marbles for play and the collectible market".

As Moore later described it: "In 1990, Mike Hall, manager of Mid-Atlantic, called me about making marbles at a site in their Ellenboro facility. After the deal in Anacortes fell through for me, I agreed but said, 'Let's make marbles – then talk money'. [Mid-Atlantic wanted to pay him $10.00 an hour as a fee.] After they started up they put me on retainer at $500 a month. Anytime I put in over fifty hours in a month, I would be compensated at $10.00 an hour. Well, they rarely called me and I got tired of taking their money so the deal was called off."

Mid-Atlantic continued to make only decorator marbles and gems for the next ten years and the skill Moore had in crafting colorful, play marbles was not called upon.

Moore reported that on November 11, 1996, he had a three hour chat concerning marbles with William Bavin from the House of Marbles (England). He said: "Mr. Bavin will be talking with Mike Hall to try to talk him into making some other type marbles. Mr. Bavin wants marbles like the ones I made at Vitro." Moore concluded by saying, "They (the House of Marbles) are good people and I hope Mike will at least try and make a pretty playing marble." Nothing is known to have come at that time of the House of Marble inquiry or Moores urging for play marbles.

In April of 1998 several hard-at-work Mid-Atlantic employees related that demand for their marbles was so great that they installed a tank and marble machine in their main glass building and planned to add more. They spoke of a possible expansion of their small marble-making building as well. Shortly thereafter, *The Glory Hole*, newsletter of the West Virginia Museum of American Glass, reported that because of increased demand for their marbles, Mid-Atlantic had in fact added two more marble machines. These relatively small marble furnaces and machines were set up inside the main handmade glass plant where a second large glass furnace had once been. Marbles were becoming a dominate line at Mid-Atlantic, where once hand blown stemware had reigned.

A visit to Mid-Atlantic by the authors on May 6, 2001, showed even more expansion. Machines running that day in the original blown crystal glass plant were making gem and utilizing four machines. In the nearby marble building, machines included three for gems and two marble machines. In a recently constructed, temporary appearing lean-to structure there was an additional machine for gems and one marble machine. This set an amazing Mid-Atlantic production record of nine machines operating at once. This 2001 observation was at or nearing the pentacle of marble and gem production for Mid-Atlantic.

In March of 2002, word was received that in September 2001, Mid-Atlantic had made its first run of marbles for play. Some were red, white, and blue. Others were red and white, and others were white and blue. The sizes are irregular, ranging from about 3/4" down to 3/8". A few are iridescent. They have no production figures as to how many were made but word has it that they burned up a tank making them.

A visit to Mid-Atlantic on May 2, 2003, showed a great reduction in the number of marble machines in operation. Only one machine was working and it was making gems. No marble production was observed, in stark contrast to 2001. A few of the machines had been completely dismantled and were not to be seen. Only the cold, empty hot glass tanks remaining in place. The authors were told locally that Chinese production had taken over sales to several large U.S. retailers who had formerly purchased from Mid-Atlantic.

This was certainly a blow to the local economy and to the marble history of Ritchie County. Mid-Atlantic had been, among other things good, a major contributor to the West Virginia Marble Festival in Cairo.

An article in the December 3, 2003, *Parkersburg News* by reporter Connie Dole states that this Ellenboro glass company has steadily lost buyers to the Chinese low-cost labor force. One of the owners, Mike Hall, stated that Mid-Atlantic will try to stay open as long as it has buyers. He further stressed that his employees know that they are struggling and that they are desperately trying to find new buyers. Hall said they have automated in the packaging department and actually shut down for a month while the equipment was upgraded, but even this effort still has not left the firm competitive enough.

Hall further noted that a glass buyer had told him that the Chinese firms hire children for 80 cents an hour so that his own one pound bag of marbles might sell for 40 cents and an equivalent Chinese bag would sell for 19 cents. One of Mid-Atlantic's biggest buyers went to China and opened a factory of its own, thus benefiting from both low wages and taxes and making money by selling in the U.S. Hall expressed his belief that the government must step in or there won't be any glass manufacturing left in this country. The West Virginia Economic Development Office contacted Hall and Spencer and has offered them their financial assistance. Hall stated firmly that it isn't financial aid that is needed, but a solid customer base.

The fires in both the hand blown and marble production facilities at Mid-Atlantic all remained cold at the end of 2004 and production had ceased. As of this writing, in the fall of 2005 no production activity has occurred at Mid-Atlantic. The company reported looking into other manufacturing possibilities, but the plans have not been revealed at the time of this writing. Hall concluded by saying, "We will be here as long as we have a customer." Activities in 2005 included selling off the remaining inventory. A local newspaper article reported later that Mid-Atlantic employees should arrange to seek employment elsewhere.

Mid-Atlantic Marbles Produced

The greatest majority of marbles produced by Mid-Atlantic are lightly colored transparents. Transparents were made in light, medium, and dark blue, amber, pink, teal green, clear crystal, and amethyst – any of these may be iridescent. The typical size range is 9/16" to 5/8" with a few irregular sizes thrown in. This line was later expanded to include opaque black, opaque white, and iridescent pearls (white opaque with iridescence).

Mid-Atlantic Glass, Ellenboro, West Virginia, production largely resembles these indistinguishable transparent and iridescent marbles, largely industrial and for the florist and crafts trade. *D. Chamberlain photo.*

The colorful marbles for play range from 3/8" to about 3/4" and were produced in a single run in September 2001.

Known color combinations include:

Red, white, and blue
Red, white
Blue, white
Yellow and white
Blue, brown, white

By far the least common color combinations are the three color ones. Prior to closing in December - January 2003/ 2004, Mid-Atlantic Glass produced a small run of light brown or tan marbles.

Mid-Atlantic Packaging

Mid-Atlantic did its own packaging and shipping. All marbles and gems were available loose, bulk, or in unlabeled cellophane bags. Plastic jars with threaded lids were also sold. Bulk sales included 50 lb. cardboard boxes and large cellophane bags of 10 lbs. None of these bear the company name, except one poly bag that was a promotional for recycled glass.

Mid-Atlantic Glass as the then relatively new marble production facility in Ellenboro, West Virginia, looked. This is the back and outside of three of their hand fed furnaces as they faced the larger glass factory facility. *L.L. Moore photo.*

Mid-Atlantic Glass marble rollers as they appeared ready for production in 1992. *Dennis Webb photo collection.*

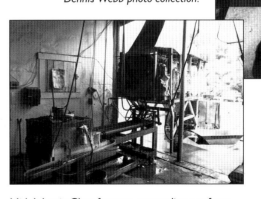

Mid-Atlantic Glass furnace, protruding out from under the shelter-like factory facility into the brighter daylight. The machine was newly in place when photographed in 1993. Covered by the roof are the marble rollers/machine and a spray nozzle for adding iridescence. Note the trough that the completed but not yet cooled marbles would roll down before dropping off the visible end into a awaiting bucket. *L.L. Moore photo.*

Mid-Atlantic Glass machine in active production. Note the small orange, hot orbs bouncing along the marble rollers. May 1994. *S. Metzler photo.*

Mid-Atlantic Glass marbles at the end of the process. Having formed on the rollers, the still exceedingly hot spheres, cooled enough to maintain their shapes only, roll down the trough and fall into the awaiting bucket. Note these are colorless marbles and the foreground shows a barrel of the same. May 1994. *S. Metzler photo.*

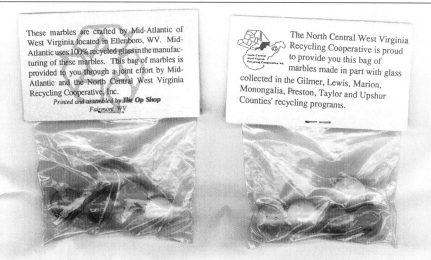

Mid-Atlantic Glass. The only known packages which Mid-Atlantic participated in producing are these promotional pieces for recycling. Note the mention of Mid-Atlantic as jointly being a provider of these packages. Shown is the front and reverse of the packaging. $10-15 each.

Mid-Atlantic Glass marble production facility as it looks from the main glass factory. Note two furnaces are fired along the building's side while one is glowing orange and fired to the far right. The backhoe in the foreground is being used to assist in readying one of the three furnaces that typically lined the building's near end. 1994 photo.

Mid-Atlantic Glass looking out from inside the marble production facility. April 2004.

THE PELTIER GLASS COMPANY

Ottawa, Illinois
1927 - marble production ceased 2002, glass production continues.

Peltier Glass Co. production examples. *Photo D. Chamberlain.*

Peltier Glass Co. production examples, including some of the most attractive and desirable. *D. Chamberlain photo.*

The Peltier Glass Company of Ottawa, Illinois, is the oldest surviving marble maker in the United States. It must be said that in the last few years production has been sporadic at best. This company was founded in 1886 as The Novelty Glass Company by Victor J. Peltier, an immigrant glass craftsman from France who had lived and worked in the United States in glass companies in New York, Pennsylvania, and Iowa before starting his own company.

The company name was changed to The Peltier Glass Company after the founder's death in 1911 and the disastrous fire of 1919. The loss sustained from the fire was estimated at $150,000. The fire was believed to have been caused by oil pipes that ignited in the furnace room. Two large buildings were destroyed, as was the attached warehouse. Firemen saved the Peltier home, which stood not over 150 feet from the flames.

Before the fire, opalescent glass novelties and other art glass products were the company's mainstay and their glass was used in Pullman car windows, lamps, and colored glass windows. After the fire and rebuilding, Victor's sons, Sellers and Joseph, took over running the firm. It was then that marble-making was first undertaken at Peltier, using the same glass recipes as for their colorful opalescent glass.

Among the colorants used was uranium oxide which, when mixed with other chemicals, produced a variety of brightly fluorescent colors. This particularly dangerous colorant became hard to obtain during and after World War II and eventually fell into disuse by the marble companies due to federal government restrictions. At Peltier white cold cream jars were brought in and recycled as a base for their variegated style marbles and for opaque marbles. Peltier's own glass formulas were used for the added striping. Other formulas were developed by Sellers Peltier to suit various needs.

At Peltier, marble production began around 1927 on a machine built and patented by William J. Miller. Later, other patents assigned to the Peltier Glen Company were made by Sellers N. Peltier and others.

The Peltier Glass Company was the defendant in a 1929 lawsuit by which the Akro Agate Company charged that Peltier's marble-making machine (William I. Miller's, 1926, Patent 1,601,699) was an infringement on Akro's Horace C. Hill machine (1915, Patent 1,164,718). The suit was decided in favor of Akro Agate, but was reversed on appeal by Peltier.

Historically, this court decision in favor of Peltier and against Akro Agate is referred to as "the breaking of the Patents," which opened up the marble industry by allowing many other companies to start up using technologies already developed without fear of patent infringement. The late Roger Howdyshell of Marble King said, "The breaking of the Patent was the most significant event in the history of the U.S. marble industry."

Around 1939, Peltier sold a marble machine to the Kokomo Opalescent Glass Company in Kokomo, Indiana. It was sold back to Peltier in the mid-1940s. (See the Kokomo chapter.)

Peak production years for Peltier were the 1930s and 1940s, when most of their collectible and recognizable marbles were made. Peltier experienced the same decline in sales as did other domestic producers due to the popularity of the Japanese cat's eye marbles in the 1950s. Peltier's total marble output for 1954 was 141 million; sales dropped by twenty-five percent the next year to 106 million marbles.

In the *Glass Factory Yearbook* of 1946 the Peltier Glass Co. of Ottawa, Illinois, is listed with "S. H. Peltier, president and general manager; E. T. Keating, secretary and treasurer; R. H. Bottom, chemist, engineer, and factory manager; J. B. Lowe, purchasing agent and sales manager. 2 furnaces, 14 pots, days tanks. Glass marbles and balls, small pressed glassware, lenses, specialties."

Like the other U.S. marble makers who survived, Peltier eventually produced a cat's eye design of its own that was unique in that it had a single thick blade in the center rather than the "X" pattern or the cage styles developed by others. These are called Banana Cat Eyes by collectors today.

At various times Peltier marbles were sold by Marble King because of a family connection in the ownership of the two companies. Sellers Peltier was one of the original incorporators of Marble King, along with Berry Pink and others, in 1949 when they acquired Alley Agate in St. Marys, West Virginia. Marble King purchased and packaged Peltier marbles in the early 1950s to fill Marble King orders. At the same time, Peltier was acquiring and packaging Marble King marbles and marketing them under the Peltier name. Any of these cross marketed packages are uncommon but can be found and have, as one might expect, caused great confusion over time.

Duncan Peltier died in 1973 and was succeeded as president by Joe Jankowski, who served as president until 1983, when he was succeeded by Karen Armstrong. Jankowski resumed the presidency in 1986. No Peltier family members remain in the company today, but the company name remains the same.

Gino Biffany related to the authors that through much of the 1980s and 1990s, the Peltier Glass Company made only industrial marbles but on occasion renewed making colorful marbles to satisfy demand generated by an interest in marbles by collectors. Peltier's big volume came from making glass gems or nuggets, which sold by the ton.

From the more recent time period of decreased production came two of Peltier's most popular new marbles, the "Nova" and the "Root Beer Float." These marbles were made on the same day, October 27, 1988, by machine operator Jerry Eich and George Zellers, who ran the furnace end at Peltier at the time. It was Zeller who named both marbles. Found in one inch size, the Nova trades around $10-30 each and Root Beer Floats can bring $50-70 in such large sizes.

In 1989 Peltier made a special run of collectible marbles for a California collector in 7/8" size.

The new owner at Peltier Glass, Boyce Lundstrum, who took over in November 2001, also purchased the Peltier family mansion and hoped to open a marble museum. As part of the glass factory purchase he obtained all the old marble machines, glass molds, and formulas. He has a safe with much old paperwork and the model of the marble machine used in the Patent suit with Akro Agate.

Mr. Lundstrum made several test runs of marbles, the first being in January 2002. These marbles were made up of blue and white vanes in a clear base – almost a cat's eye design. He made up between 200 and 225 bags with a label printed in silver that reads, "The Peltier Glass Co." Also, there is a tag attached which says, "In 2001, Boyce Lundstrum, a successful entrepreneur, purchased the Peltier Glass Company in Ottawa, Illinois." Boyce's intent is to initiate the renaissance in the art of glass marble manufacturing. These were the first marbles to come off the rollers at Peltier's in the hands of its new navigator, Boyce Lundstrum. Written on the card is "Boyce's first marbles 01/07/02." This first limited run was made specifically for the annual Ottawa Marble Show in 2002.

His second run was made in April 2002. He made two 25 lb. boxes. These turned out to be somewhat better marbles. The red marble in this run is rare because not many were made. This group of marbles resembles a kind of sparkler in a clear base with combinations of white and blue or blue and green. Some of these marbles did contain red, but most broke in manufacture. The reason for this limited run was to determine compatible glass and color. Of this run, Lundstrum took most of what he had left and scattered them in the parking lots in front and back of the factory – for the kids. He stated to plant visitor, David Tamulevich, that he believes in marbles for children and that you should give away half of what you make. Peltier stopped making gems in the summer of 2002 and sent their large gem table and customer list to Marble King.

In an August 2002 interview with marble collector, David Tamulevich, Lundstrum indicated huge plans for the future at Peltier to add a museum and test different kinds of glass and colors. Plans were elaborate, including fixing up a machine capable of making marbles up to 1-1/4" and to make a 4-color swirl with aventurine in various sizes. He had already run the pee-wee machine in a test and made some in crystal for a company that uses them to polish and grind things.

At the time of writing in 2005, no marble-making activities have occurred at Peltier since 2002. According to a report by marble collector, Ed Schubert, Boyce Lundstrum has given up his position at Peltier and now several new individuals are in charge that have little or no interest in marbles.

PELTIER Marbles
Produced

Cat's-Eye.
Character Of Comic Marbles.
Miller Swirls.
National Line Rainbos.
Opaques.
Peerless Patch.
Rainbos.
Slags.
Translucents.
Transparents.

The earliest Peltier marbles were produced on a machine designed and patented by William J. Miller. After the Akro Agate Company lost the patent lawsuit and in the flood of production by numerous companies that followed "the breaking of the Patent," probably no other company, with the possible exception of Akro Agate, produced a greater variety of marble styles and color combinations than did Peltier.

Two notes: 1. Many Peltier marbles have exploded air bubble blowout holes on their surface that are considered to be "as-made" defects. 2. Peltier marbles seem to have many variable sizes – as if concern for exact size increments was not a major issue. It appears, too, that in many of their marble types, Peltier produced many more pee wees than did most other companies.

Like Vitro Agate, Peltier generally classified their marbles for play according to opacity.

The transparent **Rainbo type** marbles have been called "Sunsets"; the translucent Rainbo types have been termed by contemporary collectors "Acme Realers," and the opaque play marbles are termed "Rainbo."

Peltier produced a huge number of marbles in styles and color combinations that would be difficult to classify as a specific type or style.

Opaques: It is known that Peltier produced one-color opaque marbles, but unless found in original packaging, it would be difficult to differentiate them from similar marbles made by other companies. It is even thought that some of these marbles in Peltier packages were actually made by Alley Agate or even Marble King. Several different Peltier packaging products have even been dug up at Marble King dumpsites.

Transparents: Peltier transparents are virtually identical to those produced by other companies, but may be identified in original packages of clearies and marine crystals. These are usually found to be in poly bags.

Translucents: Peltier produced several one-color translucent marbles. The National Milkie is similar to the Akro Agate Moonie, and the Canary is similar but has a slight greenish tint.

Slags: The Miller machine produced single stream slags and swirls and was only semi-automatic. An article on page 14 of the 1927 *The American Flint* magazine describes this machine and that it was capable of making 40 marbles a minute at Peltier.

Original packages indicate that Peltier slags were called National Onyx by the company and were manufactured in colors of brown, blue, green, aqua, purple, red, and yellow. Of all the slag marbles made, Peltier's seem to be generally the easiest to identify. The white striping most often has a fine-line feathering effect, which makes these slags distinctive.

Miller Swirls: Along with slags, these single stream swirls made on the Miller machine are the earliest made by Peltier. The swirling is random and the colors are very bright. Multicolored swirls were also produced on the machine that included a transparent base, often green or brown with swirls of several different colors; typically white, orange, yellow, red or blue.

National Line Rainbos: Possibly the most recognized and sought Peltier marbles are the National Line Rainbos. These were made in the late 1920s through the late 1930s. These marbles, usually with an opaque base, have two seams and the ribbons (or occasionally swirls) will be of one or more colors.

Collectors and especially dealers who want to give notice to various types have given these marbles descriptive names to help identify and give added value to them. Here are the names, brief descriptions, and some sense of range of value for mint condition, 5/8" sizes:

Black Panda: black with white ribbons, $30-40.
Black Widow: black base with red stripes, $40-60.
Blue Bee: yellow with blue aventurine ribbons, $30-40.
Blue Galaxy: light blue with aventurine black and yellow ribbons, $1,000-1,200.
Blue Zebra: white base with blue ribbons, $150-200.
Bumble Bee: yellow with blue aventurine ribbons, $40-50
Burnt Christmas Tree: chocolate cow brown with black ribbons, $30-40.
Christmas Tree: white base, red and green ribbons, $65-85.
Dragon: light green with red ribbons, $40-50.
Flaming Dragon: light green with red and yellow ribbons, $60-85.
Golden Rebel: yellow base, black and red ribbons, $650-750.
John Deer also called **Girl Scout:** yellow base with green ribbons, $40-50.
Ketchup and Murtard: white base, red and yellow ribbons, $30-50.
Lemon Lime: lime green with yellow ribbons, $30-40.
Liberty: white base, blue and red ribbons, $70-90.
Rebel: white base, black and red ribbons, $75-95.
Red Zebra: white with red ribbons (often with aventurine), $50-60.
Spiderman: light blue with red ribbons, $40-60.
Submarine: translucent blue with wispy white base and orange ribbons, $30-40.
Superboy: light blue with blended red and yellow ribbons, $50-70.
Superman: blue base, red and yellow ribbons, $150-200.
Tiger: orange with black ribbons, $45-60.
Zebra: white base with black ribbons, $25-30.

Note: Wasp, a red marble with black ribbons, is really an incorrect name for Black Widow.

Rainbos: Alan Basinet, marble collector and dealer, describes Rainbos as being a late 1930s and 1940s descendant of the National Line Rainbo. He states that they are usually a duller color and were made during a time of a declining marble market and cost savings. Like their predecessors, they have two seams and the base glass may be opaque, transparent, or translucent. They usually have two or four ribbons circling the marble. Most Rainbos have an opaque base with white being by far the most common. Rainbos with a translucent base are called Acme Realers. Sunsets are those Rainbos with a transparent base sometimes sparkling with air bubbles – with red, orange, yellow, white or green ribbons. Sometimes the colors are reversed. Another type of Rainbo is called a Champion Jr. and has a dark transparent base with white and yellow ribbons. Tri-color rainbos have a colored base, either transparent or opaque, with ribbons of two different colors. One beautiful type, called "7-UP" by collectors, has a beautiful dark transparent green base with white and red ribbons. It is reminiscent of the old "7-UP Uncola" bottles. Other names have been given to various color combinations of Rainbos by collectors and dealers. A "clown" has a dark transparent base with red and yellow ribbons. "Baseballs" are opaque white with blue ribbons. Rainbos are rarely seen with the oxblood color, but some do exist.

Peerless Patch: This marble, as the name signifies, is indeed a patch on a different colored base. These are similar in design to those patch marbles made by Akro Agate and Vitro Agate, although at times the patch on the Peltier version is a bit oddly misshapen. Many color combinations are known and a few 3-color hybrids can be found. One very scarce type of Peerless Patch has a satiny, almost metallic sheen, sometimes called a Pearlized Peerless Patch.

Comic Character Marbles: Sometime between 1932 and 1934, Peltier introduced its "Picture" marbles, often called "Character" or "Comic" marbles by collectors. The technique for the process to fire the characters onto the surface of the Peerless Patch marbles was developed by George W. Angerstein, who applied for his Patent in 1932 and signed a contract with Peltier the same year. This process involved applying a coating of clear glass to the marble after the character was fired on, assuring that it could not be rubbed off. The characters were printed from a graphite-like substance and were, with only a few known red exceptions, always in black. The marbles measuring between 19/32" and 11/16" featured twelve different well-known comic strip characters from the 1920s and 1930s. The characters included were Andy Gump, Betty Boop, Bimbo, Emma Schmaltz, Herbie, Kayo, Koko the Clown, Little Orphan Annie, Moonshine Mullins, Sandy Skeezix, and Agustus "Smitty" Smith. These marbles, distributed in boxes of 5, 12, and 20, were produced as late as 1938. For statistical purposes, Mr. Basinet examined 470 of these comic marbles and found the following distributions. A possible value follows the distribution numbers.

Koko – 61 in 470 – $75.
Bimbo – 58 in 470 – $65.
Emma – 49 in 470 – $65.
Annie – 37 in 470 – $125-$150.
Herbie – 36 in 470 – $100.
Skeezix – 36 in 470 – $75.
Smitty – 34 in 470 – $65.
Sandy – 34 in 470 – $125-$150.
Betty – 34 in 470 – $150-$200.
Moon – 34 in 470 – $200-$300.
Andy – 32 in 470 – $75.
Kayo – 25 in 470 – $300-$400.

Current prices are suggested by Gino Biffany. It should be noted that the prices may not reflect values for unusual color combinations on these marbles. The price of individual marbles may also depend on the general condition and the clarity and positioning of the character on the marbles as well as the presence of aventurine or other unusual characteristics of the marbles.

Even pricier than the comic marbles, are the specialty marbles:

Tom Mix, $1,500-$2,300.
Cotes Master Loaf, $800-$1,250.
Hoover for President, No price available

Franklin Roosevelt, No price available
Babe Ruth, No price available

Cat's-Eye: There seems to be some discussion as to when Peltier started making their distinctive style of Cat-eye marbles. Peltier expert Gino Biffany sets the record straight by confirming that as being 1955. Originally they were made in five basic colors: red, yellow, green, blue, and white. The size advertised were 3/8", 0", 2", 4", and 6". Biffany states that, although the 3/8" are listed, he has never seen any in person. These unique marbles are characterized by absolutely clear glass and colored interior glass with generally smooth vanes resembling a real banana but in bright colors. The vanes run generally from pole to pole and while most are relatively smooth, some have ridges down the sides and there are other oddities as well. Mr. Biffany has stated that while these marbles are called Bananas, it is a term coined by collectors and is not a company name.

Even though the Peltier cat's-eye marbles come in the standard colors, other colors are known to exist: lavender, orange, and brown. There are fat Bananas, skinny Bananas, hybrid Bananas with colored glass, marbles with aventurine and even double Bananas. There is an uncommon marble, clear red with a red center.

One uncommon and popular Peltier Banana is termed "Root Beer Float." It was made on October 27, 1988, by Peltier worker George Zellers. This marble has a dark amber base with a white vane. About 7,000 were made. George Zellers also made a marble called a Nova. About 7,000 of these were also made.

PELTIER Packaging

Peltier Glass used a variety of imaginative boxes for the packaging as well as the marketing of their marbles through the Gropper Company. Peltier marbles have also been found in certain advertising packages as well as in Marble King bags.

Among the many Peltier boxes one might find the following:

#5 box with cutouts;
Stock boxes with counts of 100, 50, & 25 in various sizes. Some are marked: National Marbles, Acme Realers, Rainbos, or Peerless;
Square deep stock boxes with 100 marbles and some are marked as above while some are marked opaque with the actual color of marbles written in;
Comic marbles in boxes of 5, 12, and 20;
Indian Head gift box with bag and beautiful graphics containing 28 marbles;
Stained glass design gift boxes with bag containing either 25 or 30 marbles;
Advertising box #224 with bag. "National Marble Set Use Coryell 70 Products" Gropper Company.

The principal jobber company distributing Peltier marbles was M. Gropper and Sons, Inc., also of Ottawa, Illinois. On some of the Gropper packages the implication is that they actually made the marbles in the boxes. The writing on some boxes clearly states, "Manufactured by M. Groper and Sons of Ottawa, Ill. USA." Some Gropper boxes are labeled as follows:

"National Onyx Toy marbles," contains 25 marbles
"Prima Agates" #50 box, contains 25 marbles
"National Milkies" #20 box, contains 25 marbles
"National Prima" #0 box, contains 25 marbles

An exceptionally appealing Gropper box is the blue #28 "Lucky Box" Champion Marble Set. This box may contain any of a number of Peltier marble types.

Peltier Glass also marketed their marbles in mesh poly and plastic wrappers. Peltier marbles are also found in bags with Marble King headers (see Marble King chapter for explanation and connections).

Known mesh bags include paper headers that read "glass marbles," 30 count and "Champion Jr." 30 count.

Known poly bags bear labels of "Champion Jr." red header, 40 count (smaller counts in these bags are known); a large poly bag containing 110 marbles including 5 shooters – this bag is marked Cat's Eye Champion." There is also a poly bag labeled "Big Boy." It contains 5 Rainbow 1" shooters and another similar one contains five 1" cat's eye marbles.

Peltier marked poly bags with headers are know to say Cat's Eyes 40 count, Champion 40 count, and Marine Crystals 8 count 1" marbles. Heat-sealed poly bags are found in 13 + 1 count cat's eyes; 19 count cat's eyes; 19 count Champion Jr.; 30 count assorted and 30 marine crystals.

There are also Peltier Morton advertising bags and cereal giveaway tubes with 5 in a tube and 6 in a tube of which all the known one bags are "Banana" type cat's eyes.

Peltier Glass Co. as it appeared in 2002. *G. Biffany photo.*

Peltier Glass Co. 3/4" "name" marbles. Includes Superman, Zebra, ketchup and mustard, Christmas tree, liberty, and Golden Rebel. A list with the descriptions is found near the end of this chapter. Can you identify them?

Peltier company letterhead noting the production of "Champion Glass Marbles" and other products.

Peltier Glass Co. factory, Ottawa, Illinois. Date and photographer unknown. *Dennis Webb photo collection.*

Peltier Glass Co. working marble machine model made for use in a patent suit. Suit brought by Akro Agate and won by Peltier. *G. Biffany photo.*

Peltier Glass Co. Big Value Marble Assortment box and contents. *Dennis Webb photo collection.* $450.

Peltier Glass Co. patent suit model and its former owner, Joseph Janowski, ex-Petlier Co. president, explaining it. The model was important in the suit that broke the patent claim Akro Agate claimed on the machinery and process.

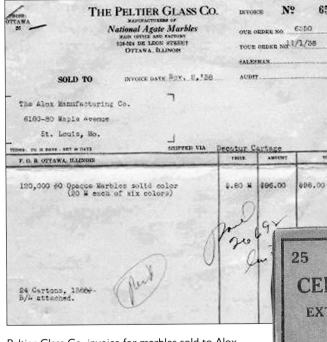

Peltier Glass Co. invoice for marbles sold to Alox in 1938. *H. de Sousa Collection.*

Peltier Glass Co. Big Value Marble Assortment box and contents. As shown, $300-400. No. 0 and 1 Bloodies, box, and original contents, $300-400.

Peltier Glass Co. Gropper jobber's box of Ceries Agates. *H. de Sousa collection.* $1,000.

Peltier Glass Co. stock box of 100 opaque game marbles. *J. Thompson photo.* $125-150.

Peltier Glass Co. jobber box lid from Gropper. *E. Schubert collection.* As shown with contents, $500-1,000.

Peltier Glass Co. job box, lid shown previously. Original contents.

Peltier Glass Co. 20 count No. 0 slag marbles in graphic lidded box. *E. Schubert collection.* $500.

Peltier Glass Co., same box and lid as previously shown, but containing National Line Rainbo marbles. $250.

Peltier Glass Co. jobber boxes from N. Gropper & Sons. *Collection of H. de Sousa.* Empty boxes, $100-200 each.

Peltier Glass Co. jobber box lids with vibrant graphics. Empty, no value determined.

Peltier Glass Co. Chinko - Checko - Marbles game box. 60 count No. 00 size. Lid in rough condition. This is a box often associated with Berry Pink, Inc. but this one is imprinted Peltier. As shown, $40.

Peltier Glass Co. National Rainbo Marbles 100 count box. *H. de Sousa collection.* $2,000.

Peltier Glass Co. National Marbles 100 count box containing 3 color Rainbos. *H. de Sousa collection.* $10,000.

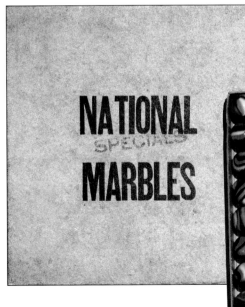

Peltier Glass Co. National Special Marbles 100 count box lid. *E. Schubert collection.* With original contents, $2,000.

Peltier Glass Co. contents of 100 count National Special box lid shown previously.

Peltier Glass Co. National Peerless Line 50 count box of Peerless patch marbles. $500.

Peltier Glass Co. box of 5 comic marbles. *H. de Sousa collection.* $850.

Peltier Glass Co. Special Box produced for Peltier for the "second run" in April 2002. $200.

Peltier Glass Co. red box of 12 comic marbles. *H. de Sousa collection.* $2,000.

Peltier Glass Co. Lucky Boy Marble Box. *H. de Sousa collection.* Value depends on the type and quantity of marbles inside. $800-2,000.

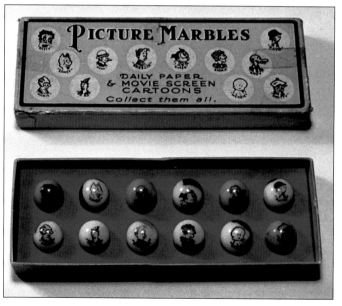

Peltier Glass Co. yellow box of 12 comic marbles. *H. de Sousa collection.* $2,500.

Peltier Glass Co. inside one Lucky Boy marble box. Selection of "favorite slags." Notice how nicely this box opens. *E. Schubert collection.* No value determined.

Peltier Glass Co. Art Deco designed lid gift box with bag and original marbles. *E. Schubert photo.* No value determined.

Peltier Glass comic marbles being offered to bakery establishments! Interesting to see how they were marketed through bakeries and couple with an ad campaign, a marble shooting contest, and a $25 prize! Note also the then cost of $12.50 per 1,000 with a minimum order of 10,000! They are out there somewhere!

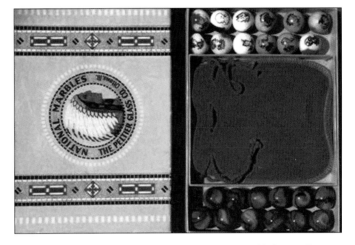

Peltier Glass Co. National Marbles gift box with marble bag and original marbles. *H. de Sousa collection.* $8,500.

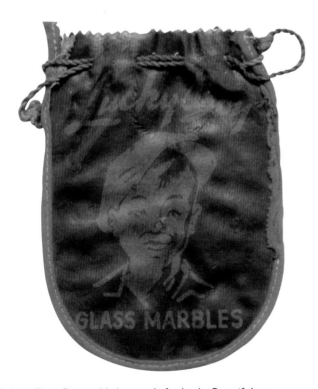

Peltier Glass Co. smaller cut out boxes. R to L: No. 10 box National Rainbo Marbles, Assorted Colors, $200-300; No. 5 box National Rainbo Marbles, Assorted Colors, $100-200; No. 106 box Rainbo Marbles, $100-200.

Peltier Glass Co. marble bag made for Lucky Boy gift box. *Marble Magnates photo.* $25-50

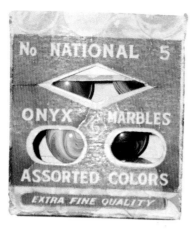

Peltier Glass Co. No. 5 National Onyx Marbles Assorted Colors cut out box. *E. Schubert collection.* $100-200.

Peltier Glass Co. 40 count "Champion" poly bag and header. *A. Rasmus collection.* $40-50.

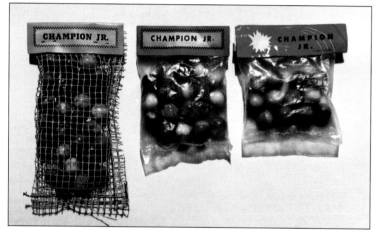

Peltier Glass Co. three variations on the Champion Jr. bags. Mesh bag, $40; poly bags, $30 each.

Peltier Glass Co. poly bags of 5/8" banana cat eye marbles. 18 count. *J. Thompson photo.* $20.

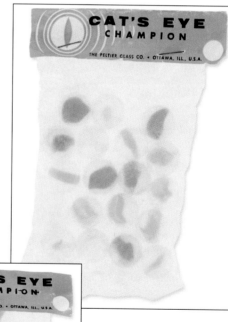

Peltier Glass Co. Morton sale advertising bags, showing both sides of header. Mesh color varies. $50-60 each.

Peltier Glass Co. poly bags of 5/8" banana cat eye marbles. *J. Thompson photo.* $20-25.

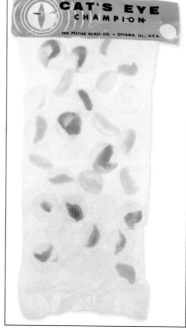

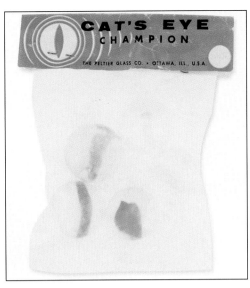

Peltier Glass Co. jobber's price list cover and terms. The actual prices are not part of the image obtained by the authors. Note the period-clothed lad shooting his "National Agates" across the US map. Price list No. 33-34 suggests it is from 1933-1934.

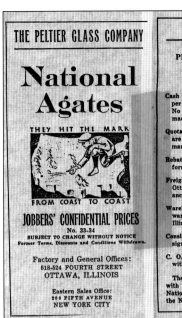

Peltier Glass Co. poly bags of one inch banana cat eye marbles. 5 count. *J. Thompson photo.* $25-30.

Peltier Glass Co. poly bag "Cat's Eye Champion 110 Marbles" bag recovered at dump site. *Marble Magnates collection.* No value determined.

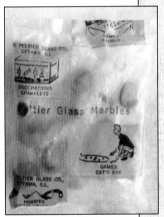

Peltier Glass Co. poly bag. Interesting suggestions for use on bag. $20.

Peltier Glass Co. banana cat's eyes in advertising hanger bag for Royal Crown Cola. *A. Rasmus collection.* $30-35.

BULK PRICE LIST
NOVEMBER, 1962
Peltier GLASS COMPANY
OTTAWA, ILLINOIS.

No.	Description		Packed In A Carton	Carton Weight	Price Per 1000 Pcs.
CAT'S EYE MARBLES					
Available in 5 colors — White, Blue, Green, Red, and Yellow.					
Packed one color per carton or assorted colors per carton.					
3/8"	CAT'S EYE	3/8 inch diameter	9,400	25 lbs.	$3.75
		3/8 inch diameter	22,500	60 lbs.	$3.75
#0	CAT'S EYE	5/8 inch diameter	5,000	60 lbs.	$ .80
#2	CAT'S EYE	3/4 inch diameter	3,000	60 lbs.	$2.90
#4	CAT'S EYE	7/8 inch diameter	1,700	60 lbs.	$4.90
#6	CAT'S EYE	1 inch diameter	1,300	60 lbs.	$5.90
MARINE CRYSTAL MARBLES					
The 3/8" dia., 1/2" dia., 9/16" dia. are available in 8 colors — Ruby, Golden Amber, Blue, Green, Flint, Purple, Aqua, Yellow. The 5/8" dia., 3/4" dia., and 1" dia. are available in 5 colors — Ruby, Golden Amber, Blue, Green, and Flint.					
Packed one color per carton or assorted colors per carton.					
3/8"	MARINE CRYSTALS	3/8 inch diameter	9,400	25 lbs.	$4.25
		3/8 inch diameter	22,500	60 lbs.	$4.25
#000	MARINE CRYSTALS	1/2 inch diameter	9,300	60 lbs.	$3.25
#00	MARINE CRYSTALS	9/16 inch diameter	7,000	60 lbs.	$1.20
#0	MARINE CRYSTALS	5/8 inch diameter	5,000	60 lbs.	$1.45
#2	MARINE CRYSTALS	3/4 inch diameter	3,000	60 lbs.	$3.60
#6	MARINE CRYSTALS	1 inch diameter	1,300	60 lbs.	$8.00
On orders calling for Ruby only add 100% to above prices.					
RAINBO MARBLES & RAINBO "BLOODIES" MARBLES					
The Rainbo and "Bloodies" marbles are available in 5 color combinations — White and Red, White and Yellow, White and Blue, White and Green, Black and Yellow. The "Bloodies" marbles contain an identifying mark of "bloodie" red glass.					
Packed one color per carton or assorted colors per carton.					
#0	RAINBO OR BLOODIES	5/8 inch diameter	5,000	60 lbs.	$ .80
#2	RAINBO OR BLOODIES	3/4 inch diameter	3,000	60 lbs.	$2.90
#4	RAINBO OR BLOODIES	7/8 inch diameter	1,700	60 lbs.	$4.90
#6	RAINBO OR BLOODIES	1 inch diameter	1,300	60 lbs.	$5.90
CHINESE CHECKER MARBLES (SOLID OPAQUE COLORS)					
Available in 6 solid opaque colors — Red, Yellow, Blue, Green, Black, and White					
Packed one color per carton or assorted colors per carton.					
#00	CHINESE CHECKERS	9/16 inch diameter	7,000	60 lbs.	$1.00

TERMS 2% – 10 – net 30 days FOB Paden City, West Virginia
 Minimum order $10.00 . . . . 25% broken package charge
No freight allowance. All prices subject to change without notice. Goods returned without authorization will not be accepted.
A charge of 1% per month will be assessed on accounts not paid in the terms specified.
GRADING: Specific tolerance – plus or minus 1/64" . . . . $.25/M
STRAPPING: Fiber Glass Tape – Domestic . . . . $.15/ctn. Export – None

Address all inquiries and orders to
PELTIER GLASS COMPANY
P. O. Box 217 ' Ottawa, Illinois

Peltier Glass Co. price list with prices dated November 1962. Note that the terms on the sheet include F.O.B. (shipping point) of Paden City, West Virginia.

PLAYRITE MARBLE AND NOVELTY COMPANY

Ellenboro, West Virginia
1945- 1947

Playrite Marble & Novelty examples of Playrite production. *M. Wilson collection. D. Chamberlain photo.*

Playrite Marble and Novelty Company was formed in March of 1945, and began producing marbles November 8 of that year in downtown Lamberton, West Virginia (now called Ellenboro), in a small building constructed of concrete blocks and a metal roof between an existing B & O Railroad siding and Highway 5. The building was rented from Isadore Tucker, who lived out of state in Cleveland, Ohio. Playrite was yet another of several small marble endeavors that sprang up in the post war years of beautiful Ritchie County. The mailing address for the company was the nearby town of Pennsboro.

The original ownership consisted of three stockholders: Jesse O. Krupp, president; Andy Long, secretary-treasurer; and Lawrence Jones, production. In the spring of 1946, Charles A. Wilson, Joseph E. Wilson, and Mary Jane Krupp-Wilson purchased stock in the company also. Jesse Krupp had no previous marble-making experience, but had a long history working in glass, first in Ohio and later in West Virginia.

Playrite's machines were made by local machinist, George Murphy, who was also responsible for the machines of several other West Virginia marble companies. Although Playrite had two machines, they generally only kept one running at any given time.

Jesse Krupp was in charge of keeping records and mixing glass. Joseph Wilson was a dairy farmer by day who packed and shipped marbles by night. Charles Wilson was a silent stockholder in the company. Clarence and Howard Jones were laborers who, for $10.00 per week each, kept the warehouse swept and cleaned. Mary Jane Wilson packaged marbles at night while watching her two small children on site. The business was largely a family operated sideline, with nearly everyone involved having another occupation.

In attempting to learn and tell the story of Playrite, we are much more fortunate than we have been regarding some other companies because two of the company ledgers have been preserved in the hands of Mary Jane Krupp-Wilson, and she has very graciously shared them with us as well as all of her memories. These written records give us some insight into suppliers of glass, equipment, and other materials; companies that purchased marbles from Playrite; and even how much the company labor cost as recorded in the payroll.

The ledger indicates frequent small transactions concerning the buying and selling of machinery and supplies with Burnell Davis (Davis Marble Company), William Heaton (Heaton Agate Company), and Carroll Jackson (Jackson Marble Company). This seems to suggest that the small marble companies of Ritchie County in the 1940s may have co-existed in a somewhat cooperative spirit.

Glass was purchased from New Martinsville, Paden City Glass, H. M. Gabbert Glass Company, Viking Glass Company, and Alley Agate Company, and was brought in by truck. Marbles were shipped by both truck and rail transport. No single-colored (i.e. Chinese Checker) marbles were produced, and no pee-wees or large sizes, all marbles produced being around 5/8", although the sizes were not as consistent as at some factories. All marbles produced were random patterned swirls in various opaque, transparent, and translucent colors.

The primary purchaser of Playrite's marbles was also one of the primary purchasers from many marble companies, both large and small, during the first half of the twentieth century, the Jerome Gropper Company. The total Gropper paid to Playrite for various orders of marbles filled in one month was close to $400.00.

Playrite marbles were packaged in mesh bags, twenty-five count and forty count, with white labels that read "Playrite Marbles." The company also sold marbles in small boxes as well, but it is unclear whether these boxes were also company labeled. Unfortunately none of this packaging has yet turned up to be photographed. Later when Ritchie County marble companies, including Playrite, Davis, and Jackson were folding, Playrite found they had more marbles than bags and labels and Jackson had plenty of leftover bags and labels. Playrite purchased remaining packaging materials and sold some of their own stock in mesh bags labeled "Jackson's Marbles".

Like other small marble companies that cropped up in the mid-1940s, Playrite was a short-lived endeavor. Operations ceased on December 31, 1947. Mary Jane Wilson states that the people involved all had other occupations claiming their time, and it seemed that "everyone else was getting into the act," meaning other local businesses were starting up, most notably in nearby Cairo. Since the factory building was rented, the equipment had to be moved out; at least one of the machines was stored for a time at the former Jackson Marble factory.

Six years after operations had ceased, in the spring of 1953, some final entries in the company ledger were made when Joe Wilson and Charles Wilson purchased from Clarence, Howard, and Laurence Jones their shares in the company. In a separate transaction in January of that same year, Jesse Krupp, Joseph Wilson, and Charles Wilson had purchased from Andy Long and the Jones' for "ten dollars and other valuable considerations, one marble-making outfit complete now stored at Jackson's marble shop near Pennsboro, W. Va." The final resting place for the Playrite machines is unknown, but it is thought that in 1953 the Wilsons decided to hang on to at least one of them for a time, just in case the market for selling marbles ever became more favorable.

The building that once housed the Playrite factory is no longer standing, and the property is now part of the Mid-Atlantic Glass Company.

Playrite Marble Identification

All Playrite marbles found are opaque, translucent, and transparent swirls with white or blue striping. These marbles, almost universally measuring 5/8", are typical of those produced in Ritchie County, West Virginia. Many of these smaller and nearby companies had their marble-making equipment made by the same people and scrap glass and cullet were purchased from the same sources. The resulting products can be strikingly similar.

Base colors for these marbles include:

Clear or milky white
Light, medium or dark root beer
Light, medium or dark blue
Light, medium or dark green
Black
Purple

Playrite Packaging

Originally the Playrite Company packaged its marbles in either red or yellow mesh bags of forty or twenty-five count marbles. The headers were white with black writing. They also sold marbles in small boxes. Unfortunately, none of these packages have turned up for photographing.

When the Jackson Marble Company went out of business, Playrite bought their remaining bags and headers. The bags were either red or yellow mesh in forty and twenty-five count size. The headers were red with black writing that read "Jackson's Marbles" in bold type and in fine print "Made in Pennsboro, W. Va. U.S.A." and can be found with Playrite marbles in them.

It is not clear if Playrite ever bought marbles from any other company or just packaged their own.

Present value ranges for Playrite packages and marbles are:

40 Count mesh bag – $200-225
25 Count mesh bag – $100-125
Single marbles – $3-5

Playrite Marble & Novelty Jesse Krupp and Mary Jane Krupp Wilson. *M. Wilson photo.*

Playrite Marble & Novelty corporate seal. *M. Wilson collection.*

Playrite Marble & Novelty December balance sheet for 1946. A rare view into the finances of the smaller marble companies from a page in the company records. Note a net loss of $292.44 on a sales of $2,548.35. Not small money in 1946. *Compliments of M. Wilson.*

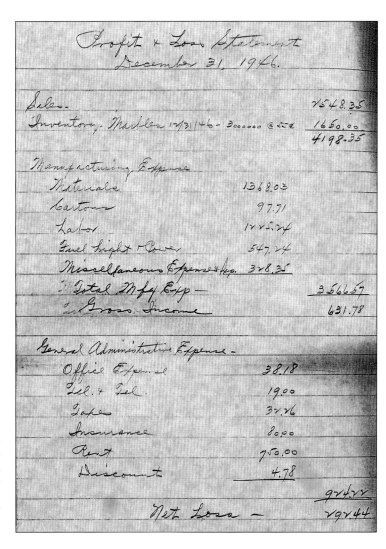

PAGE 12

COMBINED CASH JOURNAL AND DAILY FINANCIAL STATEMENT

LINE NO.	ACCOUNT NUMBER	GENERAL LEDGER			ACCOUNTS PAYABLE			ACCOUNTS RECEIVABLE			DAY	DESCRIPTION
		CHARGES	✓	CREDITS	CHARGES	✓	CREDITS	CHARGES	✓	CREDITS		FORWARDED
1								409 85	✓		1-10	Jerome Gropper Co.
2								286 74	✓		14-14	Jerome Gropper Co.
3											4	Jesse O. Krupp
4	454	776										Carrol Krupp
5	454	1030									6	Parkersburg Office Sup. Co.
6												Dr. Jas. P. Jones
7												Consumers Gas Utility Co.
8						1395						Star Lumber Co.
9											8	R. R. Lambert
10											5	Murphy Mach & Weld. Co.
11												Donald Murphy
12											10	H. M. Gabbert
13											15	Mon. Power Co.
14												Alpha E. Ancrom
15												Kenneth W. Nichols
16												J. R. Lambert
17												Mrs. Louise Bircher
18												Lawrence Jones
19												Clarence Jones
20									✓	749 17	14	Jerome Gropper Co.
21											19	Jas. Lambert Jr.
22												Kenneth Nichols
23												Alpha E. Ancrom
24		1306			1395			696 09		749 17		
25												
26		1306			1395			696 09		749 17		
27												
28												
29		14			151			107		107		
30												

Playrite Marble & Novelty cash journal, undated page. Noted here are two sales to Jerome Gropper Co., the marble jobber's for $409 and $286. *Compliments of M. Wilson collection.*

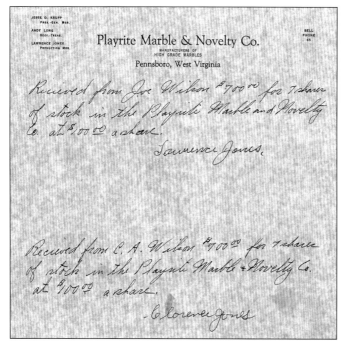

Playrite Marble & Novelty letterhead showing the principals and registering receipts where interests in Playrite were sold. *Compliments of M. Wilson collection.*

Playrite Marble & Novelty's Mary Jane Krupp Wilson appears at the West Virginia Marble Festival in Cairo, West Virginia, in 1999 and proudly shows off a bag of Playrite marbles.

Ravenswood Glass
and Novelty Company
Ravenswood Novelty Works

Ravenswood, West Virginia
1928 - 1930
Ravenswood, West Virginia
1931 - 1944, 1947 - 1955

Ravenswood production examples of brown and tan variations. *D. Chamberlain photo.*

Ravenswood production examples. *D. Chamberlain photo.*

Ravenswood Novelty Works, and it's lesser known predecessor Ravenswood Glass and Novelty Company are named for the town in Jackson County, West Virginia, where they were located.

For some time the authors operated under the assumption that there was but one marble company in this town. We put this in print in a monograph for the West Virginia Museum of American Glass and in our history exhibits at the West Virginia Marble Festival in Cairo, West Virginia. However, found in a March 1932 *West Virginia Review* magazine article is the brief note that "Charles Turnbull has leased an idle glass marble plant in Ravenswood, Jackson County, and is preparing to place it in operation as soon as new machines can be installed. The plant was built some years ago but was closed after being operated only a short time when it was discovered that the machine used was an infringement upon the patent of a rival company. The original company, composed of Jackson County people, has been dissolved."

After extensive inquiry and searching, no legal record of a patent infringement regarding any Ravenswood firm has been identified at this time. The Ravenswood Glass and Novelty Company was dissolved two years after it was formed. Documents in the West Virginia Secretary of State's office state that the Ravenswood Glass and Novelty Company was dissolved and its corporate charter returned to the state on June 4, 1930.

An additional piece of information about early Ravenswood marble history comes in 1984 from journalist Greg Matics, then with the *Jackson Star News*, who spoke with Edwin Safreed. Safreed stated he had worked for the Ravenswood Glass Novelty Works as early as 1932. The *Star News* printed an article by Matics in November 1999 that utilized that fifteen-year earlier interview with Safreed. That story, used here in part and with the permission of Matics, is as follows: "The story began in 1929 when a man named Ali came to Ravenswood and formed a small company run by Charlie Turnbull. The location of the operation was a small building, which still stands on Wood Street in North Ravenswood. Ali provided marble-making machines and produced marbles for approximately two years. It seemed that the details of the operation were kept secret for the first couple of years. Secrecy always seemed to be involved … It seems the machines Ali brought in had

infringed on someone's patent. When this violation was realized, people came into the plant one day and destroyed the machines. They smashed them with sledge-hammers and tore the shop completely apart with the workers on the site." This article goes on to say that "shortly after that episode, Turnbull purchased a marble machine from Acro Agate [sic] in Clarksburg and set it up in the Ravenswood location. A few marbles were produced, then the operation was suspended."

The "man named Ali," while sounding like a mysterious Middle Eastern gentleman, who we are told came to Ravenswood in 1929 to make marbles, is a much more obvious and important person to this story. It seems likely that writer Matics may have used a phonetic spelling and the person Safreed spoke of was the very active West Virginia marble and glass novelty manufacturer, Lawrence E. Alley, not Ali. Greg Matics, who wrote the story, tells us he was merely writing down what Mr. Safreed said and may not have gotten the spelling down correctly (note the spelling of "Acro Agate" quoted in the same article above).

Ravenswood Glass and Novelty Company has its roots in another local industry; the Ravenswood Porcelain Company. Began in 1921, the Ravenswood Porcelain Company officers were J. H. Camp, J. W. Hall, M. E. Ginther, C. E. Mason, F. D. Fleming, C. W. Turnbull, and Ed Turnbull. The local firm was later to become Trenle-Blake China Company. These companies did not manufacture glass but two of the employees, Charles W. Turnbull and C. E. Mason, would leave the porcelain business and become founders with others, including Turnbull's brother Frank, of the local glass marble factory in Ravenswood.

Corporation papers were filed with the West Virginia Secretary of States' office with Charles W. Turnbull and Frank Turnbull (secretary-treasurer) as well as Darrell Rector, W. C. Clark, Lawrence E. Alley, and Charles E. Mason (president) to charter Ravenswood Glass and Novelty Company, on April 11, 1928. The amount of authorized capital stock of the business was $25,000, which was divided into 250 shares with a value of $100. The amount of the capital stock sold with which the company commenced business was $1,000 with two shares subscribed to each of the five partners.

The chartered purpose of the company was "to mine, quarry, excavate and bore for silica sand and other materials to manufacture glass, glass novelties, and kindred products of every type and description." Transportation, access to fuel, and other natural resources made the Ravenswood area a good location for a glass factory.

Charles and Frank Turnbull were involved in the pottery business for most of their lives and brought their factory management skills to the new company. Frank had been a salesman for the Ravenswood Porcelain Company. Charles E. Mason was President of the First National Bank in Ravenswood and may have played a role limited to finances. Darrel Rector operated a wholesale grocery distribution business in Ravenswood. L. E. (Lawrence) Alley, active in a number of other marble and glass companies, was the only non-Ravenswood resident in this venture, as well as the only practical or experienced glass man. At the time of his involvement in Ravenswood, he was also operating a glass factory in Salem, West Virginia. About the remaining incorporator, W. C. Clark, no information has been found.

An article titled "Glass Marbles by the Millions" by Bill Random in the April 1945 issue of *Science and Mechanics* reads: "The plant in Ravenswood, West Virginia, using typical production methods, in which the accompanying pictures were made, was organized in 1931 as the Ravenswood Novelty Works. In 1943 it shipped about 80 million glass marbles to the trade all over the world. Its owner, C. W. Turnbull, ingenious president of the concern which makes the most of materials at hand, and who designed and built most of the equipment used, took over the business in 1932, and at present manufactures only glass marbles. He intends, after the war, to branch out into the making of general line of glass novelties. After spending a good part of a lifetime, 30 years, in the clay pottery business, Mr. Turnbull took over the plant during the depression, confident that by careful management he could build up a good business. He succeeded, with the help of his wife and two daughters, even though he admits that during the days of the N.R.A. he almost folded up; somehow, however, he managed to keep his corporate body and soul together. As a result of war conditions, considerable difficulty is being experienced in procuring the necessary materials used. In addition to sand (silica), there are some 16 chemical compounds used to control melting temperatures, brittleness, and colors. Some of the ingredients wanted cannot be obtained at all during the war, and substitutes must be used."

Charles Turnbull passed away in 1944 and his widow, Bertha, shut down the operation. In 1947 the Turnbull's daughter Edith, and her husband, Paul Cox, moved from Ohio to Ravenswood to start up the business again. Under the control of Turnbull, Ravenswood Glass Novelty Works had produced its own hot glass from mixing batch (sand, soda, etc.). During the time of Paul Cox, the company no longer made their own glass. Scrap glass was purchased from various places and remelted for making marbles. In a conversation with marble collector David Tamulevich, Paul Cox's son, Charles Cox, recalled that his father would drive to Pennsylvania, Ohio, Indiana, and Illinois to haul truckloads of scrap glass to the factory. They used rejected Pond's Cold Cream jars for their white glass, and there were always large piles of those jars outside the factory.

In a Jackson County (WV) Public Library vertical file is an interesting undated, un-sourced partial newspaper clipping. Titled "Marbles by the Millions Made at Ravenswood Plant", the information in it places the article somewhere after 1947 (the year Paul Cox joined the company) and the early 1950s.

The article states that at that time Ravenswood Novelty Works employed ten people and shipped an average of thirty-two railroad carloads of marbles a year. It estimated three million marbles to a carload – putting the average yearly production at that time at 109 million marbles per year. This same article also tells us that, by adjusting the machinery, "seven sizes of marbles can be made, ranging from 1/2" to 1-1/4"." The authors know of Ravenswood marbles as small as 1/2" but have never seen or heard reports of Ravenswood marbles as large as 1-1/4".

Earlier books on marble collecting state that the marbles as large as 1" packaged and labeled by Ravenswood as "Paul Bunyans" were all made about 100 miles away at the Master Glass Company in Bridgeport, West Virginia. Charles Cox, son of Paul Cox and grandson of Charles Turnbull, states that he recalls Paul Bunyans were in fact made in the Ravenswood factory. It is possible that 1" marbles were both made at Ravenswood and purchased from other manufacturers to go into Ravenswood packages.

Besides marbles produced as toys, some Ravenswood marbles were sold for industrial purposes. A significant Ravenswood account was the Krylon Paint Corporation, which purchased as many as a million marbles a month to use as agitators in spray paint cans. Charles Cox states that when the marble company was failing and had stopped producing marbles, his father continued to supply marbles he purchased from Vitro Agate Company to Krylon. Eventually someone at the paint company figured out that they could buy the same marbles directly from Vitro Agate at a better price.

Ravenswood stopped producing marbles in 1955, a time when a lot of marble companies were having a difficult time making a profit. Marbles were less popular with children as toys and there was competition from less expensive Japanese imports. When Ravenswood closed, only five companies remained actively engaged in American marble production.

In an interview that marble producer Jack Bogard granted David Tamulevich in 2000, Bogard reported he acquired one of the Ravenswood marble machines from the factory in the 1970s for the Bogard factory in Cairo, West Virginia. He further related that one of the machines was sold to Don Michels for Champion Agate in Pennsboro. The Ravenswood factory building sat vacant from 1955 until 1975 when Bobby J. and Virginia King purchased it for use as a storage facility. It now sits on a well-manicured lawn in the middle of a residential area without a scrap of glass anywhere in sight and very little evidence that is was once a marble factory.

Ravenswood Marbles Produced

All Ravenswood marbles of less than 1" were random pattern. Thus there are no Ravenswood patched, ribboned, spiral or cat's eye designs in sizes other than the 1" marbles.

Ravenswood Novelty Works appears to have been unique in its use of brown as a "base color." This is opposed to marbles from other manufacturers that have brown striping on a white or a different color base/underlying body color. A significant percentage, greater than twenty percent, of random pattern swirl marbles in pre-1950s groupings of marbles gathered by the authors appear to be the products of this factory. We draw no specific conclusions from this observation at this time but it may address their success on distribution and/or production.

Color combinations believed to be unique to Ravenswood swirls include opaque brown with green striping, opaque brown with blue striping, opaque green with black striping, and an opaque white with transparent green striping thinly traced with oxblood-like coloring. Other color combinations made at Ravenswood but NOT unique to the company include white with transparent orange or red striping, opaque white with opaque or transparent green striping, opaque gray with translucent lavender striping, translucent green, blue, amber or yellow with opaque white striping. Other Ravenswood's swirls are less unique to this Ravenswood. Sometimes random Ravenswood swirls are indistinguishable from those of Cairo Novelty, Heaton Agate, Playrite, Davis Marble Works, Jackson Marble Company, and Alley Agate Company.

One opinion heard from marble collectors is that there is a similarity between a Ravenswood "flame" pattern marble and the more sought-after Christensen Agate design. "Flame" is a marble collector's term for a striping that has many finger-like points dramatically leaping out of a base color.

Ravenswood Packaging

Ravenswood packaged their 5/8", "regular" sized, marbles in cardboard boxes and in mesh and later poly bags with a header proclaiming them "Buddy" marbles. Most Buddy packages do not mention Ravenswood, West Virginia, or the Ravenswood Novelty firm. Boxes were made to contain quantities of 19, 20, 25, or 30 marbles per box. There were bags with quantities of 14, 19, 20, 25, 30, 40, 50, or 100 marbles per bag. The first bags were mesh and then in the 1950s a plastic or poly bag making machine was purchased. This machine was housed and operated in the Cox family home! A single sheet of type-written text on Ravenswood Novelty factory letterhead was found left behind in the factory after closing. It survived possibly because it was attached to something else. This page appears to be a reference guide for employees who were filling orders. It might specify the quantities per size of packaged marbles to be placed in the larger shipping carton. It lists retail boxes, poly bags, and mesh bags of varying sizes as well as loose or bulk marbles of varying sizes. The authors have been led to believe that once marbles were packaged in plastic or poly bags, then the use of mesh bags was discontinued. If this is true, the mention of mesh bags refers to remaining or older stock. The sheet lists bulk marbles in only three sizes, designated as "#00", "#0", and "#6".

It is specified on the sheet that the "#6" size was a one inch marble. This is compatible with a standard marble-sizing system that originated with the Akro Agate Company and is still used by marble manufacturers operating today. The "#0" size would refer to the common 5/8th inch diameter marbles and the "#00" to a slightly smaller 9/16" diameter marble. Ravenswood is reported to not have made marbles smaller than 5/8th inch. However, actual marbles as small as 1/2" and smaller were recovered from a site where Ravenswood Novelty marbles and scrap glass were dumped. Colors and striping patterns match exactly other known Ravenswood marbles. Other marbles recovered of other sizes were perfect matches to commonly known Ravenswood production. Ravenswood made some single color transparent marbles in blue or green (called clearies), and a few single color opaque marbles in black or white (like Chinese Checker marbles), but the vast majority they produced were of a randomly swirled or striped pattern using two or three colors per marble. These very attractive swirled marbles appear in a wide range of color combinations (see known color list) and seem to be, from the various groupings available and observed, almost evenly divided in number of opaque, translucent, and transparent varieties. Almost endless combinations abound in color and opacity with striping that is crisp and tight.

Ravenswood's Charles Turnbull (left) and Paul Cox in the 1940s.

Ravenswood clearies. Owner Chamberlain has named these "Gum Drops." *D. Chamberlain photo.*

Ravenswood factory site as it appeared in April 2005.

Ravenswood Glass Novelty Co. letterhead with the principals' names: Mason, Alley, and Turnbull.

Ravenswood's Jane Safreed (left) working a marble bagging machine as Bertha Turnbull looks on in the 1940s. This is a great view of the simple, often homemade machinery utilized in the numerous smaller marble companies.

Ravenswood Novelty Works invoice.

Ravenswood marble bagging machine, still around after years of neglect, presently in a private collection.

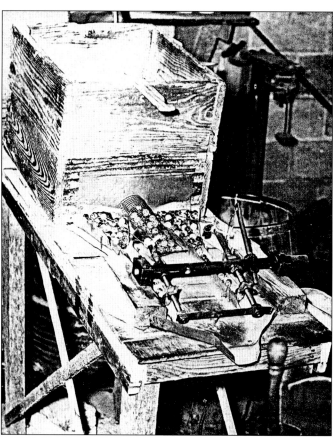

Ravenswood marbles bagging or boxing machine, foot pedal operated. The same machine and chair being used by Jane Safreed.

Ravenswood's Paul Cox holds the wood marble cross to align the marbles to begin the game. Note the visible tension in the three young ladies watching … or almost every other face! Marble tournament held in the spring of 1954, which Martin Harley won. Believed to be Huntington, West Virginia.

Ravenswood's Jane Safreed working the foot pedal on a marble bagging machine to fill jobber's. Photo 1940s, photographer unknown.

RAVENSWOOD NOVELTY WORKS
RAVENSWOOD, WEST VIRGINIA

TOY GLASS MARBLES
MADE IN U. S. A.

QUOTATION FORM

	COUNT		PACKING	WEIGHT	PER GROSS
BOXED MARBLES	19's Boxes 1 Gross Boxes to Carton			33 lbs.	$2.90
Size (0) Approx. ⅝"	30's " 1 " " " "			53 lbs.	$4.50
POLYETHYLENE BAGS	14's Bags 1 " " " "			24 lbs.	$2.75
Size (0) Approx. ⅝"	19's " 1 " " " "			32 lbs.	$3.15
	30's " 1 " " " "			50 lbs.	$5.00
	40's " ½ " " " "			33 lbs.	$6.10
	100's " ¼ " " " "			41 lbs.	$14.75
PAUL BUNYANS	5 1" Shooters, 1 Gross to Carton			33 lbs.	$6.75
					PER M.
BULK	Size 00's 6000 to Carton			60 lbs.	_____
	" 0's 5000 " "			60 lbs.	_____
	" 1's 4000 " "			62 lbs.	_____

TERMS: 2% 10 Days, f. o. b. factory

Ravenswood Novelty toy marbles "quotation form" or price list! Undated.

Ravenswood Novelty catalog page.

Ravenswood's Charles Cox shooting marbles with his cousin Lee Hudkins. Photo 1953 or 1954. Photographer unknown. See front of Ravenswood Novelty catalog.

Ravenswood Novelty catalog page.

Ravenswood Novelty catalog page.

Ravenswood Novelty Works "American Made Quality Marbles" catalog cover. Note the same image of Charles Cox and Lee Hudkins as the original photo shown above.

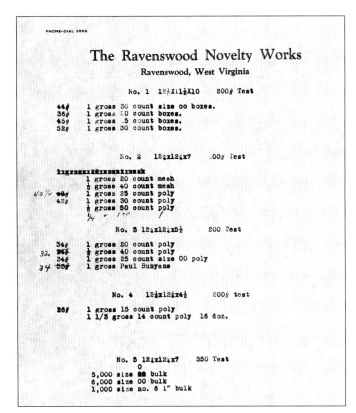

The Ravenswood Novelty Works
Ravenswood, West Virginia

No. 1   12¾X11¾X10   200# Test

44#	1 gross 30 count size oo boxes.	
36#	1 gross 20 count boxes.	
45#	1 gross 25 count boxes.	
52#	1 gross 30 count boxes.	

No. 2   12¾x12x7   00# Test

1 gross 20 count mesh
½ gross 40 count mesh
1 gross 25 count poly
1 gross 30 count poly
½ gross 50 count poly

No. 3   12¾x12½x5½   200 Test

34# 1 gross 20 count poly
32   ½ gross 40 count poly
34# 1 gross 25 count size 00 poly
34   1 gross Paul Bunyans

No. 4   12¾x12¾x4½   200# test

26# 1 gross 15 count poly
1 1/3 gross 14 count poly 16 doz.

No. 5   12¾x12¾x7   350 Test
0
5,000 size 22 bulk
6,000 size 00 bulk
1,000 size no. 6 1" bulk

Ravenswood list of marbles made at the time, including box weights and type of bags in each box. Believed to be circa 1950s.

Ravenswood marble machine in storage, later donated to JABO. *Dennis Webb photo collection.*

The Ravenswood Novelty Works
Ravenswood, W. Va.

Ravenswood marbles in jobber's cut away box. *C. Kobata photo.* Box empty, $10; as shown, $25.

Ravenswood marbles in jobber's cut away box. *D. Chamberlain collection and photo.* Box empty, $10; as shown, $25.

Ravenswood unused Buddy box. $10-15.

Ravenswood Novelty Works imprinted box of Chinese Checker. 60 count No. 00 size game marbles. *Shepherd collection.* No value determined.

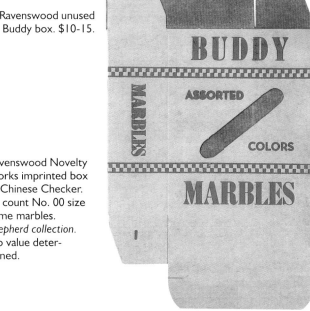

Ravenswood mesh "Buddy" 12 count bag. *Shepherd collection.* No value determined.

Ravenswood Novelty Works. Bag of 100 count swirls. Buddy poly bag. *Weekley collection. J. Thompson photo.* $150-200.

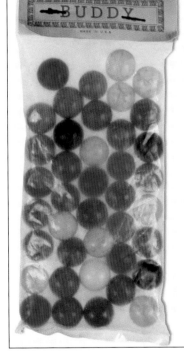

Ravenswood Novelty Works. 1" Paul Bunyans, 5 count mesh bag. *J. Thompson photo.* $25-30.

Ravenswood Novelty Works "Buddy" poly bag of glassies. *D. Chamberlain collection. J. Thompson photo.* $20-25.

Ravenswood different "Buddy" bags. *C. Cox collection.* No value determined.

Ravenswood Novelty Works. "Buddy" poly bag of 15 swirls. *J. Thomspon photo.* $10-15.

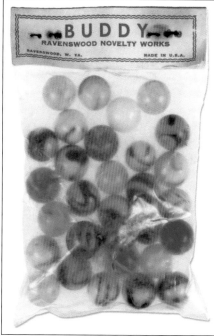

Ravenswood Novelty Works. "Buddy" poly bag of 30 count swirls. *J. Thompson photo.* $20.

Ravenswood Novelty Works. "40 Buddy 40" poly bag of swirls. *Cox collection. J. Thompson photo.* $30-50.

Selection of colorful Ravenswood production. *D. Chamberlain photo.*

VACOR DE MEXICO

Mexico City, Mexico
1934 - 1974
Guadalajara, Jalisco State, Mexico
1974 - operating at the time of publication

Vacor of Mexico production
examples. *D. Chamberlain photo.*

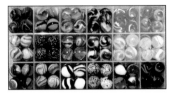

Vacor of Mexico production
examples. *D. Chamberlain photo.*

Vacor de Mexico was founded in Mexico City in 1930 and produced clay marbles for its first four years, with an output of 35,000 marbles a day. In 1934 Vacor began producing crystal marbles in four basic colors: blue, green, amber, and clear. Two standard marble machines were used and the daily production rate was 80,000 pieces.

Little is known today of the marbles produced during those early years.

In 1944, Vacor started producing a "cat's eye" marble which was primarily used as eyes in stuffed and ceramic animals. These marbles predate the cat's eyes imported into the U.S. by Japan in the post-World War II era – the same marbles that wreaked havoc on the U.S. marble industry. During this time, company production was increased to meet the demand in local markets in Mexico.

A huge step forward was taken in 1974 when Vacor decided to enter the international market. With marbles being an increasingly popular product in Europe, Vacor immediately implemented aggressive operative strategies to enlarge commercial production. They moved the manufacturing from Mexico City to a huge facility in Guadalajara, Jalisco State, where it has been since then, in the Zona Industrial. It is this post-1974 expansion into the world market and specifically into the U.S. that interests collectors today.

Vacar's success has continued, and, in part, is maintained by its ability to deliver new and fascinating lines of marbles year after year, adding them to the already wide Vacor catalog. Vacor's marble palate has expanded to more than sixty different types of marbles, generating new enthusiasts and maintaining the interest of old collectors.

With technological improvements in machinery as well as in the fabrication of glass itself, Vacor (in 2004) produces twenty million marbles a day, available in ten sizes and for different purposes: toy marbles, decorative marbles and nuggets, and industrial marbles.

Now with its seventy-four years of continuous operation, Vacor De Mexico S.A. de C.V. employs more than five hundred persons working in the following areas: Customer Service, Production, Marketing, Accounting, Computer Systems, and Research and Development.

Vacor exports its products to over forty-two countries and is aggressive in its search for the new markets and opportunities around the world.

Vacor provided the authors with these notes as a year by year highlight of production and growth:

1930 – Clay marbles
1934 – Glass machine-made marbles
1944 – Cat's eye marbles
1978 – Nuggets for the game Pente
1979 – First big size marbles (30 mm 1-1/4")

1983 – Nuggets for decorative purposes
1984 – First iridescent marbles (Silver, Diamond, Pearls)
1985 – Printed marbles (pad printing with epoxy inks)
1992 – Handmade marbles, 25mm, 35mm, 42mm
1993 – First 42mm (1-5/8") marbles, machine-made.
1997 – First 50mm (2") marbles, machine-made.
1999 – Printed marbles with decals (character and advertising)
1999 – Metallic nuggets
2002 – Re-launch of clay marbles.
2003 – Handmade marbles for collectors

Vacor also reported to the authors that in 2004 they utilized thirty marble machines operating in a building of 100,000 square feet. Their biggest customers are in the USA and Mexico. Contrary to speculation, Vacor receives no subsidies from the Mexican government. Vacor does not trade or sell marbles with other manufacturers and has a longtime working relationship with the House of Marbles in England.

The first marble machine was bought in Mexico; however, the machine came from the United States. They bought the machine not from a marble manufacturer, but from a company that had nothing to do with marbles.

Vacor does use recycled glass in the manufacture of some marbles. However, for base glass, and its uniformity, formula or batched glass is made. The proportions for each formula and the components used depend on the color desired. Yuriko Sutto, Information Director and International Sales Representative for Vacor de Mexico explained to the authors, "It is like a cake recipe. Depending on the flavor you are cooking, so depends the ingredients you use."

Vacor marbles, when found broken, appear to be found in both states: solid colors and veneered. Vacor is required by Mexican law to follow various rules to assure they do not contaminate the environment, not entirely unlike U.S. EPA standards.

In the late 1990s, Vacor's marbles were greatly improved in that the "orange peel" texture previously found on the surface had been eliminated from most marbles.

Chelly Schmidt of Mega™ Marbles related to the authors that Mega™ Marbles was established in 1992 to be the U.S. distributor for Vacor. Prior to that, Vacor marbles were distributed in the U.S. by Pioneer Balloon Co., which, like Mega, was also based in Wichita. The CFO/COO, Ron Garcia, was formerly the CFO at Pioneer and handled Vacor's marble program there.

VACOR Marbles Produced

The marbles produced by Vacor de Mexico are as varied in styles, colors, and sizes as any marbles made by any company at any period of time. Opaque solids, cat's eyes, translucent and transparent swirls, stripes, iridescents, you name it and Vacor made it. Some swirl marbles even seem to corkscrew. There are types that get confused with Akro Agate, Cardinal Reds, Christensen Agate Cyclones, and even the Peltier Superman. They even come with fantastic names – some company inspired, others tagged on by Mega™ Marbles, the U.S. importer.

Mega™ Marbles has a rich catalog of marbles and marble related items such as marble game mats, Chinese Checker boards, necklaces, and key chains. Dozens of other gift ideas in glass are available as well and the offerings grow each year.

VACOR Identification Tips

Little notice was taken by collectors before the 1990s and it is now almost impossible to determine what the early Vacor marbles were like. Company records and archives are not as complete as would be helpful to researchers.

With Vacor and its U.S. distributor, Mega™ Marbles, aggressively seeking new interest and new markets, new and creative styles are released every year, seemingly at a breath-taking pace, combining a bright color palette and interesting names. These marbles are eagerly sought by some old-time collectors who find the price range of Akro Agate, Peltier, and other big names too steep.

The best way to identify Vacor marbles is by seeing them in their original Mexican packaging or in the packages offered by Mega™ Marbles. The marbles are usually identified on the bag header by name. The Mega company catalogs are excellent aids in determining what marbles were available in what years. Examples of these are used with permission here.

Another way to identify Vacor marbles is by the oily sheen on the surface of many opaques especially. This is reminiscent of some Champion Agate Marbles of the 1980s.

Older marbles, and especially larger sizes (even today), often have what is called an "orange peel" texture. This is the result of not periodically cleaning the rollers. This problem has been somewhat eliminated in recent years as the quality of the Vacor products continues to climb.

Vacor's American logo for Mega Marbles.

Vacor of Mexico logo and address as it appears on corporate letterhead.

VACOR Packaging

Many retail outlets in the United States carry Vacor marbles for sale in a multitude of eye-catching packaging and displays. Imported from Mexico may be found all the various styles in mesh bags with colorful headers displaying the company name as well as the name of the marbles. Most of the Vacor packaging that is familiar in the U.S. is provided by Mega™ Marbles, the major distributor this side of the border.

Most bags with Mega™ headers may be seen on counter and free standing display sales racks with headers that are colorful and the style of marble is named. They even advertise the header cards as collectible and tradable. Individual marbles may be purchased from 9, 18, or 24 bin bulk display cases. Other packaging includes collector bags, tins, canisters and leather or muslin pouches. Most come with printed sets of rules for marble games.

Vacor of Mexico marbles machines in operation. Notice the exceptionally long trough for the marbles to roll down in the foreground. It ends in the square container, strikingly similar to the process used everywhere else the authors have observed. *Photo compliments of Monica Garcia.*

Vacor of Mexico factory in Guadalajara, Mexico. *Photo compliments of Monica Garcia.*

Vacor of Mexico storage facility. Nothing of this scale has ever been used by any U.S. marble manufacturer. *Photo compliments of Monica Garcia.*

Vacor of Mexico marbles packaged for domestic consumption in Mexico. "Canicas" is Spanish for marbles. *Photo compliments of Monica Garcia.* $3-5.

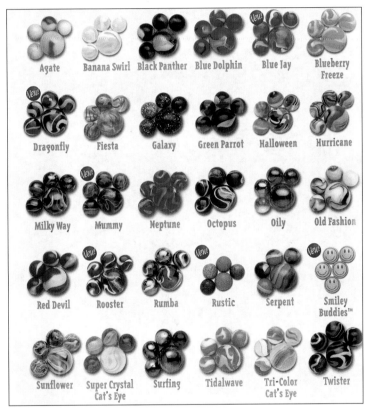

Agate   Banana Swirl   Black Panther   Blue Dolphin   Blue Jay   Blueberry Freeze

Dragonfly   Fiesta   Galaxy   Green Parrot   Halloween   Hurricane

Milky Way   Mummy   Neptune   Octopus   Oily   Old Fashion

Red Devil   Rooster   Rumba   Rustic   Serpent   Smiley Buddies™

Sunflower   Super Crystal Cat's Eye   Surfing   Tidalwave   Tri-Color Cat's Eye   Twister

Vacor of Mexico catalog spread sheet, circa late 1990s, as prepared by Mega Marble. *Used by permission of Mega Marble.*

Vacor of Mexico packaging and shipping operation. *Photo compliments of Monica Garcia.*

Vacor of Mexico products as packaged by Mega Marble for the U.S. markets, includes spinner racks and catchy individual labels for each marble style. Future collectables? *Used by permission of Mega Marble.*

Playful New Header Cards to Collect and Trade

THE VITRO AGATE COMPANY

Vienna (Paramco), West Virginia 1932-1945
Parkersburg, West Virginia 1945-1987
Anacortes, Washington 1987-1992
Williamstown, West Virginia 1992-2004

Vitro Agate, Vienna, West Virginia, examples of early production. *D. Chamberlain photo.*

Vitro Agate, Parkersburg, West Virginia, examples of production. *D. Chamberlain photo.*

Vitro Agate, Parkersburg, West Virginia, production of Blackies and All Reds. *D. Chamberlain photo.*

Few of the American marble manufacturers have histories as long, complicated, and filled with legend, interesting detail, and rumor as does the Vitro Agate Company and its name reincarnations.

However, the historical records speak for themselves. The West Virginia Secretary of State's office recorded that on April 13, 1932, George W. Johnson, Anna M. Stephenson, and Myrtle G. Smith, all of Parkersburg, West Virginia, were by their signatures, the true founders and investors in Vitro Agate. The Johnson and Stephenson families were prominent Parkersburg, West Virginia, people with social and financial connections allowing them to enter into such a business venture. The stated purpose of the company, as recorded, was "to buy, sell, decorate and manufacture transparent, translucent and opaque glassware and novelties of every description, and in all colors, blown, rolled, cast, pressed and formed."

George W. Johnson (1869 - 1944) was a lawyer and a member of the United States House of Representatives from Parkersburg, West Virginia. He served in the House of Representatives in 1923 - 1925 and again from 1933 - 1943. Myrtle G. Smith (born 1910) was a stenographer employed by Mr. Johnson. Anna M. Stephenson (born 1894) lived on the socially prestigious Juliana St. with her mother and sisters. She owned property which was valued at $80,000 at the time Vitro was begun, that is to say she was a reasonably wealthy woman. She was thirty-seven, single, and being a woman of property, was in a position to invest in a glass company. (Parkersburg City Directories)

Marble lore has centered upon Lawrence E. Alley, Art Fisher, and Prestley Lindsay as the original incorporators of Vitro Agate. This simply is not so. Much research was necessary to cleanse away old myths and misconceptions here as in much of the oral traditions that have grown in part through a lack of historical research and writing about marbles. The true identify of the original incorporators is part of the West Virginia historical record that cannot be changed.

Vitro Agate was incorporated and issued capital stock as a company with shares representing the ownership of the business. The total of authorized stock was $25,000, and not necessarily all that being sold, but it was divided into 1250 shares with a price of $20.00 each. The amount of capital with which the company commenced operations was only $15,000. This was 750 shares at $20 each.

Henry Arthur Fisher entered the picture as an enthusiastic plant manager from the Vitrolite Company, a glass company, who had an idea to start a marble company. He went to George W. Johnson's law office for help. Fisher had the knowledge to equip and operate a glass plant, but he was not in a position to finance it.

The Vitrolite Company (1907 - 1935) located in Vienna, then called Parmico, and very near Parkersburg, also employed Prestley Lindsay as a manager. This company produced colorful, heavyweight opaque architectural glass which was popular in the Art Deco Era. This glass was extensively used as bar backs, wainscoting, counter and table tops, signs, and paperweights.

Vitrolite historian, Edelene Wood, a student of Vitrolite Glass in Parkersburg said, "I was told the true story of the beginning of the Vitro Agate Company from J. Prestley Lindsay's wife. Arthur Fisher conceived of the idea to make marbles from cullet he acquired from the Vitrolite Company while he was still plant manager."

It was about this time that the services of Fisher and Lindsay were no longer required at Vitrolite. We know only that some unpleasant parting of the ways occurred and a conflict with their work at Vitrolite and their new enterprise was the root of it.

In a 1961 interview, Professor Adrian L. Headley wrote of Art Fisher in an unidentified magazine: "Henry Arthur Fisher was born in Bridgeport, Connecticut (1893), and grew up as a true Texas cowboy on a ranch near Hereford, Texas. While he was twelve years old and living at the 7 Bar Ranch, he participated in a roundup with the former outlaw Cole Younger. He knew Cash Whitsett and Tow Bassett who had ridden with Quantrill's Raiders. Fisher participated in the last roundup at the famous XIT Ranch. Two eyewitness accounts from later years tell of Fisher occasionally wearing a pair of six-shooters around the Vitro plant just to recall a more than average childhood. Fisher was a veteran of The Great War and in the early 1920s, worked as a construction superintendent in Florida, a state he grew to love and in later years vacationed there often and eventually retired to with his second wife. In 1926, a hurricane struck the Miami area leaving thousands of people homeless, including Fisher. This single event would bring him to West Virginia and a lifelong career in the glass industry. Fisher was an avid fisherman. He created lures for his own use and as gifts for friends. He fished the waters of Florida, Nova Scotia, Peru, Ecuador, Columbia, Panama, and Cuba."

As a father, Art Fisher was proud of his children. His daughter, Jackee, was an accomplished contralto soloist with the Boston Philharmonic as well as a featured star with the Radio City Music Hall. She made an appearance in a production of *South Pacific*. She was "discovered" after being seen on the "Arthur Godfrey Talent Hour." His son, Arthur Jr., made a career in the U.S. Army as an attorney with the rank of captain. He was instrumental in Vitro Agate, learning the secret of producing cat's eye marbles, and wrote the appeals to various congressional committees and government agencies that were presented to those bodies by Roger Howdyshell of Marble King.

Although Fisher is not recorded as one of the original incorporators, he is later listed as president of the company in various directories and company documents. Over the next several years after starting up, George W. Johnson is shown as vice-president and J. Prestley Lindsay as secretary. After that, Howard Hildreth is listed as vice-president and Edith Fisher as secretary.

Henry Arthur Fisher opened up the first Vitro Agate marble factory in Vienna (then called Parmico), a suburb of Parkersburg, West Virginia. The building had once been called the Old Engine House but during Vitro's tenure it was part of the Universal Glass complex. The address was on Stonewall Ave. (now called Grand Central Ave.) between 11th and 12th Streets. In those days, 11th St. was called Charlotte Ave. and 12th St. was known as Forest Ave. Today the site is part of a large shopping center and paved parking lots. Nothing remains of any part of the glass industry that once flourished there.

The name for the company, Vitro, comes from Latin meaning "in glass" and the incorporators, possibly influenced by Fisher and Lindsay, took the actual name from the Vitrolite Company. Early Vitro Agate marbles played on the Vitrolite name with names such as "Tri-lite" and "Clear-lite."

Little is known about the early days of the Vitro Agate Company in Vienna and few "I was there" accounts have been found. William Tescher was a tank man in Vienna from 1934 to 1936 and he recalled for the authors at the West Virginia Marble Festival in Cairo, West Virginia, in 1998 that early on Vitro had only one tank and one machine, but did expand later on. There was a machine shop on the premises and Mr. Fisher did a lot of experimenting making machines. Tescher told the authors he worked a twelve hour shift and was responsible for filling five 5-gallon buckets of marbles during the shift; his was a night shift.

If they were pushed for orders, they would set the buckets outside so the marbles would cool more quickly. Tescher would spend idle time putting marble boxes together and stitching and lacing marble pouches for the boxes. In 1935 he received, as a Christmas gift from Mr. Fisher, a Vitro Agate production-style lamp with crystal marbles, which he retained for many years.

Vitro Agate set the standards for survival during the Great Depression, World War II, and later during the first incursions of cheap foreign competition. Art Fisher was a man of seemingly boundless energy and ideas. Even into his last years as president, he would parade around the plant shirtless in winter breathing in the fumes of toxic production, singing opera arias, and boasting that the smell of the place made him strong.

For Fisher and Vitro Agate, much of the success came from endless research and invention. The unique method of attaching marbles to metal for the production of lamps and jewel trays and innovations in working glass and marble design served the company well.

Among Fisher's more significant innovations were the cage style cat's eye design, which helped Vitro to stay in the game against Japanese imports and developed (about the same time that Roger Howdyshell did at Marble King) a method of veneering a marble. This innovation alone revolutionized the marble industry by making it possible to use less colored glass.

Vitro Agate moved to East Street in Parkersburg in 1945, where it remained for over forty years. According to Lewis L. Moore, a longtime Vitro employee, the plant in Parkersburg started life as a barrel plant for Standard Oil in the 1920s. The place was solidly built with a concrete floor four to six feet thick. They had a dreadful time punching holes in the walls for the glass tanks. There was lots of steel in the walls and work that should have taken only a couple of hours took all day.

Both plants (Vienna and Parkersburg) had in-house machine shops. All the original marble machines were built under the direction of Fisher and could produce up to 220 marbles a minute, depending on the size and gearing.

Fisher set up a nice lunchroom (in Parkersburg) with a stove and "icebox." Fancy restrooms were installed and even the executive office was fixed up and had walls of polished knotty pine. His standing order was to keep everything clean. All work areas and glass piles were to be checked daily for orderliness according to Patty Pfalzgraf and Lewis Moore.

Mrs. Lena Moore Hunter was a Vitro Agate employee from 1955 to 1980. She told the authors that she began working at Vitro for 25 cents an hour and her shift was from 6:30 a.m. 'til 5:30 p.m. She got one whole hour for lunch and a ten minute rest break, which was timed. She later became a "floor lady" responsible for getting orders out. At one time, she had thirty-one girls and five boys working under her. She said mixing chemicals and working the "hot end" of the plant was rough on the men doing it. Art Fisher could be hard to work for and often reminded the women there that girls were "a dime a dozen" and easily replaced. The women weren't supposed to look around or engage in chatter while they worked, Hunter recalled.

Carmen Queen, in a phone interview on March 9, 2003, stated that she worked at Vitro Agate for thirty-three years, from 1957 to 1989. She worked during the winters only for the first few years during production and packaging times. Vitro had various pay scales and employees were instructed upon hire to never discuss their pay with other employees. Ones caught doing so were dismissed. She recalled that some workers got bonuses. At first she was scared to death of Mr. Fisher and kept her distance. He seemed so loud and overpowering. Once, after a small increase in the minimum wage, Fisher came into the packaging area with a stopwatch and sat in a bin of marbles and timed the girls. Lena Moore, her supervisor, instructed all the girls to have nothing to do with the men who worked there. Mrs. Queen's second job was packaging samples, the best of each kind. She sent them, in sets, to different companies. Sometimes Mr. Fisher would come by to look at them.

One source of important information on life at Vitro Agate was Patty Roberts Pfalzgraf, who started working at Vitro right out of high school in 1953 and remained until 1969, finally becoming Mr. Fisher's permanent secretary. She related two tragedies in Art Fisher's life. His first wife, Edith Campbell Fisher, died of cancer in Florida and was buried in Mt. Olivet Cemetery in Parkersburg. Son, Art Jr., disappeared in a plane crash over the Everglades in Florida. His body was never recovered. She described Fisher as a perfectionist; he wanted everything to look clean and tidy and wanted to see everyone working all the time. The East Street building was very cold in the winter. Fisher said they didn't need heat if they were working. The women wore gloves and would sit with their feet stuck in buckets of marbles to keep them warm. Once an IRS agent came to audit Vitro. He kept asking for all sorts of files. Pfalzgraf thought it was scary. After a while, the agent demanded to see this and that. Fisher finally told him "Litigate and be damned!" The agent left and they never heard another word from them.

She further reminisced that Fisher hired a lot of transient worker who never seemed to stay long. Fisher would not let the union in – it came in much later. He said anyone who was dissatisfied could go elsewhere, that the men were easily replaced. Vitro Agate bought a lot of glass from Fenton (Williamstown, West Virginia). Truckloads would come in and employees would go out and look them over. Sometimes there were virtually whole pieces, factory rejects, to be melted down. Vitro employees would take them home. She has a few pieces.

Lewis L. Moore, who worked at Vitro Agate for almost forty years, had vivid memories of what went on there and his personal notebook has been most helpful in describing activities at the plant. Here are some of his thoughts: "Most of the marble companies used lead crystal glass until 1960 when federal regulations forced them to use other materials. Art Fisher worked extensively with lime crystal until he got it perfected. It is still used in the industry today. Unless there was a specific order or deadline to meet, the shift foreman selected the marbles to be made on his shift. Vitro sold industrial marbles and one-color opaque to Ravenswood Novelty Works. Vitro also sold one-color opaque to Champion Agate. Vitro never sold 'seconds', Fisher said it was bad advertising."

Moore recalled that in World War II, 7/8" industrial crystals of hardened glass were used in the turrets of bombers. They were lighter than steel and needed no lubrication. For atom bomb tests in Nevada, the government dug holes and filled them with several truckloads of Vitro marbles. Moore, when pointedly asked, was uncertain why this strange activity occurred but recalled it clearly.

Vitro had three foot diameter fans placed by the marble machines to keep the workers cool or at least to draw away some heat. If a fan was accidentally moved or turned and blew onto the hot rollers, the marbles would pop like popcorn. In 1956, Vitro had two natural gas wells dug on the property. They saved considerable money, Moore said.

In a 1996 interview with the authors, Mr. Moore told a few more stories about his time at Vitro Agate. He recalled that Mr. Fisher could not figure out how the Japanese made their cat's eye marbles. So his son, Henry Art, Jr., who was in the army and stationed in Japan, visited one of their marble factories. They liked him and showed him everything about their process. He returned with the necessary information to help Vitro enter the cat's eye market. Of course, Fisher experimented until he came up with a pleasing cat's eye design wholly different from the others.

There are a number of newspaper accounts available for study which relate the challenge to the American marble industry by the Japanese producers. In an interview in the *Marietta (Ohio) Times* in August 1988, Lewis L. Moore stated, "Japan began to make clear cat-eye marbles in 1953, and the eight American marble companies demanded that the government raise the tariff. The government refused, but some marble makers started cutting the quality of their marbles, selling them cheaper and beating the Japanese at their own game. But Fisher refused. He didn't want to sell junk. He was going to make a quality marble. If people didn't want to buy his marbles, he was going to lock the door, move to Florida, get out his rod and reel and do some fishing."

On a similar note, the *Parkersburg News* on Sunday, November 27, 1960, reported:

"Fisher has never consented to purchase a packaging machine, for he believes that the packaging of the finished product is one of the most important aspects of sales. By using women to package the marbles, the Parkersburg industrialist is able to arrange the marbles in the most pleasing manner." This same article went on to describe Vitro's challenge to the Japanese. It tells of the development of the original "All-Red", one of the most popular and collectible of Vitro marbles today. It says in part: "Vitro Agate produces 2,164,000 marbles daily … Eighty persons of the Parkersburg area are employed by the company, and have recently set a trend which has challenged the entire Japanese marble industry … Until a short time ago, Japanese marbles had taken complete control of the world market, specializing in 'Cat-Eyes' at an exceptionally low price. Last year, after three months of research, Fisher put his 'All-Red' on the market, and the reception has been far greater than anticipated. As an example, Australian dealers have ordered more of the new marble than the company has been able to produce at the moment. The new marble is one marked by streaks of color, with red being predominant. As the marble rolls across the floor, it appears to be red. Orders have come from many parts of the world, even though the price is one hundred percent higher than that of Japanese marbles."

Several longtime Vitro Agate employees have expressed to the authors a desire to tell of their experience at Vitro Agate or of things that stand out in their minds as things worth remembering. An interview with Blaine Lemon, Vitro employee and eventual plant manager on April 28, 1999, revealed the following: Lemon was employed at Vitro from 1940 to 1941 and again from 1945 to 1967.

Lemons recalled that Vitro sold industrial marbles to Plasticote – one and a half million a year. They also sold to Milton Bradley and J. Pressman Toy Co. Art Fisher liked tight control; if something needed to be done, one had to get him to think it was his idea said Lemon. Vitro usually shut the majority of marble machines down during the summer for overhaul and routine maintenance but kept two machines running to keep the best crews employed.

Mr. Fisher, Lemon said, didn't like to keep a huge inventory stock of marbles on hand; it made him nervous, like they weren't selling any. Gradually this policy changed as the need for immediate deliveries to demanding customers became more common.

Lemon stated that it took four years to get the veneering process perfected but it helped reduce costs and kept the company competitive. Vitro got glass from many suppliers and also made their own from formula.

He also stated that Vitro spied on Marble King and Marble King spied on Vitro. They looked through windows and unattended doors. Sometimes a slingshot was used to scare lookers away. No one ever got hurt according to Lemon.

Art Fisher spent much time drafting letters to Congress about Japanese imports, which hurt Vitro for about a year before they got set up to run their own version of cat's eye marbles.

It is not widely known, but several employees at Vitro made jewelry using Vitro marbles. Necklaces, bracelets, and earrings were the dominate forms. Fisher, Blaine, Lemon, and others made and gave these but they were never a company product nor commercially produced. They used mostly crystals and fried marbles. Fisher gave a lot of jewelry away; mostly to waitresses and other service industry people. He had a lot of fun with it.

Moore remembered that Marx, Pressman, and Milton Bradley toy companies were always in touch with Fisher about his ideas for games using marbles. He said at the time Parkersburg Vitro Agate was the only major producer to allow tours. Tour were, however, limited to children only. Boy Scouts, youth groups, etc. but no adults. Adults might be able to understand or replicate Vitro processes or machinery and so were not allowed to participate in the tours. Most marble companies were secretive. At one time, Vitro had considered trying a spiral (corkscrew) design marble. Vitro, Moore said, had obtained copies of John F. Early's drawings for the spinner cup attachment used at Akro Agate. Fisher vetoed the project saying they were doing well enough without that expensive design.

Moore made the following notation for the authors concerning the Vitro Agate plant managers. At Vienna it was C. A. Fleak and Howard Hildreth. At the Parkersburg site it was:

Howard Hildreth
Blaine Lemon 1962 - 1967
Doyle I. Gandee 1968 - 1974 (Office Manager and Vice President)
Lewis L. Moore 1975
Dick Ryan 1976 - 1978
Lewis L. Moore 1979 - 1989

In December 1963, Art Fisher revised the Vitro Agate incorporation charter to include not only glassware novelties, but to include objects made of "metal, plastic or synthetic, or other substances of any kind or character."

The 1960s were not easy years for the marble industry as a whole and much of the output was industrials. However, Vitro Agate weathered the downturn in this decade well enough, as a February 7, 1966, article in the *Parkersburg News* shows: "The seven automatic marble-making machines at Vitro Agate have been working twenty-four hours a day since fall turning out three million marbles a day. (Art Fisher) The owner said that this will be a good year for marbles and he expects as much as a twenty percent gain in sales this year."

Within three years, however, Vitro Agate, with Henry Arthur Fisher at the helm, would be history. At a stockholder's meeting on January 3, 1969, with President F. Earl Martin presiding, it was determined: "Vitro Agate Company…does hereby discontinue business as a corporation and surrenders to said state its charter and corporate franchise."

It was signed by the Secretary of State for West Virginia on May 2, 1969.

Henry Fisher remarried in Florida (where he is buried). His second wife made him sell the marble factory. She reportedly thought marble-making was "low-class." Fisher was in his 70s when he sold Vitro Agate to Gladding. "He sold it ridiculously cheap through Merrill Lynch. I could have bought it. Anyone could have bought it. None of us thought that far ahead," said Patty Roberts Pfalzgraff, secretary to Art Fisher.

In 1969, Henry Fisher sold the Vitro Agate Company to Gladding of Syracuse, New York, and the name changed to Gladding-Vitro Agate Company. It is interesting to note, however, that the entity that purchased Vitro Agate at this time was actually Gladding-Kalamazoo, a West

Virginia corporation in its own right. Noteworthy is that Vitro was the first company to make flats or gems in the mid-1970s.

According to Lewis L. Moore, Vitro plant manager, "The company name was changed back to Vitro Agate when Vitro was sold to Paris Manufacturing Corporation of South Paris, Maine, in 1982. The Vitro Agate Corporation was certified as a West Virginia corporation on January 29, 1982. For the next couple of years, however, old stock was being sold and the Gladding-Vitro Agate packaging was used."

From the Paris Industries Annual Report for 1985: Paris Industries Corporation, a Delaware corporation, was organized in 1977 by Henry R. Morton, David A. Johnson, and Clifford L. Parsons in order to acquire the wood and youth products division of the Gladding Corporation. This division, which manufactured and marketed wood and plastic sleds and toboggans, had been purchased by Gladding in 1970, prior to which time it had been operated since 1861, having been founded by Henry F. Morton. In November 1982, a subsidiary of Paris acquired Gladding's Vitro Agate Division, a manufacturer of marbles. On July 3, 1984, the Gladding Corporation was merged into Paris in exchange for shares of common stock, no par value and shares of Class A Preferred Stock of Paris. After the Gladding merger, the company's name was changed from Paris Manufacturing Corporation to Paris Industries Corporation.

In a 1984 interview with Vitro Agate plant manager, Louis L. Moore, Carmen Alvis of the *Parkersburg News* writes: "The marble business has changed hands twice since 1969. Fisher sold the plant to Gladding, and then Gladding sold the plant to Paris Manufacturing Company less than two years ago. Prior to 1982, we were shut down as much as we were in operation. We only had one or two marble machines running; it seemed like all of our employees were laid off. In 1980 when the Gladding Corporation owned the plant, only 316,000 marbles were manufactured each day."

Moore said, "Gladding owned 27 divisions. We were the biggest money-maker and they just kept overlooking us and saying, 'We have got a simple little business, let's keep it that way'. They just wanted to sit back in the easy chair and wait for business to knock on the door. Because of their laziness, Vitro Agate was ready to die."

After Paris Manufacturing Corporation purchased the old marble plant, production more than doubled. Vitro's parent company had plans to upgrade and expand the operation. In 1984, the Vitro Agate Corporation added a 1-1/2" glass marble for decorative purposes to its glass products line. During 1985, the manufacture of marbles, nuggets, flat bottom glass drops used for decorative purposes, and various games continued to be expanded. Vitro Agate suffered a fiscal loss in 1985, which Paris attributed to the merger with Gladding Corporation. The Vitro Agate division's total revenues were $1,164,576, however, the total operating expenses were $1,177,176, resulting in a loss of $12,600. Paris Industries would suffer a total of $770,000 net losses.

During the period 1984 - 1986, Vitro Agate seemed to sink deeper into its slump. There were money problems even though big purchasers like the House of Marbles (England) attempted to expand their Vitro connection.

Chris Cooper, of the National Marble Museum, explained the situation, "The reason the Vitro Agate Corporation failed under Paris Manufacturing had more to do with the Paris Industries and Gladding Corporation merger than it did with Vitro. Paris lost control of just about everything; this happens sometime with a merger, if you don't have the management team and the money to back it up."

Money, materials, and labor all contributed to expanding problems. Lewis L. Moore's notebook entry for August 19, 1984, stated, "I will ask Cliff today if he wants to close the plant for a while 'til we get some material to work with." There were problems with the union as well. The Flint Glass Workers Union, brought in with Paris Manufacturing, presented Vitro with stacks of grievances. Morale problems led to absenteeism and firings. The National Marble Museum, in its Vitro archives, contains dozens of examples concerning those issues.

Paris Industries Corporation and their subsidiaries would continue to suffer problems. The Federal Government filed a lawsuit against Paris for defective children's expandable enclosures. Suppliers and vendors were beginning to have difficulty with several Paris subsidiaries, including the Vitro Agate Corporation. Vitro's cullet supplier had cut them off several times for non-payment, according to Louis Moore's personal notebook. His entry for August 20, 1984, reads:

"Gabbert [a cullet supplier – ed.] is bringing in cullet again so I suppose he won't get paid now and he will cut us off again like he did in June." An earlier entry from the notebook (on July 3, 1984) stated, "I had to lay the girls off because I don't have any cartons to pack the marbles in."

If things were bad enough for the company and its workers during this time, even plant manager Moore had troubles of his own. He relates this story from 1986: "In my office at the plant I had a picture of Art Fisher hanging on the wall. I figured it should still be part of the company even though it has had several owners since. A general manager from one of these later owners came into my office and tossed the picture in the wastebasket. I took it out, dusted it off, and hung it back on the wall. When the manager noticed it was hanging up again, he warned me that the company's president wouldn't appreciate this show of rebellion. I said that if the picture was taken down again, I'd take my check and finish out the day. The picture stayed."

The *Parkersburg News*, in recounting the story of the situation at Vitro Agate in an article dated Wednesday, March 2, 1988, wrote "Production at Vitro Agate was shut down for three months last summer (1987) when Paris Industries of South Paris, Maine, the former owner, filed for Chapter 11 bankruptcy. When production resumed in the fall, the marble industry had lost it's only unionized labor force."

The law firm of Ronning and Brown of Parkersburg, West Virginia, submitted documents on August 11, 1987, to Tim Sullivan and Dick Ryan of the Viking Rope Company of Anacortes, Washington, outlining the purchase of the Vitro Agate Corporation. Included was an accounting of delinquent property taxes from the previous owner, Paris Manufacturing, and a listing of other judgments against Vitro Agate. On September 29, 1987, the Viking Rope Company became a West Virginia corporation.

Dick Ryan had been plant manager of Vitro Agate from 1976 to 1978 and it was his experience and awareness that led him and the Viking Rope Corporation of Anacortes, Washington, to be interested in Vitro Agate.

On July 22, 1988, Ronning and Brown informs the office of the Secretary of State of West Virginia to issue a trade name registration to Viking Rope Corporation/Vitro Agate Corporation. The DBA name Vitro Agate became effective on July 26, 1988. The net purchase price for the Vitro Agate Corporation was $360,246.43, which included an assumption of a West Virginia Economic Development loan for $140,000. The balance due on the economic development loan was $110,440.54. Viking Rope Corporation on July 26, 1988, applied for a certification of registration to transact business in West Virginia under the assumed name of Vitro Agate Corporation. The application was signed by Timothy G. Sullivan and Richard Ryan.

In October of 1989, Sullivan and Ryan begin to move the old marble plant and inventory to Washington State. Paul La Pann, a reporter for *The State Journal* writes, "Parkersburg has lost its marbles. Tim Sullivan and Dick Ryan, co-owners of Vitro Agate, decided to move the company to Anacortes, Washington, where they are building a marble factory. The Washington town is the site of the Puget Sound Rope Company, which Sullivan and Ryan own. The marble plant is being built in the same building as the rope company, thus reducing cost."

Sullivan and Ryan bought the Parkersburg marble plant at a bankruptcy auction in September 1987. Ryan, with his prior experience as Vitro plant manager (1976 to 1978), felt he could run a profitable marble plant. But, said Ryan, Vitro Agate continued to lose money and his company did not have the capital to improve the plant facilities. It came down to a decision of which operation to consolidate. Because the Washington State rope plant was profitable and the West Virginia marble plant wasn't, the western state won out.

Lewis L. Moore, former Vitro Agate plant manager and longtime employee, summed up what was happening toward the end of Vitro Agate in Parkersburg. "It takes people to run a marble business. It is done by feel and experience. Ryan and Sullivan wanted their system fully automated and run by computer. They actually had the system in place at the old plant in 1989 when they decided to move to Anacortes." In the author's final interview with Mr. Moore, he summed up his feelings about all that had happened: "They wanted me to pack up and go to Washington and I told them I hope I never get hungry enough to work for Vitro Agate again. I told them the fishing was just as good in West Virginia as there. So I retired. I still have dreams about the old place."

The convoy west from West Virginia to Washington State consisted of twenty-two semi-trailers of many items from the Parkersburg plant. Included in the move was 80 million finished marbles, both packaged and bulk. There was machinery and tools, six regular marble machines, two machines capable of making 3/8" marbles, one machine for 7/8" to 1" marbles, the large machine for making up to 1-1/4" marbles, that was owned by the House of Marbles (England). Also moved was two nugget machines and one new duplex machine.

An interesting interview recorded in the *Skagit County Business Pulse* (in Washington State) in April 1990, with Tim Sullivan and Dick Ryan, gives insight as to why Vitro Agate was relocated away from traditional marble country. "The Vitro Agate Company used to be neighbors with other marble manufacturers in the rolling country of West Virginia. That made it difficult to keep trade secrets in a locale where everyone is related. If, not in fact, at least by feeling."

"It was also a company mixed in tradition. New technology and an outsider's ideas made little headway in an 'it's always been done this way' workforce. So when the company filed for bankruptcy, Ryan and partner Sullivan bought the outfit lock, stock, and marble barrels. The move took twenty-two semi-truck loads and a lot of blood, sweat, and tears. Vitro Agate seeks to market its product to quality-conscious consumers. Like many other American manufacturers, Vitro Agate faces stiff competition from outside the country. The biggest business adversary is based south-of-the-border, in Mexico. Imports take up seventy percent of the total U.S. marble consumption."

Once they had relocated to Anacortes, Washington, Vitro Agate commenced operation in mid-1989. Their line included game marbles, decorative and industrial marbles, and Vitro Grow kits.

The multi-colored mix of transparent to opaque swirls called "Classics" were introduced in 1991. At least twenty varieties have been identified to date. Cage style cat's eye marbles in one, two, and even three colors were produced, starting in 1990. Frosted, carnival glass, and iridescent marbles were produced as well as gems.

Raelyn Dolton – marble collector, researcher, and dealer, who generously donated her great Vitro find to the National Marble Museum – has gleaned some information from the Anacortes owners of Vitro Agate that deals with the day to day operations there.

Her observations include: Vitro in Washington made their own glass from formulas, they had plans for marble machines drawn by John F. Early (Akro Agate) and Oris Hanlon (Cairo Novelty Works), revenues in Anacortes totaled less than $10 million a year, and they employed an average of twenty-six workers in eight hour shifts. The rule that Lewis L. Moore employed in Parkersburg "clean the rollers two hours into the shift and again two hours before ending the shift" was followed. The big ruby red marbles were made on the House of Marbles (England) machine. The frit for the Anacortes confetti marbles came from Germany."

Regarding production, she learned that the pink cat's eye marbles were made on May 20, 1990 – less than 200 produced. Vitro Agate (Anacortes) by 1990 was rolling out about 400,000 marbles a day and carried an inventory of about 100 million marbles. An estimate for production in 1991 was between 300 and 500 million marbles.

An article in the June 4, 1990, *Puget Sound Business Journal* states: "Most of the company's dollars have gone into efficient, high-tech equipment that produces a better product for less. Ryan and Sullivan have one marble-making machine up and running, but intend to expand their capacity. The additional machinery is on hand, but Vitro still needs to build the furnaces that heat sand into molten glass … By the end of the year, Vitro will be capable of producing 1 million marbles daily; eventually, says Ryan, its capacity will reach seven million per day."

An article in *The Anacortes Port District Newsletter* (September, 1989) states:

"New furnaces are being manufactured and much new equipment has been ordered." Ryan and Sullivan will rebuild most of the original equipment from the factory. By next spring, when construction is complete and everything is running smoothly, Vitro Agate will offer tours of the plant and an outlet store. 'Both the Port of Anacortes and the City have been very supportive with the move,' said Dick Ryan. 'Vitro Agate will make an excel-

lent addition to the City. It should become a tourist attraction, as we plan to make some beautiful marbles interesting to collectors'."

That bright day never came for Vitro Agate.

Rolf and Jenie Wald, glass artists, reported that they had made arrangements with the owners of the Anacortes marble plant to set up a glass oven and make the only Vitro Agate handmade marbles. The deal fell through as the marble operation there ceased before they could get started. Anacortes production stopped in early 1992 and stock on hand was being sold as late as September 1992. The final closing of the Anacortes plant was 1993 and a letter from Viking Rope Corporation to the Washington Department of Licensing dated March 17, 1993, requested the cancellation of the trade name Vitro Agate Corporation. Inventory lists show many truckloads leaving Washington for Ohio on Vitro's long journey back to the shores of the Ohio River. J. B. Hunt Motor Freight Lines did the job between December 7, 1992, and May 6, 1993.

Marble historian, Dennis Webb, once stated that "Anacortes marbles, packaged or loose (when properly identified), are now considered highly collectible because of the short lifespan of the factory there." National Marble Museum president, Chris Cooper, suggests that the reason the Anacortes people wanted to get out of the marble business was that they lacked a sufficient market for their marbles. Cooper observed, "they did make a profit in Washington, but it still did not meet their original projections."

Vitro was operated by a number of owners, as is apparent. The outline of ownership after it ceased to be independent, simplified, is: Gladding-Kalamazoo Sled and Toy, Inc. 1969 - 1971; Gladding Corporation 1971 - 1982; Paris Manufacturing Corporation 1982 - 1985; Viking Rope Company 1987 - 1992; and JABO, Inc. from 1992 to present. The Vitro Agate name is today owned by JABO and was used by them until 2000 when they adopted a new label, JABO V, a label introduced in May of 1999 at the West Virginia Marble Festival in Cairo, West Virginia. Jabo had used the Vitro name to designate their production facility outside of Williamstown, West Virginia, where Jack Bogard continued his pursuit of industrial marbles as a part of the JABO firm. That facility ceased production circa 2004.

The story of how it came about that JABO, Inc. of Reno, Ohio, purchased the Vitro Agate Company has been related in the chapter on JABO, Inc.

Many thanks must be given to the many individuals who helped sort out the voyages of Vitro Agate. The chief contributor is Chris Cooper of the National Marble Museum, whose determination and resolve to see it through got to the very roots and sorted out the beginnings of this company.

VITRO AGATE Marbles Produced

Identification of Vitro Agate marbles is oftentimes made easier by the fact that this company was a prolific user of factory-made packaging and it is even possible to give approximate timeframes to some marbles by their packaging. There is a huge number of original Vitro boxes and bags that have been made available to researchers for the purpose of marble identification.

Vitro graded their marbles by opacity using the following designations:

A = Opaque
B = Translucent
C = Transparent
The majority of Vitro marbles were C grade.

Industrial Marbles: Over the years, Vitro Agate probably produced hundreds of millions of industrial marbles for various uses including, interestingly, one inch glass ball bearings used in the turrets of World War II bombers and in the 1950s in Nevada A-bomb test sites. These type marbles, virtually identical to those produced by other companies, are of no particular value to collectors.

One Color Opaque: Commonly called Chinese Checker marbles – as seen in Vitro's original Chinese Checker boxes – these marbles came in at least ten different shades. In some boxes, rows of transparent or translucent marbles were used. However, none of these marbles are easily identified outside the original packaging unless one is very familiar with the Vitro color palette.

Transparents: Nice variety of rich see-through colors – packaging helps to identify, but are difficult to identify when found "in the wild." These are variously packaged as "Aqua Jewels" and "Exotic Glass Gems."

Brushed Patch: These marbles are among the oldest, yet most common of all Vitro marbles. They were produced at both the Vienna and Parkersburg sites. They are often found in older mesh bags. These marbles have either an opaque white or clear base with a colored patch seemingly "brushed" upon the surface. The patch comes in a wide variety of colors, including green, yellow, red, blue, lavender, and white. Japanese game pieces are sometimes confused with these, but an experienced eye can tell the difference.

Victory Agates and Conquerors: These marbles were primarily made during World War II, as the military names suggest. This being the case, most were probably made at the Vienna site. They usually are found, when packaged, in very old mesh bags. Lewis L. Moore, a former Vitro plant manager, once remarked that the Conqueror was not really the name given to a specific marble but was made to go with a game of that name invented by Art Fisher that never got off the drawing board because of wartime paper (cardboard) shortages. Nevertheless, both Victory Agates and marbles packaged as Conquerors are variations of brushed patch marbles; Victory Agates having an opaque color patch on a transparent base. The rounded patch sometimes has a "V" shape wedge coming off one side. The Conqueror – or the marble usually packaged as such – is very similar but the non-patch side is brushed white.

Patch with Whispy Threads: As the name implies, these marbles have an opaque patch on a clear base with filaments of white "glass threads" running lengthwise through the interior. The patches are usually found in red, orange, yellow, rust, blue, and green.

Multicolor Patch: Some call this marble a three-color patch with white and others simply call it a four-color patch. This marble nearly always has white with a combination of three other colors. These marbles have a transparent clear base and the patches, almost ribbon shaped, are usually found in various color combinations, including any three of the following: orange, blue, green, lavender, or yellow. A thin line of oxblood is sometimes found on these marbles.

There is another multicolor patch marble, much less common, that may have as many as six or seven different patches on an opaque white base. These marbles appear to be veneered, as often the white opaque base may be seen. The colored patches are those which are usually associated with Vitro Agate, although on this marble the patch colors seem to be brighter than usual.

Helmet Patch and other Akro look-alikes: Vitro Agate produced a marble with similar color combinations as the Akro Agate "Popeye" patch, but the typical Vitro seams make the differences easier to spot. Another Akro look-alike is the so-called Helmet Patch – so-called because when viewed in one way, resembles a football helmet with a bright patch right down a symmetrical center. The mostly straight-line patch is typically red or orange or yellow and occasionally green or blue. The base glass may be opaque white or clear. Mesh bags labeled "Spinners" frequently contain Vitro helmet patches.

Transparent Clear with Opaque Colored Patch: These marbles are often confused with an old Alley marble of the same design. The typical Vitro colors are easier to detect and the patch sometimes forms a "V".

Blackies: According to Lewis L. Moore, Vitro plant manager, Vitro Blackies were made in two different styles during the 1950s. The older style, more common and easier to identify, is very distinctive. These marbles have a black (or dirty brown) equatorial ribbon and a same-color patch on either pole. Dark blue seem to be the most common, followed by orange, yellow, green, light blue, red, white, and – the hardest of all to find – lavender. In fact, after inquiries were made of many Vitro collectors, only one lavender Blackie is known to us. Sizes of older Blackies are 5/8" to 1". Larger sizes are harder to find. The newer style Blackie appears muddied, as the colors are not as sharp and appear to run together. They tend to

resemble newer Marble King patch marbles and two-color patch marbles produced by Vacor in the 1990s. These newer Blackies have been found only in 5/8" size.

Whities: Whities seem to be a newer addition to Vitro than Blackies and typically have opaque white on either pole with a colored equatorial band. They also seem to be harder to find than blackies.

Anti-Blackie: This is a name given by us to a group of Vitro Agate marbles that somehow otherwise have never been given a name. Typically, these marbles have an equatorial color and either one or two different colors at the poles. Typically the colors are bright and, in the opaque colors, these appear to be very stunning to view.

Type I Opaque: Equatorial ribbon may be white, red, blue, yellow, or green. The poles may be the same color blue, light blue, light green, brown, or other colors. The dissimilar colored poles may contain a range of color combinations of red/yellow, green/red, green/brown, yellow/blue, blue/white, or yellow/green.

Type II Translucent: The equatorial ribbon may be typically blue, yellow, orange, green, black, or white. The poles may be the same color white, blue, green, orange, or yellow. Differing colored poles include blue/white, yellow/lavender, white/lavender, blue/lavender, and yellow/green.

All-Reds: Introduced October 9, 1959, the All-Red covers two time periods: Old All-Reds from the 1950s and new All-Reds from the 1980s. As the name suggests, all of these marbles contain the color red – along with other colors as well. All-Reds Old Style are marbles that have a black band at the equator and red at one pole and another color at the opposite pole. Opposing pole colors include: dark blue (the most common), green, orange, white, yellow, and light blue. These marbles range from 5/8" to 1" and, as with Blackies, the larger sizes are more scarce. All-Reds New Style are marbles that have been found in Vitro packaging from the Gladding Corporation era. They lack the black equatorial band, which in this case is white. Pole colors are always one red pole with the opposite pole being: yellow, orange, green, brown, light blue, or dark blue.

Mystery Marbles Type I: As far as the authors can determine, these marbles, said to be made by Vitro Agate during the 1980s, include two-color opaque patch marbles and are rather like the old style Akro, Vitro, and Peltier half and half. These marbles include color combinations of dark blue/green, light blue/red, green/red, brown/green, and light blue/brown (5/8" only).

Mystery Marbles II: These are also from the 1980s, but from the Paris Manufacturing era, and have been found in size 5/8" and 7/8". These Vitro Agate marbles are eighty percent clear with colored patches that seem to float inside, just below the surface, but sometimes dive into the center. These beautiful marbles appear to be uncommon. The interior patches are in either one, two, or three color combinations. Blue/red, green/red, brown/red, blue/red/brown or green/red/brown seem to be most typical.

Parrots and Parakeets: One of the most popular Vitro Agates is one that has come to be called Parrot, largely because its varied colors resemble several species of that bird. These tend to be larger marbles, 3/4" up to 1", and usually contain four or more typical Vitro opaque colors. A classic Vitro-style "V" pattern in one of the colors enhances the value. These marbles are white-based and the colors include: yellow, green, red, lavender, black, and light blue. The green color will sometimes contain aventurine. The Parakeet is a small version of the same marble using the same basic color combinations. These are not the same marble as the similar styled transparent patch type.

Frosted: Vitro Agate was among the first marble companies to "frost" marbles using a lightweight acid. These marbles were used in the late 1950s and early '60s in the making of experimental lamps and in jewelry.

Ruby Reds: Art Fisher worked for ten years before creating in 1958 what he called the "perfect red marble." He called it the Ruby Red. These are made in 5/8" and 1" sizes. JABO, Inc. has recently used this same recipe in some marbles.

Spotteds: Lewis L. Moore created this marble, as explained earlier. He originally made fifty-one. Later, the House of Marbles

(England) contracted Vitro to make them and provided the colored frit for these. Only several small runs were made. Vacor de Mexico makes them now. They were also made experimentally in Anacortes and very scarce.

Four Fingers: Not exactly a Cat's Eye, but rather like one. This marble has a transparent base color with four finger-like bands extending from opposite sides of the marble. The fingers are white and the base may be purple, yellow or red. The greatest number of these has been seen in the collection of Blaine Lemon, a former Vitro plant manager. Although these marbles appear to be very rare in the world, he had hundreds of them.

Cat's Eyes: In order to compete with the popular Japanese cat's eye – copied wholesale by Marble King – Vitro Agate developed a unique cage style design. It was introduced in 1954. When examining two very different cat's eye extruders (part of the marble machine that inserts the colored vanes) from the Parkersburg Vitro site, it is possible to come to the conclusion that Vitro must have produced several different designs. Indeed they did. Their earliest cat's eye had four to five wavy vanes and the colors included red, light blue, dark blue, orange, yellow, white, light green, and dark green. Rarer colors do exist, including black and pale lavender. There are also in-between colors. It was at one time assumed that the marbles tipped with a second or third color were rare accidental hybrids, but since there seems to be so many of them, "accidental" may not be the case. The second generation of Vitro cat's eyes, produced beginning in the 1970s, contained up to eight vanes. Many of these are multicolored as well.

Vitro marbles larger than 1" were made exclusively for the House of Marbles in England. Most are multicolor opaque patch marbles.

Hybrids: Within virtually all these types of marbles are many variations of color and style that may be considered hybrid. Many of these are extremely rare and command interest and value that goes beyond common value.

Anacortes Vitro Agate Marbles Produced

When Vitro Agate moved to Anacortes, Washington State in 1989, they took much of the technology with them and the marbles they produced strongly reflect that West Virginia heritage. Among the marbles produced were:

Cat's Eye marbles were made in several sizes, comparable to those made in Parkersburg. The multicolor ones are positively spectacular, notably the color combinations of blue/red in clear, yellow/red in clear, and yellow/black. There are other combinations just as stunning. The National Marble Museum has a collection of Vitro Agate (Anacortes) cat's eye marbles in original cans that are dated and marked as to the particular shift and number of pounds produced. The change of color within the cans demonstrate the adding of different chemicals for different colors.

Classics: It was in Anacortes that Vitro Agate first produced the marbles known as classics, a tradition carried on by JABO, Inc. in Reno, Ohio. These marbles are mostly of the random swirl type with combinations of transparent, translucent, and opaque. There are even a few that show a metallic sheen. The colors are generally bright and deep but seem to have that same oily appearance as seen in newer Champion marbles. As far as is known by the authors, only one of these marble types has been named by collectors. This marble, called a "Blue Moon," is a beautiful transparent blue with a soft white patch covering about a third of the marble and extending into the interior of the marble.

Pink "Horseshoe" Cat's Eye: This is a unique and rare marble produced on May 20, 1990, in a run of about 200 marbles. With known and such limited production, this is a marble that qualifies as rare.

Solids & Transparents: These are regular and iridescent unique frosted that seem to glow in light. Oversize marbles were produced on the House of Marbles machine. The quality of these is inconsistent.

Spotted: The Anacortes operation made no more than a few of these and they are very scarce. Spotteds were efforts to create a marble with powdered or small chunks of an opposing color on the exterior surface.

Vitro Agate Division of JABO, Inc. Marbles Produced

Dave McCullough, Vice President of JABO, Inc., began producing his own version of Classics in September 1991. Since that time, until the year 2000, JABO, Inc. produced a great variety of Classics. In the year 2000, the name Vitro Agate was dropped by JABO.

Since 1932, the various incarnations of the Vitro Agate Company have produced a huge variety of marbles in many color combinations, styles, and sizes. The list includes Brushed Patch, Cat's Eye, Half and Half - 2 color, Fried, Frosted, Iridescent Opaque, Iridescent Transparent, Multicolored Patches, Opaque Swirls, Patch and Ribbon, Patch Opaque, Patched Translucents, Patched Transparents, Solids, Spotted, Translucents, and Transparents.

Notes: At the Anacortes, Washington, site, an attempt was made to produce the first machine-made sulphide superhero characters, starting with "Spiderman". After only five attempts, it became clear that this would not work. Also at the Anacortes, Washington, site, experimental spotted (confetti) were produced: Blue – only 105 produced; Red – only 49 produced; Purple – only 31 produced; Turquoise/yellow on clear – only 25 produced. Examples of these have sold for $200.00 each at auction.

Some of the factory and/or popular names of the more well-known Vitro marbles and packaged marbles include: Four Fingers, Parakeet, Shooters, Yellow Jacket, Helmet Patch (a.k.a. Elites), Conqueror, Seniors, Pee Wee, Ringer, All-Red, Deco-Mates, Tri-Lite, Spinners, Victory Agate, Hi-Lite, Clear-Lite, Buddies, Blackie, Classic, Tiger Eye, Spotteds, Whitie, Parrot, Aqua Jewels, Ruby Red, Sunny Boy, Exotic Gems, Cat Eyes, Eight Fingers, Transparent Patch with wispy threads, and Four-color Translucent Patch.

Over the last few years, intensive research has brought to light literally dozens of Vitro Agate marbles that had previously been unidentified.

VITRO AGATE Packaging

Vienna (Parmico), West Virginia, 1932 - 1945

The time Vitro Agate spent in Vienna, West Virginia, the earliest of the long company history, is less well documented than all of the later versions and reincarnations of this company. It is known that the production-type lamps and the Fisher Jewel trays were assembled during the Vienna days, but specific marble packaging remains elusive. Vitro used a general Parkersburg address at the time. The earliest known mesh bags and boxes were products of this era. At least two eyewitness accounts point to the fact that marble bags for use in gift boxes of Vitro Agates were put together in Vienna.

It is possible that the relatively common Vitro 60 count Chinese Checker boxes are as early as the Vienna/Parmico era. The game of Chinese Checkers was introduced in 1937 and Vitro, like the other leading companies, was eager to cash in on this craze. The Vitro Agate logo appears on these and several other early boxes.

The main focus of Vitro Agate packaging, both in terms of original production and today's collecting, is centered in Parkersburg, West Virginia. Some of the packaged goods described in this section were surely from the Vienna days of Vitro Agate, 1932 - 1945. It is impossible at present to pinpoint Vienna or Parkersburg as the location for most early packaging. Much of the information that follows relies on the research of Al Rasmus (bags) and George Sourlis (boxes). Their efforts to preserve and share this aspect of the Vitro Agate story are greatly appreciated. Some of the original packaging, both bags and boxes, are completely without company identification, but the seasoned Vitro marble collector will spot these marbles in a flash.

There are several Vitro Agate boxed sets of marbles. Several Marble Champ boxes were Vitro Agate company issues and Pressman Toy Co. of New York issued the others. The Vitro Agate Marble Champ boxes are in two sizes: No. V110 contains a bag and 63 marbles and No. V59 contains a bag and 36 marbles.

The Vitro Agate name and "Parkersburg, W. Va." make them identifiable as those words appear on the lids. The Pressman Marble Champ boxes are identified by that company's name on the lids and by the box numbers 1190 and 5990. No. 1190 comes in two sizes. Each has a marble bag. The larger box has 63 marbles and the small one contains 36 marbles. The No. 5990 series also comes in two sizes and again, each contains a bag. The larger of these boxes has 39 marbles and the smaller one has 35 marbles.

There are also two Marble Champ boxes that have cellophane cut-outs in the lids so that the contents may be at least partially seen. One has a blue lid and one has a red lid. With these two boxes, the trays that hold the contents slide out of either end when the end flaps are opened.

There are other large gift-type boxes with variously colored lids. All contain a one or two-color marble bag and 68 Vitro Agates.

Vitro Agate or its jobber also put out small gift boxes, only one of which has the Vitro logo on the lid. The others have no identification whatsoever. These boxes contain 26 or 28 marbles and a bag. One old-time worker from the Vienna days remembered lacing up the strings for the bags that went to those small boxes when he wasn't moving glass to the tanks.

Three other Vitro boxes carry the company logo: the 60 count Chinese Checker box, a deep box stating that it contains "more or less 100 Vitro Agates," and one other box with a splashy red design on the lid within which is imprinted the logo. As discussed earlier, the Vitro logo seems to have been short-lived and probably disappeared in the late 1930s.

One other small gift box has a lid with an almost tapestry look about it.

During his time, Art Fisher was in constant contact with game manufacturers with new ideas for games using marbles. One that did not receive a patent was the 1939 game of "Jumpcheck." It was deemed too similar in layout to Chinese Checkers. One game that is known, however, is called Circle X and touted as "the new marble game for old and young." One version of the game has a lid with "Vitro Agate Co." and "Parkersburg, W. Va." printed on it. Another rendition of this same game, with the same box and same graphics, but in small print on the lid, says, "Marietta Games, Inc. Marietta, Ohio." No date for this game has been established.

The Vitro Agate double-width sleeve box is the first package featuring All-Reds, a Vitro line that lasted for many years. This sleeve is virtually identical in make-up to the Master Marble #13 box from around 1937. The 25-count Vitro tournament box is most likely from the 1930s. These are the only two slotted Vitro boxes to surface to date.

Vitro Agate also had a number of cellophane-lidded slide out boxes or sleeves. These boxes are each size specific, each one containing only one size. The boxes are colored red, blue, orange, or green. The lettering is the same style on all of the boxes.

The red Vitro AA Agate No. 1-35 box contains 35 - #1 shooters. A slightly smaller version of the red box contains 30 - #1 shooters. The blue box contains 24 - #2 shooters. The orange box holds 16 - #4 shooters. The green box comes with 12 - #6 shooters. All five of these slide boxes are identical with Vitro Tiger Eye marbles – a type of patch and ribbon marble. A Vitro ad from 1954 shows these marbles.

The black and silver Vitro Agate sample or display box contains an assortment of Vitro marbles, probably from the 1950s. Some contain sample poly bags with labels which identify them from this era. This is verified by Vitro ads from the period.

Vitro Agate Marble Bags: offer challenges to collectors in variety. The oldest known Vitro Agate marble bags were mesh style with stapled-on paper headers. The bags were usually red, yellow, white, or tan and the paper headers were yellow, red, or tan. All printing seems to have been in black ink.

The few older bags we have seen thus far have been in the following counts: 60, 40, 30, 25, and 5. The 5-count bags have contained shooters. The headers contain the colorful names – although not necessarily the names of specific marbles: Sunny Boy, Seniors, Spinners, Buddies, Shooters, Victory Agates, Conquerors, Pee Wees, Vitro Agate, and Agates.

These marbles could have been packaged in Vienna (1932 - 1945), or for a few years in Parkersburg, but no city is listed on the headers. Most of the marbles seen in these bags are patch on transparent types or helmet patches.

Vitro Agate poly bags from the 1950s (while Art Fisher still owned the company) are among the most interesting and sought after because of the marbles they contain. These poly bags have a seam down one side and the marbles are quite often Blackies (2 styles), Whities, All-Reds, Yellow Jackets, Tiger Eyes, and the first of the unique Vitro Cat's Eye marbles – so different from those of other companies. Other more common types of this era also found in poly bags include patch marbles, patch with wispy threads, patch on transparent, and Chinese Checker opaque marbles.

The labels or headers came in a variety of color combinations and styles. The following wording may be found in addition to the name of the marble type: Made in U.S.A. Vitro Agate Co., Parkersburg, W. Va. Five Star Brand The Pride of Young Americans.

Marble counts may vary widely as Vitro used a great number of packaging arrangements; these include the numbers: 4, 6, 8, 10, 12, 14, 15, 19, 22, 25, 26, 29, 30, 40, 50, 60, 70, 80, 85, 90, and 100.

There is one unusual early poly bag of Victory Agates with a paper header on each end. Vitro also put out a 9 count cellophane tube as a cereal box giveaway premium.

During the 1950s, Vitro Agate put out a few large poly bags with draw-strings and bright graphics. These include a cowboy on a horse – 100 count containing Cat's Eyes; Shooters and Ringers; an Indian on a horse – a very large bag 8" x 11" (must have held 200 marbles or more); a standing cowboy – 8" x 11", contains 250 All-Reds; and The Black Cat (large bag 8" x 11") contains Cat's Eye marbles.

After the Gladding Corporation bought Vitro Agate in 1969, many of the older-style marbles and packaging went out of production. Cat's Eyes, Aqua Jewels (also called Exotic Gems by Gladding), and opaque of one, two, or three-color became the standard fare of the company. A new style of All-Red was introduced, although it is not as popular with collectors as the older ones.

The poly bags seemed to have changed during this time as well from having a seam on one side to having no seam at all. Both types are found, however, with Gladding-Vitro headers. The headers changed too. The American flag with no star in the blue field was added to many headers as well as the now-familiar "Not recommended for children under 3 years" warning. The colors of these first flag headers were a vivid red, white, and blue. Most of these bags say "Gladding-Vitro Agate" as well as "Made in U.S.A." and/or "Parkersburg, West Virginia." Of interest to some collectors is the header written in French, probably for the French Canadian market.

Poly bag counts under Gladding-Vitro downsized in amounts to 8, 25, 45, 50, 60, 75, and 80.

Gladding-Vitro Agate also marketed two sizes of large drawstring poly bags and both used "The Pride of Young Americans" slogan. The smaller of these bags contains 75 marbles: 72 + 3 shooters. The larger bag had 135 + 5 shooters. Most of these bags are found to contain cat's eye marbles.

After the corporate merger of Gladding and Paris Manufacturing, around 1982, Gladding packaging supplies continued to be used until exhausted. The Paris Manufacturing Company called their marble operation the Vitro Agate Corporation. The marble bag headers they produced will say that and will have the Parkersburg, West Virginia, address. Some of these headers will read "Subsidiary of Paris Manufacturing Corporation".

The red, white, and blue color scheme was retained as well as the American flag. The blue field, instead of being plain, now contained one large white star.

The poly bags contained no seam and many of the headers contain three staples instead of the usual two. The marble counts are: 8, 25, 45 + 1, 50, and 75.

In 1988, when Viking Rope Corporation of Anacortes, Washington, purchased Vitro Agate Corporation, the first noticeable change was the radical reconfiguration of the poly bag headers. The headers were now a bright silver/gray with red, black, and white accents. The American flag was greatly reduced in size. It is not known at this time if this header was ever used in Parkersburg. The only ones we have seen have the Anacortes, Washington, address.

Vitro Marbles in Advertising Packages: Marble bag collector, Al Rasmus, has put together a sizable collection of marble packages that advertise products, services, or companies. Many of these use Vitro Agate marbles as the premiums or giveaways as a component of that advertising. Vitro Agate marbles used include: Whities, Brushed Patch, Opaque Patch on Transparent, Tri-color Patch, and All-Reds.

Besides the standard poly bags with headers of various counts, cellophane tubes were used as well as bottle hangers for soda six packs. Listed here are some of the known advertising using Vitro Agate marbles, although a complete listing might be next to impossible: Get-Up Soda, Gladiola Mixes, Pepsi Cola, Double Cola, Penny's, National Dust Hydrofilters, Mountain Laurel Brand Meat Products, High Impact Polyethylene Film, Royal Crown Cola, Tom Sawyer Apparel.

The Fisher Jewel Trays: Dennis Webb did much of the original research on the Fisher Jewel Trays, being among the first to realize interest in them as a marble collectible. The patent dates put them in the area of the mid-1930s. They first appeared as "Design Patent 99857" and were applied for on October 21, 1935, and granted on June 2, 1936. A second patent (2,094,529) was applied for on September 20, 1935, and granted on September 28, 1937. The latter patent addressed the fabrication of the tray and other miscellaneous objects to include reflectors for automobile fenders.

Don Miller, writing in the newsletter of the West Virginia Marble Collector's Club (November 2003), reported the following: "Over the years, several varieties of trays were made, which makes it an interesting collectible. One can find trays that have different patent and design numbers and some that are plain. These (latter ones) may have been sold before the patent was granted. Some are marked "Vitro Agate Parkersburg, West Virginia Patent Pending." The trays marked Vitro Agate and the plain ones are scarcer. In 1939, a souvenir jewel tray for the World's Fair (New York) was marketed containing the Trylon and Perisphere symbols. This tray is rare and brings the most interest due to it being a crossover collectible to both marble and World's Fair collectors. All the jewel trays mentioned so far contain 12 - 5/8" marbles taken from Vitro stock and the trays are approximately three inches wide. The trays may have either a smooth or textured brass finish.

Author's note: Be aware that jewel trays containing JABO, Inc. "Classics," Marble King, or Vacor marbles have been seen for sale at several marble shows and often the old trays can be found with replacement or partially replaced marbles from several sources. This alteration dramatically alters the tray value.

An additional tray was marketed that is about five inches wide and contains 14 - 7/8" marbles. These trays are marked on the back in large letters "Fisher Master-Jewel-Tray" and usually have the patent and design numbers. These larger trays are scarcest of all and are rarely seen for sale. It is difficult to tell how long the jewel trays continued to be made. It is possible that wartime metal shortages dampened production and the majority were probably made from 1935 to 1941. That would place their manufacture while Vitro Agate was located in Vienna. It appears that the Fisher jewel trays – the small ones at least – were sold singly or in boxed sets of four. The interesting thing to a marble collector is the marbles used in the trays. It appears that the vast majority have one color opaque marbles, some have multicolored patch marbles, Vitro helmet patch, and some of the opaque marble trays use more than just one color of marbles such as four red, four white, and four blue. In addition to the regular trays, there exists trays with clock inserts, certain customized ones like the U.S. Marine Corps or advertisements for businesses. There are some trays that come with transparents of different colors. There are definitely enough colors, styles, and types of these jewel trays to keep a collector busy.

Vitro Agate Lamps: The Vitro Agate regular production lamps date from the mid-1930s. William Tescher, a tank man at Vitro Agate from 1934 to 1936 told us that he received, as a Christmas gift from Mr. Fisher in 1935, a production-style lamp with 7/8" crystal marbles. Tescher allowed the authors to photograph it while on display at the West Virginia Marble Festival in Cairo in 1999. These lamps are uncommon and the three we have seen are chrome metal, sixteen inches high with a six inch base. The marbles are 7/8" and we have seen clear crystal, black, and opaque marbles in these three lamps. The marbles, forty-five in all, are arranged in the same fashion as on the Jewel trays. Thirty-three are in a trylon arrangement, making up the slender center pole. Twelve are arranged around the base. On the bottom of the lamp it is written: "The Vitro Agate Co., Parkersburg, W. VA. Patents Pending."

Experimental Lamps: In 1959, Art Fisher, ever an innovator, made four experimental lamps. He used old, used table lamp parts for one and made up a batch of "fried" marbles for it. For two others he used formed sheet metal as the center for hanging lamps. What makes these two lamps interesting is that for the twelve inch one he used Vitro's first ever run of frosted marbles. For the eighteen inch lamp he used Vitro's first successful run of Ruby Red marbles. The fourth lamp has been lost and not even a known description of it remains.

During the brief time Vitro Agate was located in Anacortes, Washington, many of the types of packaging seen today for marbles were utilized by this company. Standard packaging for all marbles includes small mesh bags containing 100 pieces (25 pieces for 7/8" size) with header card. Plastic jars of clear plastic containing 350 pieces (80 pieces for 7/8" size) with white lid and label. Large poly bags containing 1,000 pieces (250 pieces for 7/8" size) per bag were used and shipped four bags to a carton. Bulk heavy-duty cardboard cartons containing 6,100 pieces (1,600 pieces for 7/8" size) were another option in packaging.

Cat Eyes Size and Count and Package notes:

5/8" marbles / 25 pieces poly bag w/header
5/8" marbles / 50 pieces poly bag w/header
7/8" marbles / 8 pieces poly bag w/header
5/8" and 7/8" marbles / 45 + 1 pieces poly bag
5/8" and 7/8" marbles / 72 + 3 pieces poly bag
5/8" marbles / 4,500 pieces bulk carton
7/8" marbles / 1,600 pieces bulk carton

Classics: These marbles, currently produced by JABO, Inc., were first introduced by Vitro Agate in Anacortes. The size, count, and packaging is the same as for Cat's Eye marbles.

Chinese Checker Marbles: 60 pieces, 9/16", six distinctive colors. 10 pieces: Poly bag with header; also available without label and in bulk for game manufacturers.

Deco Mates: These are 9/16" and 7/8" marbles in a wide range of colors packed in tubs of 350 and 80 and in bulk cartons of 6,100 and 1,600.

Other Packaging: included the Vitro Grow Hydroponic Kits. This is a plastic tub containing 350 - 9/16" clear marbles, a package of hydroponic plant food, and the complete instructions for use.

We have found several interesting types of packaging or labels not listed in company sales brochures: Mesh bag with 80 - 16 mm marbles, 2 - 25 mm Shooters, 2 display rings. This bag has a large round header that reads "Official Cub Scout Marbles." It has the distinctive blue/yellow colors on a white background and carries the official Cub Scout logo.

Another form of packaging not listed is a plastic tub 6-3/4" in diameter and 2" high. The tub is sectioned off into quarters and opposite sections contain either 5/8" size or 7/8" size marbles. Each tub is individually placed in its own cardboard box.

Vitro Agate, Division of JABO, Inc., packaging is covered in the chapter on JABO, Inc.

VITRO AGATE COMPANY
Employees

Based on Polk's City Directory 1961 (Parkersburg, West Virginia):

Anthony, Leo W., Machinist; Callahan, Garnet C., Lab; Chaddock, Charles E., Employee; Dotson, Max F., Employee; Fisher, Henry Arthur Jr., Secretary-Treasurer; Flowers, Eleanor, Bagger; Fredericks, Wm. C., Lab; Gandee, Doyle I., Office Manager; Grady, Rondall, Foreman; Lemon, Blaine E., Plant Superintendent (Hired 1940); Mays, Frank G., Machine Operator; McCray, Donald, Machine Operator; Moore, Lena (Hunter), Forewoman; Moore, Lewis L., Foreman (Hired 3-9-50); Roberts, Patricia A. (Pfalzgraf), Office Secretary; Fisher, Edith, Secretary; Fisher, Henry Arthur, Owner.

Other employees we have heard of include: Burrows, R.; Byers, Byron M.; Byrd, Arthur; Dailey, Robert; Dye, Mrs.; Flowers, Deel; Goudy, Catherine; Higgens, Howard; Hildreth, Howard; Littlejohn, Ella; Lott, Violet; McPherson, Scott; Small, Edith; Thiel, Jane; Trescher, William 1934 - 1936, Tankman.

From Polk's City Directory for Parkersburg, 1942: While the plant was in Vienna, we find employed:

Mrs. Lulu Davis, Forewoman; Virgil C. Davis, Foreman; Denver Deem, Shipping Clerk; Henry A. Fisher, President; Edith Fisher, Secretary/Treasurer; Chest A. Fleak, General Manager; J. Howard Hildreth, Vice President; Kathleen Rogers, Forewoman; Paul W. Ward, Clerk.

Vitro Agate Employees Listed by Hire Date from information in the Vitro corporate papers, National Marble Museum collection:

Canfield (Monroe), Laura L. 11-9-51: Moore (Hunter), Lena. 12-11-52; Queen, Carmen, F. 12-31-57: Dawson, Macel M. 12-3-59; Buckley, Evelyn 2-14-62; Cale, Blondena 2-17-62; McCray, Leroy G. 9-12-62; Sims, Ruth 1-17-63; Lipscomb, Edward 11-18-67; Mason Sr., Elbert 10-27-69; Carpenter, Lloyd H. 8-11-70; Cantwell, Charles 3-7-71; Cantwell, Terry L. 6-6-72; Courtney, James F. 5-11-74; Stewart, Mattison 12-12-74;

Eddy, Albert E. 1-4-75; Smarr, Delford Lee Jr. 5-11-75; Gribble, Mark 8-9-75; Cantwell, Ronzil Lee 8-26-75; Moore, David 7-13-76; Arthur, Stephen 7-13-76; Barringer, Monty 10-25-76; Braham, Mabel 4-22-77; Burrows, Ada 6-9-77; Cox, Dennis 6-25-77; Chipps, Ronald 7-18-77; Williams, James 7-20-77; Dooley, Jeffrey 7-26-77; Roger, Harold 9-2-77; Sams, Richard 9-27-77; Draper, Larry 10-19-77; Smith, Marc 10-25-77; Conkle, Gerald 11-21-77; Wolverton, Stephen; 12-22-77; Shively, Jim 4-3-78; Moore, Steven P. 5-30-78; Sams, John H. 7-79; Scarberry, Herman 10-9-79; Starcher, Louie 12-7-79; Vincent, Kevin 12-10-79; Hammel, Kevin J. 12-31-79; Pruney, Jeffrey 1-17-80; Shephard, James 1-22-80; Church Larry Joe 1-23-80; Kerns, Ronald 2-7-80; Wagoner, James 2-7-80; Riel, John D. 4-14-80; Collins, Roberta K. 5-5-80; Monroe, Charles W. 5-10-80; Tichnell, Gregory L. 5-6-82; Starcher, Marvin 9-26-82; Cantwell, David W. 3-7-83; Miller, William M. 3-11-83; McCray, Gregory 3-30-83.

There were no doubt hundreds more Vitro Agate employees throughout the many years that the company was in business, but this list contains only those who have been positively identified.

Vitro Agate, Anacortes, Washington cage-style cat's eye production of first shift, May 17, 1990. *D. Chamberlain photo.*

Vitro Agate, Anacortes, Washington, confetti marbles.

Vitro Agate's plant in Vienna, West Virginia, was a part of the manufacturing complex of Universal Glass. The Vitro building is the one in the very foreground. The diagonal street in front of the factory is now Grand Central Ave. (then Stonewall Ave.) and the flanking streets are 12th Street (then Forest Ave.) and 11th Street (then Charlotte Ave.). Photographer and date unknown. *Photo courtesy Bob Enoch.*

Vitro Agate, Parkersburg, West Virginia, factory site as it appeared in 1984.

Vitro Agate, Parkersburg, inside the factory, Art Fisher inspects hands full of agates. 1987.

Vitro Agate, Parkersburg, West Virginia, factory site as it appeared in May of 2005. Note that the building was destroyed by fire the May 17, 2005, only six days after this photo was taken.

Vitro Agate, inside of the factory, showing the rear of the furnaces and the gravity fed batch feeders. 1987.

Vitro Agate, Parkersburg, West Virginia, Art Fisher's office as it looked in 1987.

Vitro Agate furnaces with hot liquid glass flowing out to cool and then form cullet to be used in later batches for marbles. Vitro batched or made their own glass, a practice limited generally to the larger marble factories. *D. Simmons photo.*

Vitro Agate factory stockpiles of cullet, glass made on site to be later re-melted to create marbles. *D. Simmons photo.*

Vitro Agate's Louie L. Moore chats with author Michael Johnson about marbles, of course. *1996 photo by S. Metzler.*

Vitro Agate marble sorting machine. Compare this to earlier ones shown in the Master Glass or other chapters to appreciate the sophistication of Vitro. *D. Simmons photo.*

Vitro Agate, Anacortes, West Virginia. Note the Vitro Agate sign above the door. 1990. *D. Simmons Photo.*

Employees at Vitro Parkersburg sorting and bagging marbles, note the poly bags sliding down the conveyor belt.

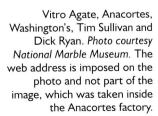

Vitro Agate, Anacortes, Washington's, Tim Sullivan and Dick Ryan. *Photo courtesy National Marble Museum.* The web address is imposed on the photo and not part of the image, which was taken inside the Anacortes factory.

Vitro Agate Anacortes facility included this shipping warehouse. Imagine the marbles!

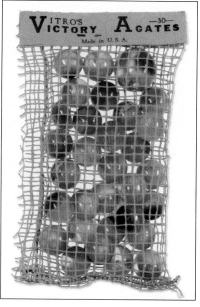

Vitro Agate mesh bag of "Victory Agates," 30 count. Possibly circa 1945? *Jeremy Thompson photo.* $100-125.

Vitro Agate, Anacortes, Washington, marble machine in operation. Note the oversized globs of glass that were not going to make good marbles. 1990 photo.

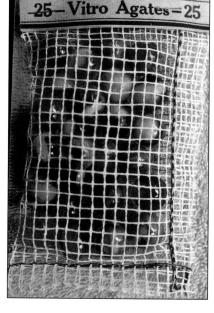

Vitro Agate mesh bag. *Dennis Webb collection.* $100.

The well-traveled House of Marbles machine for making marbles in excess of 1", machine-made at Vitro Parkersburg and now is on display at House of Marbles, England. *Photo 2005 courtesy of William Bavin.*

Vitro Agate All Reds poly bag. Contains "old style" 70 count No. 0 agates. 30 count bag, $30-50. *Jeremy Thompson photo.* As shown, $60-80.

Vitro Agate "Vitro Blackies Five Star Brand" 1950s poly bag Type I, 19 count. *Marble Magnates collection. Jeremy Thompson photo.* $150.

Vitro shooters" Tri-color patches. 1" shooters, six count. *Jeremy Thompson photo.* $20-25.

Vitro Agate "Vitro Blackies" 1950s poly bag Type II, 19 count. *Jeremy Thompson photo.* $30-50.

Vitro Agates 7/8" opaque shooters. *Jeremy Thompson photo.* $10-15.

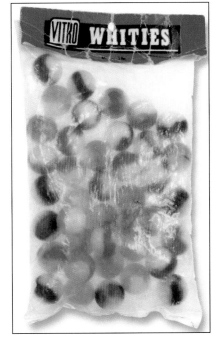

Vitro "whities" poly bag and header. *Jeremy Thompson photo.* $200-300.

"Vitro Cat Eyes" 12 count poly bag. 5 cents pre-printed price. *D. Six collection.* $10.

"Vitro Cat Eyes" 30 count bag, pre-priced 10 cents. *J. Thompson photo.* $15-20.

Vitro Agate poly bag of 100 count "Vitro Cat Eyes" cage style. *J. Thompson photo.* $50-60.

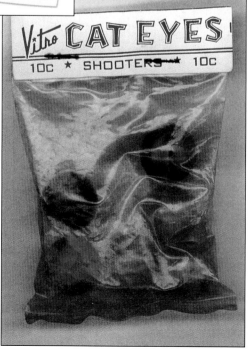

Vitro Cat Eyes shooters with less common yellow header. Five count poly bag. *J. Thompson photo.* $20-30.

Vitro Cat Eyes. 1" cage style. Red, white, and blue header. *J. Thompson photo.* $15-20.

Vitro Aqua Jewels. 7/8", 12 count, pre-priced 10 cents in poly bag. *J. Thompson photo.* $10-15.

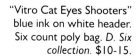

"Vitro Cat Eyes Shooters" blue ink on white header. Six count poly bag. *D. Six collection.* $10-15.

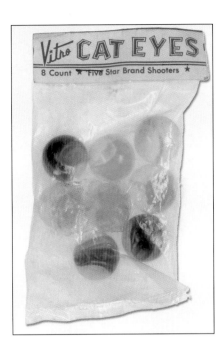

"Vitro Cat Eyes" 8 count Five star brand shooters" 1". *J. Thompson photo.* $15-25.

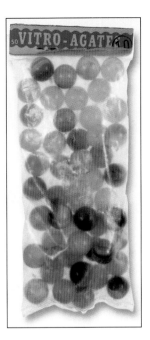

Vitro Agate 50 count patch and wispy thread marbles in poly bag. Circa 1950s. *J. Thompson photo.* $25-40.

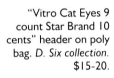

"Vitro Cat Eyes 9 count Star Brand 10 cents" header on poly bag. *D. Six collection.* $15-20.

Vitro Agate 4-color translucent patch marbles in ply bag, 14 count. *J. Thompson photo.* $15-25.

Vitro Agate, Parkersburg header on previously shown bag, showing the headers reverse "The Pride of Young Americans."

Vitro Agate, two eras of Chinese Checker game marbles, No. 00 in poly bags. Note that the earlier bag has solid color throughout the marbles while the newer bag contains veneered marbles. Older bag Vitro Agates, $40; newer Gladding-Vitro bag, $15.

Gladding-Vitro cat eyes "tournament grade" 10 count poly bag. Note the excessively oversized bag used. *D. Six collection.* $15.

Vitro Agate "Vitro Finest Quality 8 pieces marbles." 7/8" unusual cat eye shooters circa 1980s. *J. Thompson photo.* $30-40.

Vitro Agate unusual cat eyes of the Paris Manufacturing/1980s era. "Vitro Finest Quality Marbles 45 + 1." *Marble Magnates collection. J. Thompson photo.* $25-35.

Vitro Agate "Vitro Finest Quality 25 pieces" cage style cat eye's. Contains some of the multi-colored cat eyes commonly called "hybrids." $10-15.

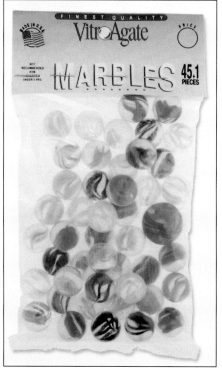

Vitro Agate, Anacortes, Washington, addressed label. The reverse of this looks like the silver label below with the address changed and without JABO mentioned. Contains 45 + shooter "Classics." *J. Thompson photo.* $15-20.

Gladding-Vitro Billes packages intended for export with French captioning. Contains new All-Reds. *J. Thompson photo.* $15-20.

Vitro-Agates black cat logo bag for cat's eyes, poly with drawstring. Empty, $15; full, $50.

Vitro Agate Division of JABO labeling on 50 piece poly bag. This silver label, adopted during the Vitro Anacortes, Washington, time (see previous) was continued by the company after acquired by JABO and was used until 2000. Found with 8 piece bag as well. As show, front and reverse of 50 piece bag, $10.

Vitro-Agates "The Pride of Young Americans Parkersburg W. Va." poly bag with drawstring and bronco busting cowboy. 6 x 10 in. bag. *Jeremy Thompson photo.* As shown, empty, $15; $30-50 with original marbles.

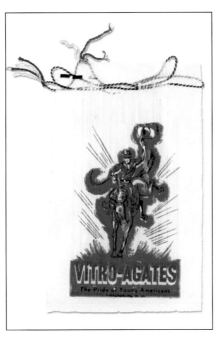

"The Vitro Agate Company The Pride of Young Americans." Showing period boys shooting marbles in a circle. Drawstring poly bag circa 1960s. Empty, $25; Full, $50.

Left:
Vitro-Agates 250 All Reds poly bag with drawstring and cowboy. As shown, empty, $20; with original contents, $50.

Right:
Gladding-Vitro Marbles, 22 marbles + 3 shooters. "The Pride of Young Americans." Poly bag with drawstring. Circa 1970s. Empty, $25; Full, $35.

Gladding-Vitro poly bag with boys shooting marbles. *Dennis Webb Collection.* $25.

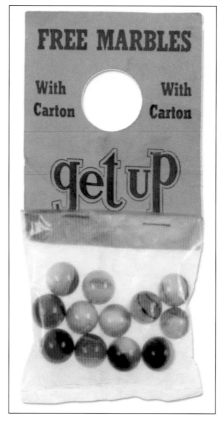

Vitro Agate marbles packaged "Free with carton Get Up" bottle hanger poly bag. Contains four color patch marbles. *Marble Magnates collection. J. Thompson photo.* $25-30.

Vitro Agate Marbles, 72 marbles + 3 shooters. Poly bag with cartoon boys shooting marbles. "The Pride of Young Americans. Vitro Agate Corporation, Anacortes, Washington," printed on front. *Marble Magnates collection.* $40-45.

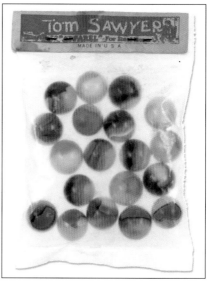

Vitro Agate marbles in advertising bag for Tom Sawyer Apparel. *J. Thompson photo.* $10-15.

Vitro Agate packaged as "With Every Carton Royal Crown Cola" bottle hanger poly bag. Contains four color patch marbles. *A. Rasmus collection.* $25-30.

Vitro Agate, Anacortes, Washington, plastic mesh bag and circular label, circa 1990. White opaques. *Marble Magnates collection.* $25-30.

Vitro Agate, Anacortes, Washington, "Official Cub Scout Marbles." *Marble Magnates.* $50.

Vitro Agate blister pack "Out of this World" with rocket graphics. Contains "new" All-Reds. 1960s packaging. $250-300.

Vitro Agate, Anacortes, Washington, Hydroponic Plant growing kit all in one plastic tub with lid – another "great" use for marbles. *Dennis Webb Collection.* $80-100.

Vitro Agate unmarked gift box with bag and 26 patched translucents. $200.

Vitro Agate "Marble Champ" gift box with bag by J. Pressman Co. $1,000.

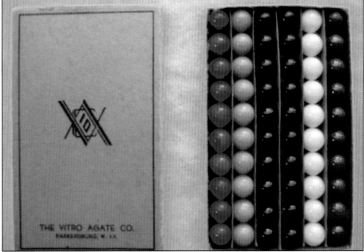

Vitro Agate logo lidded box containing No. 00 Chinese Checker game marbles. See below. $30-60.

Vitro Agate logo wood grain No. 10 box with bag and marbles. $450-650.

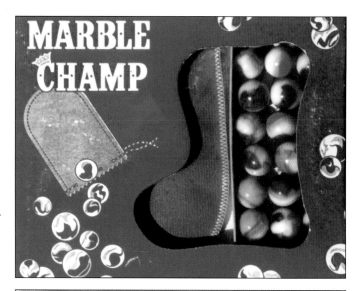

Vitro Agate blue Marble Champ gift box with cut out lid. *Brandstetter collection*. $500-600.

Vitro Agate contents of No. 10 wood grain box shown previously.

Vitro Agate Marble Champ blue box shown previously, contents.

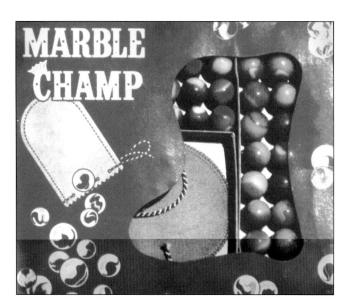

Vitro Agate red Marble Champ gift box with cut out lid. *Brandstetter collection*. $650-750.

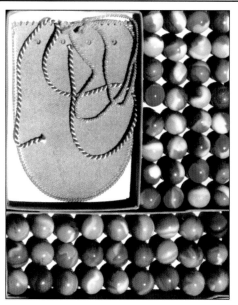

Vitro Agate Marble Champ red box as shown previously, contents.

Vitro Agate tan box with red logo and printing. *Brandstetter collection.* $400-500.

Vitro Agate red splash with logo box containing game marbles. *L. Jones collection.* $350-500.

Vitro Agate tan box contents.

Vitro Agate red splash logo box, lid shown previously and contents shown here.

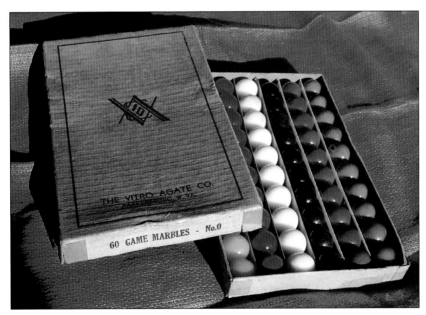

Vitro Agate logo lidded box for 60 count No. 0 game marbles. *H. de Sousa collection.* Note this and the similar box shown previously. This image is of size 0, the other is size 00, a significant difference. Only three of the size 0 boxes are known, while the size 00 box is more common. $300.

Vitro Agate No. 1 red sliding box with cut out lid containing 30 shooters. *B. Shultz collection.* $300-400.

Vitro Agate No. 2 blue sliding box with cut out lid containing 24 shooters. *Brandsteter collection.* $200-300.

Vitro Agate No. 4 orange sliding box with cut out lid containing 16 shooters. *B. Frede collection.* $250-350.

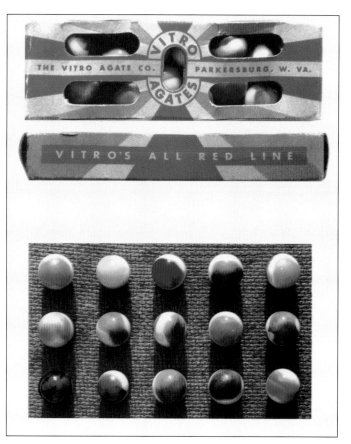

Vitro Agate double window sleeve marked "All Red Line." Cut away box front, side, and contents. *G. Sourlis collection.* $100-150.

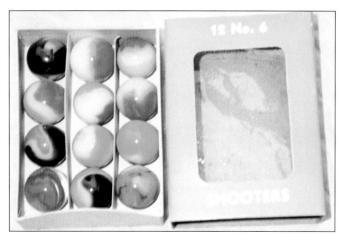

Vitro Agate No. 6 green sliding box with cut out, shown open. 12 shooters. $200-300.

"Vitro – AA – Agate" double window box containing 25 No. 1 shooters. *B. Schultz collection.* $250-400.

Vitro Agate Tournament box with cut out top. *B. Frede collection.* $100-150.

Gladding Vitro Agate "Blackbeards Treasure Chest of Marbles. 242 piece plus 8 shooters." *Dennis Webb collection.* $250.

Vitro Agate "more or less 100" count bulk box. $200-250.

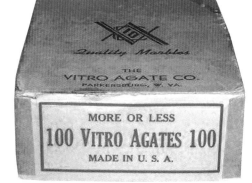

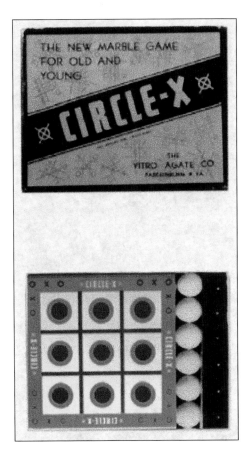

Vitro Agate Circle X game box. *D. Goddard collection.* $75-125.

Vitro Agate Fisher Jewel Tray bottom of tray embossed 1939 New York World's Fair. In original box, $200-250.

Vitro Agate Fisher Jewel Tray. *Dennis Webb collection.* No value determined.

Vitro Agate sample box, lid. *S. Key collection.* No value determined.

Vitro Agate sample box shown previously, the contents.

Vitro Agate Fisher Jewel Tray embossed for the 1939 World's Fair. $100-150.

Vitro Agate Fisher Jewel Tray, a selection showing the variances in marbles used. Each, $20-30.

Vitro Agate advertisement for products including gift box, bulk box, and mesh bags. Circa 1940s. $75.

Vitro Agate salesman's sample box. *S. Kaye collection.* No value determined.

Vitro Agate chrome and marble electric lamp. Given as a 1935 Christmas present from Art Fisher to William Tescher, the tankman at Vitro in Vienna, West Virginia. Tescher worked at Vitro for three years in the mid-1930s. No value determined.

Vitro Agate, Anacortes, Washington, plastic jar of marbles made on second shift 1990.

Vitro Agate lid and information recorded on the jar of marbles.

Vitro Agate production lamp of the 1930s. This chrome and marble "masterpiece" typifies the creative uses for marbles Art Fisher found. $1,000-1,400.

Vitro Agate Whities. *D. Chamberlain photo.*

Vitro Agate multi-colored cat eyes. *D. Chamberlain photo.*

Vitro Agate produced this 8 1/2" x 11" booklet to celebrate its 30th anniversary. The colorful 8-page item is both informational and full of interesting images of the factory, products, and people. Shown here is the cover and back, opened flat. $20-25.

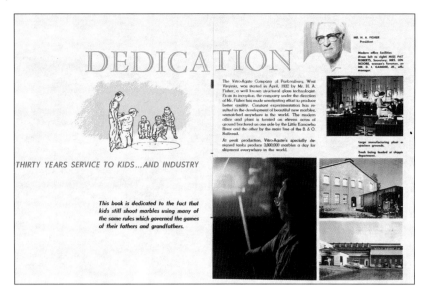

Vitro Agate 30th anniversary
booklet, pages 2-3.

Vitro Agate 30th anniversary booklet, pages 4-5.

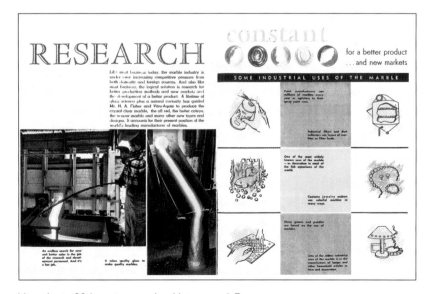

Vitro Agate 30th anniversary booklet, pages 6-7.

Marble Clubs, Events, & Museum Directory

Akro Agate Collector's Club. Roger Hardy, Claudia Hardy, 10 Bailey Street, Clarksburg, West Virginia 26301

Badger Marble Club 410 W. Hickory Street, Lancaster, WI 53813

Blue Ridge Marble Club 3410 Plymouth Place, Lynchburg, VA 24503

Blue Ridge Marble Club, Southwest Virginia Chapter 101 McArthur Street, Galax, VA 24333

Buckeye Marble Club 10380 Taylor Road, S.W., Reynoldsburg, OH 43068

Canadian Marble Collectors Association 59 Mill Street, Milton, Ontario, Canada L9T JR8

Great Plains Marble Society 9206 Ruggles, Omaha, Nebr. 68134

Indiana Marble Club 4803 Ridge Road, Kokomo, IN 46901

Kansas City Marble Collector's Club 5913 NE 45th Terrace, Kansas City, MO 64117

Knuckledown Marble Club 3112 Amherst Road, Erie, PA 16506

Maine Marble Collectors 47 Gorham Road, Gorham, ME 04038

Marble Collectors Society of America P.O. Box 222, Trumbull, CT 06611

Marble Collectors Unlimited 503 West Pine Street, Marengo, Iowa 52301

Midwest Marble Club 23265 Lawrence Way, Hastings, MN 55033

Oklahoma Marble Collectors 16328 South Peoria, Bixby, Oklahoma 74008

Sea-Tac Marble Collectors Club, Ruth Van Dyke, STMCC, P.O. Box 65, Fernley, NV 89408

Suncoast Marble Collectors Society P.O. Box 60213, St. Petersburg, FL 22784

Texas Marble Collectors, Inc. 417 Marsh Oval, New Braunfels, Texas 78130

The Marble Connection P.O. Box 132, Norton, MA 02766

Tri-State Marble Collectors Club P.O. Box 18924, Fairfield, OH 45018

West Virginia Marble Collector's Club 531 Third St., Marietta, OH 45750

The marble clubs shown here probably represent only a few of the formal and informal gatherings of marble lovers. Clubs are known to change, form or disappear. A good way to find a marble club is to check the computer/internet as many clubs are now listed in that medium. Many marble clubs hold regular meetings, have shows, and publish newsletters. For the beginning marble collector as well as seasoned veterans connecting with a club enables the collector to make useful contacts for education, buying, selling, and trading.

For those marble collectors interested in more than just buying and selling, the authors recommend the following marble festivals that feature historic displays, presentations, and the opportunity to meet with vintage marble factory workers, owners, and many local people with knowledge of the toy glass marble industry.

West Virginia Marble Festival in Cairo, West Virginia. Contact Dean Six: 304-628-3321. This grandfather of marble festivals is the original and is held yearly on the first Saturday of May in the small, historic marble town of Cairo, West Virginia. Held in a community hall, this is an event where exhibits and history are highly valued. Also included is the showing off of collections, trading, buying, selling, marble ID, and the swapping of much marble history. The festival begins Friday night with an informal session of show and tell, visiting, and story telling. Most events are held Saturday. The event has been featured on CNN, a syndicated television documentary, and independent film documentary!

The Sistersville Marble Festival is held in Sistersville, West Virginia. Contact Jim King: 1-800-296-4030. This festival is held yearly the last full weekend in September, Friday, Saturday, and Sunday. This is a relaxed outdoor event in a historic marble town featuring trading, buying, selling, marble auction, and a marble tournament for children. Includes a live demonstration of handmade marbles from a tank and from flame work. This is a festive outdoor street fair event.

An interesting stop for marble traveler is the Toy and Miniature Museum of Kansas City. It is located at 5235 Oak St., Kansas City, Missouri. The phone number if 818-333-2055 or toynmin@swbell.net. This museum counts, among its many treasures, the marble collection of Larry and Cathy Svacina, a combined eighty years of marble collecting experience, and a whole room is dedicated to marbles of all kinds from antique to contemporary art glass.

The West Virginia Museum of American Glass located on Main Ave. in Weston, West Virginia, has nationally prominent displays of many kinds of glass, some of which includes products made by marble companies and marble-related artifacts. It has in its collection contemporary marbles as well as those from various factories and sites contained in this book. www.allaboutglass.org or 304-269-5006.

The National Marble Museum is a nonprofit corporation dedicated to the preservation of history of marbles and objects of the game. The organization's purpose is to develop a museum for the vintage marbles, related historical artifacts, and contemporary art glass orbs. The founder and president of the museum is Chris Cooper. While still working to establish a public, physical space, the Museum may be contacted by writing to P.O. Box 1093, Yreka, CA 96097-1093 or via e-mail at marblemuseum@marblemuseum.org.

Other Marble Resources

Since 1999 JABO jobber packaging has been created by Mike Warnelis. These attractively packaged items may be purchased by contacting Mike Warnelis at chard123@aol.com, 902 Mahone Drive, Winchester, VA 22601.

An attractive 11 x 13" color poster of all the known Vitro Agate boxes can be purchased by contacting George Sourlis 308 W. Elizabeth Street, Pierre, Indiana 46374.

An award-winning documentary by filmmaker Jake Forbes on the West Virginia marble industry, including now historic footage of production at Mid-Atlantic and other locations, entitled *Jim Davis: A Man and His Marbles*, chronicles much about the marble industry in addition to the handmade marbles of Davis. VHS format only. Contact West Virginia Museum of American Glass as noted above.

Significant Patents In The Marble Industry

Dennis Webb, a pioneer in glass marble history, has done much of the original work on the subject of patents and the evolution of this industry's technology. Our discussion of patents includes some, but not all, of the patents covered in Webb's and other books.

Martin F. Christensen of Akron, Ohio, designed a marble-making machine in 1902 that required much by-hand labor. It was what might be called a transitional apparatus, but it set the stage for the establishment of the machine-made marble industry. This was patent 802,495 (granted October 24, 1905) for a "machine for making spherical bodies or balls."

This device used a pair of wheels with semi-circular grooves on the edges. The wheels turned so that the rolls moved in opposite directions at their "working point" (the edge where they almost meet). A gob of hand-gathered molten glass was dropped onto the wheels at the working point, and their turning worked the glass into a spherical shape as it cooled and hardened. When the gob of glass was sufficiently hard, the wheels were levered apart and the marble dropped away from the wheels. This machine produced only one marble at a time.

Since the 1905 Christensen patent, improvements have continued. Some of these "improvements" were simply experiments with machines that while not entirely successful, did produce some remarkably beautiful and unusual marbles. Other improvements were genuine advances that remain in use today.

Patent number 1,164,718 was granted December 21, 1915, to Horace C. Hill of Akron, Ohio, and assigned to and used by the Akro Agate Company. Hill, a former employee of the M. F. Christensen Company, and certainly not an inventor or engineer whatsoever, is often reported to have taken, in addition to company cash assets, glass formulas, customer lists, and the actual plans for Mr. Christensen's next generation marble machine.

The improvements over the original Christensen machine were obvious. The two wheels were replaced by a pair of cylinders with helical peripheral grooves arranged so that the grooves were exactly opposite each other at the working point. This arrangement allowed a gob of glass to automatically move away from the beginning point, rounding and cooling as it moved toward the other end. In this way, additional marbles (though still hand-gathered) could begin forming while the previous ones were still working. The final length of the grooves was widened and deepened so that the finished marble automatically dropped off the cylinders, thus relieving the necessity of levering the cylinders apart by hand.

Howard M. Jenkins of Pittsburgh, Pennsylvania, was responsible for patent number 1,488,817, granted April 1, 1925. His machine was similar to Hill's 1915 model, but had eight pairs of grooved wheels and a mechanism to distribute the gobs of glass to each set of wheels. This machine was also adjustable to make marbles of different diameters. Jenkins became an officer in the Christensen Agate Company of Payne and (later) Cambridge, Ohio. His machine was used by that company.

An infringement of this patent may have been involved in the downfall of the first incarnation of the marble factory in Ravenswood, West Virginia. More research is required to determine what happened in that early Ravenswood factory and efforts to locate patent suits, as often reported, have to date found nothing.

Patents 1,529,947 and 1,529,948 were granted March 17, 1925, to Ira H. Freese of Clarksburg, West Virginia. This machine was used by the Akro Agate Company. Freese used a main melting tank for clear glass with a number of smaller tanks within the main furnace with each of the smaller tanks having a nozzle designed to inject a stream of colored glass into the center of the clear glass as the glass was discharged from the melting tanks toward the marble-making machine.

William J. Miller of Swissvale, Pennsylvania, received patent 1,601,699 (granted September 28, 1926) for a marble machine that was not significantly different from the 1905 Christensen machine, except for the replacement of the two wheels with grooved cylinders and minor differences in the arrangement of the rollers. This design was used by the Nivison-Weiskopf Company of Cincinnati from 1921 to 1924 and later by the Peltier Glass Company of Ottawa, Illinois. This became known as the Miller Machine.

John F. Early, an engineer and designer for the Akro Agate Company, was granted several important patents to be subsequently assigned to that company. Patent 1,761,623 (granted June 30, 1930) had a significant design change in that the alignment of the grooves on the cylinders was offset just a little. This offset improved the roundness of the marbles by causing them to rotate, constantly changing their axes, while forming and hardening.

Early's patent 1,880,916 (granted October 4, 1932) was also assigned to the Akro Agate Company, but curiously this came after he and three other Akro employees had left that firm to found an authentic competitor, the Master Marble Company. The improvement contained in this patent doubled the output of each marble machine by adding a second set of grooved rollers, along with a guide for directing the gobs of glass alternately into the grooves of either pair of cylinders, thus, twice the number of marbles could be working at the same time.

Patent number 1,993,235 (March 5, 1935) was actually a shearing machine for use with marble machines. The design was the work of Russel U. Adams and Clyde Hibbs of Sistersville, West Virginia. This mechanism cut gobs of glass from a continuously falling stream and discharged them alternately along two different directions for use with a two-paired machine. This device was assigned to and used by the various marble factories of Lawrence E. Alley.

Another significant patent (number 2,422,413), granted June 17, 1947, to Oris G. Hanlon of Massillon, Ohio, was used by the Cairo Novelty Company. Hanlon's design claimed a "novel shearing mechanism" designed to increase production by the movement of a cutting blade over a series of holding cups. The molten gobs of glass were then dropped alternately into two pairs of rollers as in the 1932 Early patent. This device was reminiscent of the Adams/Hibbs 1935 design. This complex machine encountered a number of operating difficulties and breakdowns during its lifetime due in part to the wearing out of soft brass parts that needed continual replacement. One time this machine spit out not marbles, but glass objects that more resembled doughnuts. Nevertheless, when working properly, this machine produced some of the most eye-pleasing marbles of its era. Mr. Hanlon was proud enough of his invention that he carried a copy of his patent certificate in his pocket at all times.

There were other patents significant to the marble-making industry, but the ones presented here represent an overview of the evolution of technology important to the industry.

It is important to remember that patent numbers are assigned by the U.S. Patent Office sequentially, according not to the date of application, but rather to the date granted. Oftentimes there was a gap of several years between application and patent granting and there is little doubt that the inventor or his designee could have been using the machine for some time prior to the date of the patent grant.

Finally, and perhaps most significantly, patents, including specification and detailed illustrations of equipment and processes, once filed for patent protection are available to the public. All secrecy is lost when a patent is granted. Even though a patent grant is to protect its owner's rights, there were clear cases of patent infringement. Suits often took years to reach settlement, cost amazing sums in litigation, and for several of the disagreements, never reached a definite resolution. During such times a competitor might have been using the original inventor's own designs in competition against him. Obviously, it was not always in the best interest of the inventor to make public his new designs. Some inventors or their marble company designees chose not to patent, but to use their inventions or improvements without patents, relying on secrecy for protection. This was certainly the case in the machine-made marble industry.

To search on line for specifics of the mentioned patents or others go to http://patft.uspto.gov/netahtml/srchnum.htm and put in the patent number in the search or "query" box.

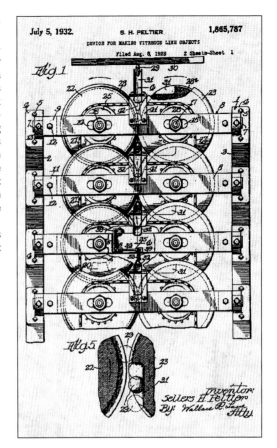

Peltier patent illustration.

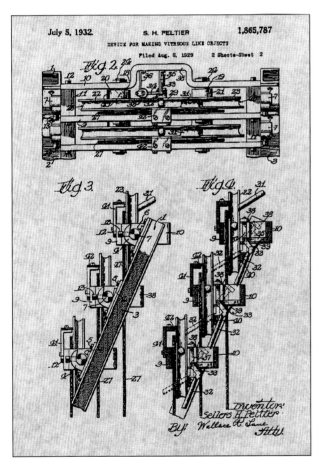

Peltier patent illustration.

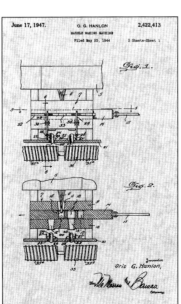

Hanlon patent illustration.

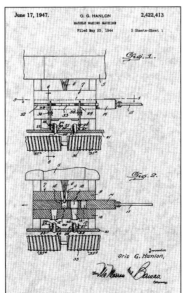

Hanlon patent illustration.

Bibliography

Barrett, Marilyn. *Aggies, Immies, Shooters, and Swirls: The Magical World of Marbles.* New York: Little, Brown and Company, 1994.

Block, Robert. *Marbles: Identification and Price Guide.* Atglen, Pennsylvania: Schiffer Publishing Ltd., 1996.

Block, Stanley A. *Marble Mania.* Atglen, Pennsylvania: Schiffer Publishing Ltd., 1998.

Castle, Larry and Marlow Peterson. *Collecting Machine-Made Marbles: Identification and Price Guide.* Ogden, Utah: Utah Marble Connection, 1989. Second Edition 1995.

Castle, Larry and Marlow Peterson. *Marbles: The guide to Cat's Eye Marbles.* Ogden, Utah: Utah Marble Connection, 1998.

Cohill, Michael. *M.F. Christensen and the Perfect Glass Ball Machine.* Akron, Ohio: Group Ideate Publishing, 1990.

Cooper, Chris. *The Vitro Agate Company.* Yreka, California: The National Marble Museum, 2005.

Grist, Everett. *Everett Grist's Big Book of Marbles.* Paducah, Kentucky: Collector Books, 1993 and later editions.

Hardy, Roger and Claudia. *The Complete Line of the Akro Agate Company.* Clarksburg Publishing Company, 1992. Second Edition 1998.

Nentwig, M. Ruth. *Machine-Made Marbles: A Beginner's Guide.* Self-published. P.O. Box 244, East Flat Rock, North Carolina. 28726. 2004.

Randall, Mark and Dennis Webb. *Greenberg's Guide to Marbles.* Sykesville, Maryland: Greenberg Publishing Company, 1988.

Webb, Dennis. *Greenberg's Guide to Marbles.* Sykesville, Maryland: Greenberg Publishing Company, Second edition 1994.

Index